The Boundary Hunters

The Boundary Hunters

Surveying the 141st Meridian
and the Alaska Panhandle

LEWIS GREEN

UNIVERSITY OF BRITISH COLUMBIA PRESS

VANCOUVER AND LONDON

The Boundary Hunters

Surveying the 141st Meridian and the Alaska Panhandle

© The University of British Columbia 1982
All rights reserved

This book has been published with the assistance of the
Canada Council and of the Government of British Columbia
through the British Columbia Cultural Fund and the British
Columbia Lottery Fund.

Canadian Cataloguing in Publication Data

Green, Lewis, 1925-
   The boundary hunters

   Bibliography: p.
   Includes index.
   ISBN 0-7748-0150-6

   1. Alaska — Boundaries — Canada. 2. Canada —
Boundaries — Alaska. 3. Surveying — Alaska —
History. 4. Surveying — Yukon Territory —
History. 5. Surveying — British Columbia —
History. I. Title
FC190.G73   979.8'03   C82-091008-2
F912.B7G73

INTERNATIONAL STANDARD BOOK NUMBER 0-7748-0150-6

Printed in Canada

To the men of the field parties

Contents

Photographic Credits

Negative or photograph numbers in brackets

Public Archives Canada: Plates 2 (PR-12159), 3 (PR-12151), 4 (74924), 12 (21425)

Provincial Archives of British Columbia: Plate 16 (62460); Barraclough collection: Plates 39 (95249), 45 (95246)

International Boundary Commission (Canadian Section): Plates 5 (3969), 10, 11, 22 (4925), 28, 30, 34 (2092), 37 (3289), 38, 46, 47

International Boundary Commission (U.S. Section): Plates 33 (Leland 1907, 9665 h3), 36 (Riggs 1907 n. 8), 41 (Riggs 1910–23), 44 (Riggs 1912 n. 46), 48 (Baldwin 1913-3), 49 ibid. 20, 50 ibid. 16, 52 ibid. 52

The Canadian Surveyor and M.K. Nelles (D.H. Nelles collection): Plates 24, 25, 26, 27, 35

Historical Photography Collection, University of Washington Libraries, Pratt collection: Plates 6, 7; Hegg collection: Plate 9

Library of Congress, Hay papers: Plate 14

John Stewart (A.G. Stewart collection): Plates 18, 19, 20, 21, 32, 40, 42, 46 insert

H.C. Hammond (A.G. Gillespie collection): Plates 17, 31

Vancouver Public Library: Plate 8 (VPL 32809)

University of British Columbia Library, Special Collections: Plate 15

Plate 1 is reproduced from Frederick Schwatka, *A Summer in Alaska* (St. Louis: J.W. Henry, 1894).

Plates 43, 51, 53 are from the 1918 Report and plate 23 from the 1952 Report of the International Boundary Commission.

Plate 29 is a portion of a photograph of ice worms taken by E.W. Grove of specimens collected on the Leduc glacier (east of B.P.s 20 and 21) in 1968. The complete photograph appears as Plate VB in Edward W. Grove, *Geology and Mineral Deposits of the Stewart Area, British Columbia,* Bulletin 58, British Columbia Department of Mines and Petroleum Resources (Victoria: Queen's Printer, 1971).

Illustrations

Acknowledgements

My interest in writing on the boundary surveys dates back to 1975 when I had the good fortune to accompany Hugues Salat of Aquitaine Company of Canada on a geological reconnaissance from Dawson, Yukon, north almost to the Arctic coast. During it, our helicopter landed at many points close to the boundary, and having worked with horse parties over similar terrain some twenty years earlier, I had some conception of the problems the surveyors had overcome. Hugues very kindly modified his planned programme somewhat to allow me to visit or fly over a number of points of particular interest.

Later, the hospitality of good friends John and Nora Wheeler, then living in Ottawa, made possible extended visits at the Public Archives of Canada and the International Boundary Commission. Both the Canadian and the United States Sections of the International Boundary Commission have supplied material and permitted me to examine their holdings.

Much of my work was done in the library of the University of British Columbia, and as with an earlier book, I consider myself a beneficiary of the policy that makes the stacks of this excellent facility available to the public. Fishing expeditions for information would be difficult if not impossible if the many publications consulted had to be requested individually. Unfortunately, increasing amounts of historical material have disappeared into storage as the library attempts to make the best use of their now inadequate shelf space. Librarians everywhere have been helpful, but two deserve special mention for assistance in locating obscure publications and maps: Mary Akehurst of the Geological Survey of Canada's Vancouver office and Anne Yandle of the university's Special Collections.

A chance encounter with Gordon Stead on the summit of a local mountain elicited the information that he had once worked for the Geodetic Survey of Canada and was interested in many aspects of surveying. Subsequently, he read my manuscript and made many valuable suggestions about preparing it for publication.

Later, G.S. Andrews, retired Surveyor General of British Columbia, read the manuscript as a critical reader and became an enthusiastic supporter of the project. He has helped with the technical aspects and brought a wealth of new material to my attention.

Permission from W.W. Taylor to make use of his father's diary and from H.C. Hammond, the material on his father-in-law, Alexander Gillespie, is gratefully acknowledged. Photo credits are given elsewhere but special thanks go to G.B. Leech, R.G. Schmidt, John Stewart and George Wood for their help in locating or supplying them. Generous grants from the Corporation of Land Surveyors of the Province of British Columbia and the following firms made it possible to expand the photo coverage: Goudal and Associates; Justice, Chicalo & Young; Matson, Peck & Topliss; McElhanney Surveying & Engineering Ltd.; Thomson, Isaak & Osman; Underhill & Underhill.

John D. Spittle, interested in longitude determinations using lunar observations, did his best to explain some of the mysteries of this subject to me. He made many valuable suggestions used in preparing my simple description of the method.

Dr. Jane Fredeman, senior editor of University of British Columbia Press, edited the manuscript with care, picking up many loose ends and insisting on fuller explanations of some of the surveying techniques. It has been a great pleasure to work with her.

Finally, there is the continual encouragement I have received from my family, especially my wife, over the past six years.

Preliminary Note

On the accompanying sketch maps an attempt has been made to show many of the topographic names referred to in the text despite limitations imposed by page size. Names used are those in present day use. The reader wishing a better idea of the terrain involved should examine larger scale topographic maps of the region. Best are the modern 1:250,000 maps (about one inch to four miles) with their contour interval of five hundred feet or less. Some idea of the magnitude of the boundary surveys may be drawn from the fact that thirty-one such maps are needed to form a mosaic covering the Alaska boundary from the tip of the Panhandle to the Arctic Ocean, a north-south distance of roughly 1,040 miles.

When the boundary surveys were underway, the Canadian surveyors were commonly referred to as "British" and the commissioner as "His Britannic Majesty's Commissioner." In accord with current usage, they are referred to as "Canadian" in the text. This seems more straightforward since their work was both organized and paid for directly by the Canadian government. On technical matters, the United States commissioner dealt directly with his Canadian counterpart. In contrast, diplomatic negotiations between Canada and the United States were handled through the government of Great Britain.

The Alaska boundary surveys were done using metric units, but the final reports on both the 141st meridian and the Panhandle sections give horizontal distances in metres and vertical elevations in feet above sea level. The use of metric units was confined to the technical aspects of the work. In descriptions of field travel, such as from a camp to a survey station, distances are invariably given in miles. The final maps of both sections are a compromise, printed on a scale more appropriate to the metric system but with a contour interval expressed in feet.

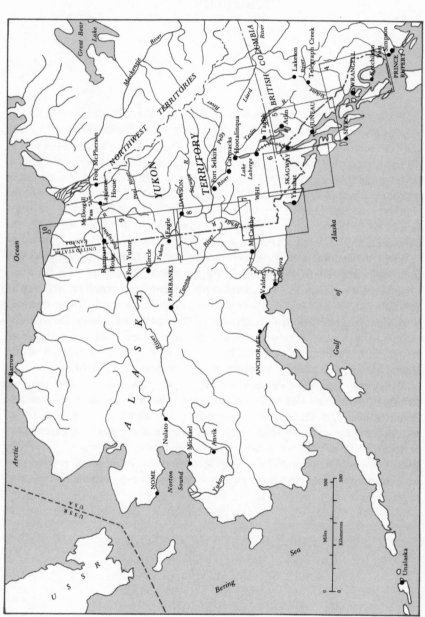

Map 1: Alaska, Yukon Territory, and adjacent portion of British Columbia showing location of detail maps (4 to 10)

Foreword

Most Canadians assume that the Alaska Boundary means the Panhandle, that incongruous strip of territory that cuts off almost half of British Columbia from the Pacific Ocean. For them, it exists because an English lord sided with the Americans and, by doing so, gave away Canada's interests on the Pacific Coast.

Like many things in this world, it is not that simple. The Alaska Boundary was described in the Anglo-Russian Treaty of 1825, and the southern limit of the Panhandle was fixed at that time. At the Alaska Boundary Tribunal of 1903, both sides accepted this limit, and the main issue was Canada's claims to the heads of the longer inlets cutting into the Panhandle. Regardless of what Lord Alverstone did or did not do, the Panhandle would still be there; the loss was not so much territory as the snatching away of Canada's only hope of saving face in the settlement.

A great deal has been written on the political history of the issue but little on the work of the surveyors, both Canadian and American, who marked the boundary on the ground. I have concentrated on the latter, ignoring much of the polemics. Negotiations that led nowhere are mentioned briefly, or in a few cases, not at all. Nor has the boundary dispute been considered as part of the complex interaction between Canada, Great Britain, and United States on the North American continent. Instead, it is treated as a nagging issue that had to be resolved before the surveyors could set to work.

The surveyors involved were tough, competent men. So much so that, despite the great physical difficulties they worked under, there are no epic tales of heroism in the face of self-inflicted disasters. Between 1869 and 1920 about 150 government field parties did work along the Alaska Boundary. Most parties had at least six men and a few had over thirty. Yet of the hundreds of men involved, only three lost their lives through accidents in the field.

Today, when any part of the Alaska Boundary can be reached in a few hours by helicopter, it is easy to forget how remote it once was. For the surveyors there were steamers along the coast and on the larger rivers, but beyond they used canoes, poling boats, pack-horses, or hand-drawn sleds and, at times, back-packed. Even the outboard motor was a luxury, first available in 1920, the final year of the survey. Once in the bush or out on the glaciers the parties were thrown on their own resources without as much as a radio to call for help in an emergency.

Theirs was a remarkable achievement; one that both countries can be proud of.

On the maps, the boundary is shown all along by nice little dotted lines, but the work of putting this line on the ground is still in progress, and both American and Canadian surveyors are putting forth their best to establish a boundary which will stand the test of time; so that when a hundred years hence the engineer of the period throws in his equilibrium clutch, turns on the gravity and air current absorber and brings his huge "dirigible" to a stop above some one of our stations, he may look through his improved surveying instruments along the vista . . . and pronounce the line laid out by the old-timers straight and good.

Thomas Riggs, Jr., 1909

Your news regarding the rumor of a "Geodetic Conference" and the bringing together of the Alaska Boundary hunters is news indeed and for which I am greatly obliged.

J.F. Pratt to O.H. Tittmann, 14 November 1893

1

Britain and Russia Establish Their Boundary
(1825-67)

The Anglo-Russian Treaty fixing the boundary between British and Russian possessions on the North American continent was signed in St. Petersburg on 28/16 February 1825, the second date according to the Julian calendar still in use in Russia.[1] Signatories were Count Nesselrode, Russia's foreign minister, Pierre de Poletica, formerly Russian ambassador to the United States, and Stratford Canning, Britain's ambassador to Russia. The boundary description, given in Articles III and IV of the treaty, continued unchanged when the United States purchased the Russian possessions in 1867 and Canada took over the British possessions in 1870 and 1871. Years later, differences between the United States and Canada over the 1825 description of what is now the Alaska Panhandle culminated in the Alaska Boundary Tribunal of 1903.

Need for an agreement between Britain and Russia went back to Tsar Alexander's Ukase of 1821 closing the North Pacific Ocean.[2] Under it foreign ships were prohibited from approaching within 100 nautical miles of the coast in a huge arc that swept from 51° North Latitude on the North American coast, north around the Bering Sea and along the Siberian coast almost to the Japanese Islands. Any ship seized was to be taken to Petropavlovsk on the Kamchatka Peninsula of Siberia where it and its cargo could be confiscated and disposed of. Crews would be sent overland to the Baltic Sea, and, after the expenses of the trip had been deducted, the proceeds were to be divided with a one-fifth share for the Russian government and the remainder going to the captors, either the Russian-American Company or officers of the Russian Navy.

Soon after negotiations began in the late summer of 1823, there was general agreement that the land boundary should be in the form of a Panhandle, and that from some point the line would follow a meridian of longitude north to the Arctic Ocean.[3] The Panhandle would protect the Russian settlements on the islands of the Alexander Archipelago, while the line along a meridian would protect the mouth of the Mackenzie River and British fur-trading interests there. There was surprisingly little give and take. From the beginning, Russia insisted that her southern boundary should lie about 55° North Latitude and refused to budge. Tsar Paul had given this boundary in his Ukase of 1799 granting rights to the Russian-American Company and his son, Tsar Alexander, had no intention of settling for anything less.

By July 1824, George Canning, Britain's foreign secretary, was prepared to accept Russia's claim in order to obtain a treaty. A draft treaty, describing a panhandle much like the one in the final treaty, had been forwarded to Sir Charles Bagot, Britain's ambassador in St. Petersburg. But now the Russians objected to conditions governing freedom of navigation and trading privileges, in part originally offered by the Russians themselves. Bagot, despairing of a compromise, broke off the negotiations.[4]

In December 1824, George Canning tried again. He had a new negotiator, his cousin Stratford Canning, and a new draft treaty with the two sections dealing with navigation and trade lifted almost word for word from the Russian-American Treaty of 1824.[5] Surely Russia would offer the same terms to Britain! The new approach succeeded, and the final, signed treaty had only a few minor changes from his draft. For Russia, it meant recognition of her claim to the Panhandle and a chance to back down from the Ukase of 1821 without losing face. Britain had gained something too; originally she had been willing to settle for a boundary along the 135th meridian of longitude, but it had gradually shifted westward to 139, 140, and finally the 141st meridian. Unknown to the negotiators, the Klondike goldfield lay in the strip added to British territory. Two articles of the treaty described the new boundary:

III. The line of demarcation between the possessions of the High Contracting Parties, upon the coast of the continent, and the islands of America to the north-west, shall be drawn in the manner following:
Commencing from the southernmost point of the island called Prince of Wales Island, which point lies in the parallel of 54 degrees 40 minutes, north latitude, and between the 131st and 133rd degree of west longitude (meridian of Greenwich), the said line shall ascend to the north along the channel called Portland Channel, as far as the point of the continent where it strikes the 56th degree of north latitude; and from this last mentioned point, the line of demarcation shall follow the summit of the mountains situated parallel to the coast as far as the point of intersection of the 141st degree of west longitude (of the same meridian); and, finally, from the said point of intersection, the

said meridian line of the 141st degree, in its prolongation as far as the Frozen Ocean, shall form the limit between the Russian and British possessions on the continent of America to the north-west.

IV. With reference to the line of demarcation laid down in the preceding Article it is understood:

1st. That the island called Prince of Wales Island shall belong wholly to Russia.

2nd. That whenever the summit of the mountains which extend in a direction parallel to the coast, from the 56th degree of north latitude to the point of intersection of the 141st degree of west longitude, shall prove to be at the distance of more than 10 marine leagues from the ocean, the limit between the British possessions and the line of the coast which is to belong to Russia, as above mentioned, shall be formed by a line parallel to the windings of the coast, and which shall never exceed the distance of 10 marine leagues therefrom [about 34.5 miles or 55.6 kilometres].

At the time the treaty was signed, neither country had trading posts close to the new boundary. Those of the Russian-American Company were strung out along the islands and the northern coast while those of the Hudson's Bay Company, spreading westward from the Mackenzie River, were still far inland. But the latter company, strengthened by a merger with the North West Company in 1821, was about to enter a period of expansion under George Simpson, their new governor. On his first inspection trip to the recently acquired Columbia Department, Simpson was present at the dedication of Fort Vancouver on the Columbia River on 19 March 1825. Included in the many changes he planned was a northward expansion along the coast to close the gap with the Russians, and the brig *William and Ann* had already been purchased for the northern coastal trade.[6]

Surprisingly, the first attempt to locate the new boundary on the ground was made along the shore of the "Frozen Ocean" in the summer of 1826. Word of the new boundary had reached Captain John Franklin in January 1826 at his winter camp on Great Bear Lake. Early in July, Franklin and fifteen of his men, travelling in two open boats, cleared the Mackenzie River delta and began to work their way westward along the Arctic Coast. If all went well they would rendezvous with Captain Beechey of the Royal Navy working eastward from the Pacific. Progress was slow, but when the sun burned off the fog about noon on 27 July 1826, Franklin saw open water about half a mile offshore which the party were able to follow for about eight miles to the mouth of a wide river flowing out of the British mountains.

This being the most westerly river in the British dominions on this coast, and near the line of demarcation between Great Britain and Russia, I named it the Clarence, in honour of His Royal Highness and Lord High Admiral. Under a pile of drift timber which we erected on the most elevated point of the coast near its mouth, was deposited a tin box, containing a royal silver medal, with an account of the proceedings of the Expedition; and the union flag was hoisted under three hearty cheers, the only salute that we could afford. This ceremony did not detain us longer than half an hour; when we launched into a larger space of open water than we had seen since the 9th of the month. This circumstance, together with the appearance of several seals, and the water becoming more salt, created a hope that we should soon enter upon a brisker navigation. But this too sanguine expectation was dispelled in little more than an hour, by a close and heavy field of ice, which obliged us to pull to the shore.[7]

It took until the morning of 31 July to reach Demarcation Point, about 12 miles to the west, named by Franklin for its location close to the 141st meridian. There was no rendezvous that summer; both Franklin's and Beechey's parties had to turn back the way they came, the way ahead blocked by pack ice. The gap, of about 180 miles, was finally filled in 1837 by Peter Dease and Thomas Simpson of the Hudson's Bay Company.[8]

In mid-June 1834, there was a boundary incident between Hudson's Bay Company traders and the Russians at the site of present-day Wrangell.[9] The former, led by Peter Skene Ogden, arrived aboard the brig, *Dryad,* intent on establishing a post on the Stikine River inland beyond the ten-marine league limit. Forewarned, the Russians were at work on their Fort Dionysius, and their brig, *Chichagoff,* with fourteen guns and a crew of eighty-four was standing by. No one could interpret, but Ogden was certain that the Russians were prepared to use force to keep him from ascending the Stikine. An appeal to Sitka, dispatched by Russian whaleboat, brought a letter in French from the deputy governor. Once again, Ogden was refused permission to proceed, and there was a suggestion that he visit Sitka after Governor Wrangell returned there at the end of August. An added complication was the arrival of a party of Tlingit Indians, who made it quite clear that no one was to interfere with their role as middlemen in the trade with the Interior Indians on the Stikine. Ogden gave up his attempt and recriminations between London and St. Petersburg followed. The Russians denied threatening to use force, holding that the British party had turned back through "an excess of caution on the part of the persons in charge of it."[10] The incident was finally closed when the Hudson's Bay Company abandoned their claim for £22,000 in damages as one of the conditions of a lease that gave them control of the mainland portion of the Panhandle lying south and east of a line from Mount Fairweather to Cape Spencer.[11]

The lease was signed at Hamburg on 6 February 1839 by George Simpson, governor of the Hudson's Bay Company, and Baron Wrangell for the Russian-American Company. It was for a ten-year period beginning on 1 June 1840. Under its terms the Russians would give up their trade along the mainland coast in return for an annual rent of two thousand land otter skins taken or hunted on the west side of the Rocky Mountains. In addition, the Hudson's Bay Company were to offer up to five thousand otter skins per year at agreed prices and supply agricultural products including flour, pease, barley, salt beef, butter and pork hams at fixed prices and quantities. Payment would be by bills of exchange prepared in triplicate on delivery by the agent of the Russian-American Company and payable at St. Petersburg. The lease, without the provisioning clause, was later extended for a nine-year period and then shorter periods until the United States purchase of Alaska.

Even before the lease was signed, Hudson's Bay Company activity had spread northward along the Pacific coast. A northern depot at Port Simpson, moved to its present site about 1834, lay within 20 miles of the southern tip of the Panhandle. With the lease in effect, Fort Dionysius became Fort Stikine, and a new post, Fort Durham, was established at Taku Harbor, about 10 miles south of Taku Inlet. At both, the Indians proved "difficult to deal with and so treacherous" that it was decided to abandon the posts and collect the furs by steamer.[12] While complying with the lease in the south, the Company trespassed on Russian territory in the north by building Fort Yukon at the junction of the Porcupine and Yukon Rivers. The new post, founded in 1847, lay almost on the Arctic Circle and about 120 miles west of the 141st meridian.[13] Apparently, Governor Simpson was willing to gamble that the traders of the Russian-American Company would never penetrate far enough inland to challenge the *fait accompli*. It was simply one more step in the series of moves that gave the Hudson's Bay Company a virtual monopoly on the fur-trade throughout what is now British Columbia and the Yukon.

The challenge to their monopoly came from gold-seekers rather than rival trading companies. Try as they might, there was no way of keeping out the miners who were gradually working their way north, testing the streams as they went. In 1861, the first discovery was made in the Panhandle area, on the Stikine River about four miles downstream from today's Telegraph Creek.[14] The paydirt, carrying tiny flakes of flour gold, lay on benches a few feet above river level. Initially, one or two men working with a primitive rocker could recover almost $100 a day at the going price of $20.67 per ounce of pure gold.[15]

The following summer, Captain William Moore, a colourful character associated with every gold rush from the Cariboo to the Klondike, brought his sternwheeler, *Flying Dutchman,* into Wrangell Harbor.[16] She had 125 miners on board and pushed a barge loaded with freight. The trip upstream to the new finds took three days. Later, on his return, Moore faced an angry meeting with the Tlingit Indians who were convinced that his fire canoe would drive away the moose and the salmon. Finally, after many words and the gift of two hundred dollars' worth of Hudson's Bay blankets, Moore was given permission to navigate on the Stikine. Even the Russians took an interest, and in the summer of 1863, a boat party from the corvette *Rynda* ascended the river to a point above

Little Canyon to make certain that none of the mining was in Russian territory.[17] The first rush was soon over, but it was merely a precursor of those to follow. Some would prove important; others little more than a flash in the pan.

There were political changes too. The United States purchased Alaska in 1867, and after the summer of 1871, the Dominion of Canada lay across the boundary line. North of 60° Latitude was part of the North-West Territories administered by the federal government, and to the south, the Province of British Columbia.

The boundary area was still remote, and, for the moment, the exact location of the boundary line was of no concern to the natives, traders, and miners living near it. But, if mining activity increased or governments took a greater interest, there would soon be a need for the surveyors to mark the line on the ground.

2

Canada and United States Mark the 141st Meridian
(1869-96)

THE UNITED STATES EVICTS THE HUDSON'S BAY COMPANY FROM FORT YUKON, 1869

It was almost two years before the United States government dealt with the trespass across the Alaska boundary at Fort Yukon. The Hudson's Bay post had been built by Alexander Murray in 1847, and even at that date, the company must have known it lay west of the 141st meridian, in flagrant violation of the 1825 Treaty.[1] Any doubts, genuine or feigned, vanished with Robert Campbell's explorations in the summer of 1851.[2] Setting out by boat from his post at Fort Selkirk, Campbell travelled downstream to Fort Yukon, proving that his Pelly River and the Yukon River were one and the same. From Fort Yukon, Campbell followed the supply route to Fort Simpson, depot of the Mackenzie River District, by way of the Porcupine River and over the divide to the Mackenzie drainage. Later that season, he retraced his route to Fort Selkirk. Results of his explorations were incorporated in Arrowsmith's map "British North America 1854" published in London.[3] The map shows the junction of the Porcupine and Yukon Rivers far to the west of the boundary but tactfully omits Fort Yukon itself. With the nearest Russian post about four hundred miles to the southwest, there seemed no reason for serious concern. In the summer of 1863, Ivan Simonsen Lukeen, in the employ of the Russian-American Company at St. Michael, reached Fort Yukon, but this does not appear to have been widely known and there was no official protest.[4]

In the spring of 1868, there was a confrontation between American traders and Hudson's Bay men at the trading ground at the mouth of the Tanana River, close to three hundred miles below Fort Yukon. The Americans, who had wintered nearby, met the British when they came downriver on what had become an annual trip, contested their right to trade in United States territory, and informed them that any further attempts to purchase furs would be resisted by force, if necessary.[5]

Protests through "official channels" made their way to Washington. On 27 January 1869, General J.M. Schofield, secretary of war, forwarded a letter of protest to William H. Seward, secretary of state. The letter, from an American trader, claimed that the Russians had been aware of Fort Yukon for many years but "owing to either lack of energy or faithfulness of employees of the Russo-American Company, have failed to report it to the home government."[6] Seward, in his reply, concluded that the problem could be handled using existing legislation:

"The act of 30th June 1834 defines the Indian country as, in part, 'all that part of the United States west of the Mississippi and not within the states of Missouri and Louisiana, or the Territory of Arkansas.' This, a happy elasticity of expression, widening as our dominion widens, includes the territory ceded by Russia." And under the provisions of that act no one could trade with the Indians without a licence, which could be granted only to United States citizens. Offenders risked the loss of all merchandise, fines, and, if all else failed, the president was authorized to use military force for their removal. But first it was necessary to confirm that Fort Yukon was in United States territory.

The task fell to Captain C.W. Raymond, Corps of Engineers, United States Army. Early in April 1869, he was ordered to proceed to Fort Yukon by Major General Halleck, commander of the Military Division of the Pacific, with headquarters in San Francisco. His main duty would be to determine the latitude and longitude of Fort Yukon, but he was also directed to report on the amount of trade carried on by the Hudson's Bay Company within Alaska and the quantity of goods brought in from British territory.[7] In addition, he had the general's permission to act as a temporary representative of the Treasury Department should this prove necessary.

There were no delays. Raymond and his assistant sailed from San Francisco on 6 April 1869 on the brig *Commodore* bound for St. Michael on Norton Sound, not far from the mouth of the Yukon River. The ship carried employees and supplies for one of the new trading companies planning to establish posts along the Yukon River. On her decks she carried the *Yukon,* about fifty feet in length, for use on the Yukon River. With stops at Sitka and Unalaska and delays caused by ice and gales, the *Commodore* did not reach St. Michael until 29 June.

The little sternwheeler, *Yukon,* launched in 1 July, passed her trials with flying colours. In his report to the chief of engineers, published two years later, Raymond described setting out from St. Michael:

Having obtained two large open boats, which we loaded with supplies and trading goods, and having constructed a small rough pilothouse upon the [*Yukon's*] deck, we prepared for departure. Early on the morning of the 4th of July, taking our boats in tow, with flags flying and guns firing, we started on our voyage to the upper mouth of the great river. . . . Our course lay through the narrow channel which separates the island [St. Michael] from the mainland and along the coast for about seventy miles. We accomplished this portion of our journey without much difficulty, although our little vessel was hardly fitted for this sort of navigation, and early on the morning of July 5 we entered the upper mouth of the Yukon River.

A native, well acquainted with the lower portion of the river, had been engaged at St. Michael and under his guidance we groped our way among the islands and shoals, occasionally grounding or turning back to seek a more favorable channel. As there was a bright twilight during the short time that the sun was below the horizon we travelled night and day, only stopping occasionally to obtain wood or to purchase a few skins or a little game at some native village. Our approach was usually the occasion of considerable excitement. As we drew near a village, we were accustomed to herald our coming by a vigorous sounding of the whistle, and this was usually followed by general stampede of men, women, children and dogs. Our little steamer, which puffing about the bay of San Francisco, had seemed a mere toy, appeared to them a huge monster, breathing fire and smoke. Curiosity would, however, bring the more daring ones to the river's bank, and having won their confidence by a few judicious presents, we would soon find our boat surrounded by a score or two of noisy and excited natives.[8]

The *Yukon* proved a success on the river and was able to ascend Halls Rapids near Anvik and the Ramparts above the mouth of the Tanana without serious difficulty. She reached Fort Yukon on the afternoon of 31 July after travelling an estimated 1,040 miles in a running time of twenty-three days, including two or three stops a day to cut wood for the boiler. Throughout the trip, Raymond and his assistant alternated in taking notes and bearings needed for the preparation of a map. Their work went on night and day. It was often impossible for the off-duty man to find a place to sleep. The tiny *Yukon,* not intended as a passenger ship, had only makeshift quarters for her own crew.[9] With thirteen men aboard, some had to sleep on the open deck, regardless of the weather. For Raymond, there could be no rest on reaching Fort Yukon. A preliminary longitude determination was needed quickly in order that the traders could make their plans and send word downstream on the *Yukon* before the river dropped too low for travel.

Aside from excitement and wonder over the *Yukon* herself, it must have been an emotion-packed moment as the little ship worked her way to the riverbank in front of Fort Yukon. On board, Yankee traders coveted the neat white buildings with their red trim, and, on shore, John Wilson, a young Scot temporarily in charge, worried over the threat to the Hudson's Bay property left in his care. Despite the awkward situation, the newcomers were given a cordial welcome by Wilson and Reverend Bompas, a roving Anglican missionary visiting the post.[10] Raymond and his assistant were installed in one of the buildings while the remainder of the party stayed aboard the *Yukon* or camped on shore nearby.

Work on the observatory began the next day. Raymond's instruments, hurriedly assembled in San Francisco, included a transit, an old zenith telescope in poor condition, two sextants and six chronometers. Raymond hoped to determine the longitude of Fort Yukon by using astronomical and chronometer observations to establish the difference between local time and that at Greenwich, England, the reference meridian of longitude. The observatory was housed in two wall tents, pitched end to end, with specially designed observation slits on both sides of the tent's ridge. In the centre of one tent the zenith telescope was mounted atop a twenty-inch diameter spruce log, and, in the other, the transit was erected on two spruce logs fastened together with wooden tree nails. Raymond's instruments had been carefully stowed for the trip up river, the chronometers in one of the large boats, the smaller instruments in the wheelhouse of the *Yukon,* and the transit and zenith telescope, in four large boxes, stored under cover in the forward part of the boat, as far as possible from the heat of the furnace.

During a stormy night, some of the men who had to sleep on deck, exposed to the weather, conceiving, perhaps with reason, that their bodies had quite as good a right to protection as my boxes, removed the instruments from their shelter, and placing them near the furnace, disposed themselves in their place. The arrangement was soon discovered and the boxes were replaced; but on our arrival at Fort Yukon I found that considerable mischief had been done. Two of the seven threads had been broken from the reticle of the transit, and both of the levels of the zenith telescope were utterly ruined; so much ether had evaporated that the bubbles could not be read.

As soon as I discovered these injuries I set about repairing them. The reticle-frame was fixed in the tube of the transit in such a way that, in the absence of the proper tools, it could not be removed without danger to the remaining threads. Having procured some fresh thread from a spider, I made a little frame of paper, with a handle bent vertically, and fixing the lines to it, lowered them into position, adjusting them with my pocket-microscope, and finally securing them in place, by means of a little shellac varnish, with which I was fortunately provided. After a great many trials, I finally succeeded in adjusting them to my satisfaction; and I found afterward that the intervals were quite as good as those fixed by the instrument-maker.[11]

In contrast, attempts to add ether to the damaged levels of the zenith telescope ended in failure, and Raymond was forced to improvise using a level from another instrument lashed with copper wire to a block of wood cut to fit the place of the damaged level tube.

Finally, on 7 August the weather cleared enough for Raymond to observe a solar eclipse. Despite floating clouds and difficulties with the telescope, Raymond was able to obtain sufficient data for a longitude determination. Next day, the chronometer error was computed, and the longitude calculation, begun the same evening, was completed at six the following morning. It was still approximate, but it confirmed that the fort lay in Alaska, a considerable distance west of the 141st meridian.

At noon on 9 August, Raymond took the next step, acting on his instructions from the Treasury Department. "I notified the representative of the Hudson's Bay Company that the station is in the territory of the United States; that the introduction of trading goods, or any trade by foreigners with the natives is illegal, and must cease; and that the Hudson's Bay Company must vacate the buildings as soon as practicable. I then took possession of the buildings and raised the flag of the United States over the Fort."[12]

John Wilson, overwhelmed by the turn of events, poured out his feelings in a letter to his superior, Chief Trader MacDougall, away on a trip to Fort Simpson:

My dear Jim: The boat starts tomorrow morning for Lapierre's House with the returns, 40 packs fur, 20 ditto leather [hides], 2 kegs castorum, and the red mud for Simpson.

Everything was going on in the usual way till the latter part of last month, when a Yankee made his appearance with a skin boat for the purpose of purchasing this place. His name is Mr. Paul Zandt, agent for the firm of Hutchinson, Kohl & Co. of San Francisco. But as he could get no satisfaction he took himself off very quietly. . . .

[Raymond] today gave orders to a Yankee firm to take possession of what buildings they may require, but not to put the HB Co to any inconvenience. So their goods are in our new store. The name of this firm is Parrott & Co. They appear very nice, gentlemanly fellows, but I assure you that I felt my heart come to my mouth when I stood and looked on; but what could a few of us do, for the Captain told me it would be foolishness to make any noise. . . . They purpose also to purchase the buildings. . . .

'Oh'!! my dear Mac, what would I not give to have had you beside me today. I can neither eat nor sleep for thinking. . . . Hurry on, for God's sake, for I expect some more of these Americans here yet, for they tell me that a boat started nine days from St. Michael's before the steamboat.[13]

For the first time the position of the 141st meridian, an arbitrary line chosen on another continent forty-four years before, had affected the lives of those living near it. For the Hudson's Bay Company it would mean a withdrawal up the Porcupine River and the building of a new post to block the American traders from invading the Mackenzie River drainage. About half their trade, that with the Tanana natives, would be lost, but if all went well, natives living upstream on the Yukon and Porcupine Rivers might continue to trade at the British Post.

The *Yukon* had gone downriver on 10 August, leaving Captain Raymond and his party with the problem of making their own way to St. Michael after the necessary observations were completed. Their solution was a small skiff, the *Eclipse,* designed by Moses, a French-Canadian now working for the American traders. The craft, such as it was, was built of well-seasoned timber sawn from drift-logs, calked with rags and finally thickly coated with pitch. "On the evening of the 26th she was completed, and we placed her in the water, fastening her with a strip of moose-hide. On the next day we intended to dismantle our observatory, and, toward evening, begin our journey. But in the morning we discovered that the hungry dogs of the station had eaten the moose-skin fastening, and our boat started off on an independent voyage to the coast. A pursuit was immediately instituted, and toward evening the party returned, bringing with them the *Eclipse,* in a somewhat dilapidated condition. In excuse for the dogs, it should be added that they are fed but once a week during the summer."[14]

Raymond's party of three, plus two natives returning to Nulato, finally got away on the afternoon of August 28th: "Our journey down the river was too monotonous to require much description. We felt the necessity of travelling with rapidity, and unless the weather was unfavorable we were at the oars from sunrise until it became too dark to proceed with safety. We then landed and went into camp for the night. When the wind was favorable a small sail . . . proved of material assistance. We were occasionally compelled to land to repair our boat, which it was almost impossible to keep reasonably tight, and we were much delayed by this cause."[15]

When the party pulled in at Nulato about noon on 8 September it found that the traders had gone to St. Michael leaving the post in charge of a native.

> Our [natives] could not be persuaded to accompany us farther, nor could others be obtained, and, after a delay of an hour or two, we started again, somewhat disconsolately, in our battered and leaky boat, with our force seriously weakened, and the most laborious part of our journey still before us.
>
> On the 12th . . . a sudden turn brought us to Halls Rapids. A strong breeze blowing against the current made this portion of the river very rough. Suddenly, and almost without notice, our boat was swept into the rapids, and it was only by great exertions that we were able to reach shore in safety. This last trial was almost too much for the *Eclipse.* She was now very nearly a wreck. Nevertheless, not being in a condition to choose, we re-embarked early the next morning, one man bailing and the two others at the oars, and swiftly passing the rapids, worked our way slowly down the river. At 4 P.M. we pulled the *Eclipse,* now thoroughly useless, upon the shore near Anvik, where I

presume she still remains, unless the process of disintegration has at length been completed.[16]

Hopes of continuing downriver ended when the Anvik natives refused to risk the trip owing to the lateness of the season. The only other alternative to wintering at Anvik appeared to be to follow a summer route up the Anvik River and across a portage to a village about eighteen miles east of St. Michael. The party, using six canoes and a local crew, set out on the afternoon of 14 September, leaving most of their provisions behind in the rush to get away. A native sent back that evening with a message asking for five days' supplies returned with a note from the trapper left in charge of the post that he could not read the handwriting but presumed the party wanted something to eat. "The provisions accompanying this epistle consisted of about sufficient hard-tack for a single meal, which we proceeded to eat upon the spot, making up our minds to live upon the country thereafter. Fortunately we had plenty of tea."[17]

Luckily, the party came across native villages, and at a critical time when they had gone all day without food: "a welcome sight greeted our eyes. It was the smoke of a camp-fire, and, as we drew nearer we saw a little hut covered with hides, and near by rude frames, from which were suspended great sides of reindeer meat. . . . On approaching the hut we found that it was the habitation of one of the natives of the coast. Earlier in the season he had penetrated to this valley to hunt, but, having been seized with a severe attack of rheumatism, he had been compelled to remain later than usual, until his friends should come for him. His wife was with him. . . . He begged so earnestly for 'American medicine' that we had not the heart to refuse him, although we had nothing of that character except a Seidlitz powder. We gave him the contents of the blue paper, and, to our astonishment, he soon declared that he felt much better."[18]

In return, the party was offered all the meat they could use, and after feasting they prepared a substitute for pemmican consisting of small pieces of boiled meat placed in a bag and covered with boiling grease. Unfortunately, much of the meat used was tainted, and the product left much to be desired.

Finally, on 23 September, the exhausted party climbed the hills west of the Anvik River and sighted the waters of Norton Sound in the distance. The next day's journey of about twenty miles was the worst: "The ground is covered with hummocks and deep moss, and it is nearly all a swamp. Through this terrible region we floundered until eight o'clock in the evening, when our troubles were terminated by our safe arrival at Ikikiktoik." The village was temporarily deserted and the party was unable to cross to St. Michael that night. Fortunately, they had killed a rabbit on entering the village. "With this and some seawater, we made a soup, which we fancied delicious, as we had not tasted salt for more than a week."[19] Taken to St. Michael the following evening, the party sailed for San Francisco aboard the *Commodore* on 27 September. Delayed by gales and unfavourable weather, it was 6 November before they reached San Francisco, exactly seven months after starting out.

Raymond's trip had taken care of the immediate problem, and it would be twenty years before United States surveyors returned to locate and mark the 141st meridian on the ground.

LIEUTENANT SCHWATKA, U.S. ARMY, RAFTS THE YUKON RIVER, 1883

First Lieutenant Frederick Schwatka, of the Third Cavalry, was ordered to Alaska by Brigadier-General Nelson A. Miles, commander of the Army's Department of the Columbia, on 7 April 1883. The lead paragraph of his orders stated:

> In view of the frequent reports of the disturbance of the peace between the white and Indians in Alaska, and the indications that the present condition of affairs must lead to serious hostilities between the two elements in the near future, you are hereby directed to proceed to that Territory for the purpose of gathering all information that can be obtained that would be valuable and important, especially to the military branch of the Government.

Miles, much involved in the Indian campaigns of the American West, probably anticipated a new one in Alaska. Four following paragraphs outline the information Miles wanted. First, Schwatka was to find out as much as possible about the Indians, their numbers, tribes, attitude towards the government and whites, means of communications, and weapons. Second, he was to learn the character of the country and the best means of using and sustaining a military force, making "especial inquiry as to the kind and extent of the native grasses that would sustain animals ordinarily used in military operations." A fifth paragraph contained the only restriction: "You will endeavor to impress the natives with the friendly disposition of the Government, and in no case will you move in any section of the country where you cannot go without provoking hostilities or inciting the natives to resistance, as you are not authorized to exercise any control of affairs in that Territory."[20]

On paper, everything was left up to Schwatka; nothing in the orders suggested what parts of Alaska he should visit. In a way, it was to be a secret mission hidden from both the United States and Canadian governments. At the time, the United States Navy was responsible for what government there was in Alaska, and the expedition might have been in violation of the presidential order that withdrew the Army from the Territory in 1877.[21]

Schwatka, if not the promoter of the expedition, was an enthusiastic supporter. About thirty-three years of age at the time, he had already established his reputation as an explorer by leading an expedition to the Canadian Arctic in 1879–80 to search for traces of the lost Franklin expedition. Other Army personnel assigned to the Alaska party were a surgeon, a topographer who was also a photographer, an artist, plus two other ranks. In addition, there was one civilian, a miner who had lived and travelled in Alaska.

In his popular account, published in 1894, Schwatka wrote of their departure:

> The expedition was therefore, to avoid being recalled, kept as secret as possible, and when, on May 22nd, it departed from Portland, Oregon, upon the *Victoria,* a vessel which had been specially put on the Alaska route, only a two or three line notice had gotten into the Oregon papers announcing the fact; a notice that in spreading was referred to in print by one government official as "a junketing party," by another as a "prospecting" party, while another bitterly acknowledged that had he received another day's intimation he could have had the party recalled by the authorities at Washington. Thus the little expedition which gave the first complete survey to the third river of our country stole away like a thief in the night and with far less money in its hands to conduct it through its long journey than was afterwards appropriated by Congress to publish its report.[22]

The party landed at Pyramid Harbour, near the head of Chilkat Inlet on 2 June 1883. Schwatka hoped to use sixty to eighty Chilkat Indians and to start packing his outfit over Chilkoot Pass within a few days. Unfortunately for his plans, a chief had died about the time of Schwatka's arrival, and the funeral, mainly a series of feasts, was expected to last for a week or ten days. Treated as a chief, Schwatka was invited to join in the ceremonies, but he declined, suspecting that the Indians' real interest was in protecting their packing jobs until after the concluding cremation. By acting determined, he managed to persuade enough Indians to leave the funeral to pack his outfit in two trips. With that, resistance caved in and enough packers came forward to do it in a single trip.

A steam launch belonging to one of the two newly completed canneries took his outfit to the mouth of the Taiya River. Behind it bobbed a long string of about twenty Indian canoes, tied to one another by their tow ropes and each carrying two to four of the prospective packers. From the mouth of the river, the loaded canoes were lined to the head of canoe navigation on the Taiya, a direct distance of about ten miles but perhaps half as much again along the twisting channel.

Five days after leaving Pyramid Harbour, Schwatka watched his packers on the final ascent of Chilkoot Pass:

> On the morning of [11 June] about five o'clock, we commenced the toilsome ascent of this coast range pass . . . and by seven o'clock all my pack train was strung up the precipitous pass, making one of the prettiest Alpine sights that I have ever witnessed, and as seen from a distance strangely resembling a row

of boulders projecting from the snow. Up banks almost perpendicular they scrambled on their hands and knees, helping themselves by every projecting rock and clump of juniper and dwarf spruce, not even refusing to use their teeth on them at the worst places. Along the steep snow banks and the icy fronts of glaciers steps were cut with knives, while rough alpenstocks from the valley helped them to maintain their footing. In some such places the incline was so steep that those having boxes on their backs cut scratches in the icy crust with the corners as they passed along, and oftentimes it was possible to steady one's self by the open palm of the hand resting against the snow. In some of these places a single mis-step, or the caving in of a foothold would have sent the unfortunate traveller many hundred feet headlong to certain destruction. Yet not the slightest accident happened, and about ten o'clock, almost exhausted, we stood on the top of the pass, enveloped in a cold drifting fog. . . . How these small Indians, not apparently averaging over one hundred and forty pounds in weight, could carry one hundred pounds up such a precipitous mountain of ice and snow, seems marvelous beyond measure. One man carried one hundred and thirty-seven pounds, while boys from twelve to fourteen carried from fifty to seventy pounds.[23]

Descending from the pass, they reached a campsite at the head of Lindeman Lake late in the evening after fourteen hours on the trail. To Schwatka's amazement, the packers insisted on being paid off and started back immediately, some insisting they would make the mouth of the Taiya River without stopping.

Over the next few days, the party built a raft, fifteen by thirty feet, using the best logs available, mainly stunted spruce and contorted pine. Cross logs, holding the raft together, were notched at the contact with the underlying logs, much like the corners of a log cabin, and secured by stout wooden pins driven in auger holes drilled through both logs. Other lashings were made using the ropes that had secured the loads carried by the Indian packers. The raft, completed on the evening of 14 June, proved too small to float the entire party and their outfit.

Next morning, the raft, with three men and half the gear aboard, was swung out into the current where a small stream entered the lake. The crew hoisted a sail improvised from a wall tent, but after the wind got up, they had to take it down and lash it over their gear as protection from the spray coming over the rear. By now, a gale was blowing and the lashed load presented enough surface to the wind to drive them along at a good rate. The three men aboard had a hard time of it, but by late afternoon, the raft was safe at the foot of the lake and the rest of the party had made their way along the shore to it.

To reach Bennett Lake, the raft had to be run through a small river about fifty to seventy-five feet wide and a little over a mile of "shallow rapids, shoals, cascades, ugly-looking boulders, bars and a network of drift timber."[24] Despite some anxious moments, the raft was taken through with the only damage being the loss of a side log or two. The party set to work to improve their craft using sound dry logs, larger than any in the raft, but still too short for side logs. The redesigned raft, sixteen by forty-two feet, now had heavy oars on each side as well as steering oars at the ends. The party's equipment and supplies, weighing about three tons, were carried on two elevated decks built fore and aft of the side oars.

On 19 June they set out again, this time with all the party and outfit aboard. By mid-afternoon, a fair wind had turned into a howling gale, and the raft, lacking logs running its entire length, was working like an accordian. Wooden pins were beginning to snap, and Schwatka, worried that "in her peculiar explorations she might spread herself over the lake, and her crew and cargo over the bottom,"[25] headed her for the eastern shore of the lake at the best angle they could make running before the wind. Using an Indian canoe carried on the raft, they carried a line through the surf to the boulder-strewn beach. Then, while some of the crew stayed aboard using poles to keep the raft off the rocks, the rest tracked it back along the shore for about half a mile to reach the shelter of a small crescent-shaped cove.

They were in luck; the timber skirting their haven was "the largest and best adapted for raft repairing of any we saw for many hundred miles along the lakes."[26] Four large logs running the full length of the raft were added, two as side logs and two in the centre. On 21 June, the party was away again in a good breeze, and their now-rigid craft passed the test with flying colours.

In short order, Schwatka and his crew gained the skill and confidence needed to handle their awkward craft through the many obstacles along the Yukon waterway. On it, they travelled the chain of lakes below Bennett Lake, shot Miles Canyon and the Whitehorse Rapids, and continued on to a point just below the mouth of the Tanana River, a total distance of about thirteen hundred miles. At that point, on 6 August 1883, they abandoned the raft in favour of a river schooner made available by the Alaska Commercial Company.[27] On the trip, the raft was pried off innumerable bars, but only once did they come close to abandoning it and building another. That happened on 25 July when they chose the wrong channel in the maze about seventy miles upstream from Fort Yukon and hung up on a long spit with about a foot of water running over it. Fortunately, their predicament was not as serious as they first thought, and after about four hours of heavy work, they succeeded in carrying their gear to shore and working the raft upstream against the swift current and into a deeper channel.

Charles Homan, Schwatka's topographer, mapped the party's route from Pyramid Harbour to the mouth of the Yukon River. While they were rafting on the river, bearings were taken by prismatic compass and distances estimated by dead reckoning. Total river distance from Crater Lake, just below Chilkoot Pass, to the mouth of the Apoon Channel in Norton Sound is given as 2,043.5 miles. The method proved surprisingly accurate, which Schwatka attributed to the exactness of the dead reckoning when the raft was being carried along by a steady current. He put the cumulative error between Pyramid Harbour and Fort Yukon, both locations fixed by earlier astronomical determinations, at less than ten miles, or about 1 per cent.[28]

Schwatka did not make a serious attempt to determine or mark the Alaska Boundary. On 19 July 1883, camped on the future site of Dawson and believing himself close to the 141st meridian, he planned to take the day off and make astronomical observations. However, the weather was poor and "after getting a couple of poor 'sights' for longitude, I ordered camp broken, and we got away shortly after eleven o'clock."[29] From his report and maps, Schwatka appears to have placed the 141st meridian about six miles too far to the west.[30] Later, when preparing his report for General Miles, he concluded that he had crossed into Canada at the summit of the Chilkoot Pass.

With single-minded determination, Schwatka had led his party the length of the Yukon River in one season. Quite possibly this is what General Miles expected him to do, but, if so, he was careful not to state it in his orders to Schwatka. Perhaps the main achievement of the expedition was the knowledge that river steamers could operate from the mouth of the Yukon river upstream to Whitehorse Rapids, a distance of about 1,865 miles according to their maps. With the publication of Schwatka's reports and maps, an invaluable guide to travel on the Yukon River became available. His highly readable accounts are still relevant.

For many years, Schwatka's accomplishments were overlooked or denigrated. It was Schwatka's own fault for ignoring much of the earlier exploration and for tossing off geographic names as freely as a politician's promises. It was worst between Chilkoot Pass and Fort Selkirk where most of the local names were ignored and many features were named after prominent geographers, explorers, or U.S. Army officers.[31] Not even Chilkoot Pass escaped; it became Perrier Pass in honour of Colonel J. Perrier of the French Geographical Society. Fortunately, that change did not survive, but many of the others did.

Surprisingly, the main dispute was over the use of the name "Yukon River." Robert Campbell had been there first, naming it the "Lewes River" above Fort Selkirk some forty years before.[32] After ascending the river from Fort Selkirk in 1887, George M. Dawson of the Geological Survey wrote: "I need have no hesitation in stating my belief, that [Schwatka's] desire to affirm that he had started at the source of the Yukon and followed it to its mouth, caused him to fail to observe that Lake Lindeman is not even on the main source of the Lewes, and to change the name of Lewes which had already appeared on the maps for about thirty years to that of Yukon, a quite arbitrary and unjustifiable proceeding."[33] Regardless, the name Yukon River continued in common use for the upper river, and finally, in May 1945, the Canadian government conceded and changed the official name.[34]

Other than a host of names there were no consequences from Schwatka's journey. Nevertheless, a military expedition had entered and explored Canada without prior permission. An official protest of sorts was delivered by the

British ambassador in Washington in September 1887. Whatever impact it might have had was undercut by a concluding paragraph: "I may add, however, that Her Majesty's Government do not attach any importance to this fact, and that no doubt had their acquiescence been asked it would not have been refused."[35]

WILLIAM OGILVIE LOCATES THE 141ST MERIDIAN ON THE YUKON RIVER, 1887-88

Following the expulsion of the Hudson's Bay Company from Fort Yukon in 1869, trading along the Yukon River was left to the Americans. The company covered their retreat by building a new post near Howling Dog Rock, close to 150 miles up the meandering Porcupine River.[36] There was nothing to the south; their post at Fort Selkirk had been abandoned after it was pillaged by the Chilkat Indians in August 1852.[37]

The Americans, interested in gold as well as furs, prospected the country at every opportunity. Fort Reliance, the first American post east of the 141st Meridian, was established by Leroy N. "Jack" McQuesten in 1874.[38] It lay about six miles downstream from the mouth of the "Trundeck" River, now known as the Klondike. At the time, McQuesten was employed by the Alaska Commercial Company, but in the following year, McQuesten and his partners, Arthur Harper and Albert Mayo, took over the company's Fort Yukon and upriver trade on a commission basis. To the south, the first white man crossed the Chilkoot Pass about 1878, and by 1880, prospecting parties were crossing it each season.[39] Creeks were tested for gold by panning the gravels, and traces or "colours" of gold were found on many of them. Then, in 1885, workable deposits, where a miner could make as much as $100 a day, were found along the Stewart River.[40]

The Canadian government, aware of some of the mining activity and Schwatka's reconnaissance, undertook the Yukon Expedition in 1887-88. The work, directed by George M. Dawson of the Geological Survey of Canada, involved three field parties. Dawson's party would ascend the Stikine River, cross to the Liard drainage, follow the old Hudson's Bay route to the upper Pelly River, and descend that river to the site of Fort Selkirk. There they would meet William Ogilvie's party and retrace that party's route from the coast. The second party, led by R.G. McConnell, also of the Geological Survey, would map the course of the Stikine River, cross the divide to the Liard River, and descend it to the Mackenzie River. Originally, he was to return to the south along the trade routes up the Mackenzie. However, after unexpected delays, he was ordered to winter on the Mackenzie and then descend it and cross to the Porcupine River the following spring. From Fort Yukon he would ascend the Yukon River to its headwaters and cross Chilkoot Pass to reach the Pacific Coast at the head of Lynn Canal. The third party, led by William Ogilvie, DLS, a government surveyor, would cross Chilkoot Pass and descend the Yukon River to the 141st

Meridian, making a careful instrument survey of their route. At the boundary, Ogilvie was to complete an astronomic determination of the meridian, and the following spring and summer, he would continue his surveys northeast to the Mackenzie River and south along it to connect with previous surveys at Lake Athabasca.

The three field parties left Victoria, B.C., aboard the sidewheel steamer, *Ancon,* on 12 May 1887. The steamer, never fast and now loaded to the gunwales with equipment and supplies for the mining and fishing industries along the coast, "excelled herself in slowness on this voyage."[41] Dawson and McConnell and their parties were dropped at Wrangell on the 18th and Ogilvie and his six men landed at Haines Mission at the head of Chilkoot Inlet on the 24th. Some twenty years later, Ogilvie wrote of that moment: "At 11 A.M. . . . the boat left us on the threshold of our exile, for it proved that for fourteen months from that date we heard no news from any person or place, except the news of the district around us. As the steamer blew us a farewell, and dipped her flag to us, there was a lump in my throat I could not swallow, and a moisture in my eye that would not dry as long as she was in sight."[42]

Already there was an unexpected worry:

> The first news I received on landing was that there was trouble in the interior on the [Yukon] River in the vicinity of where I intended to go. A miner, who had recently arrived from the interior, stated that there had been a fight between the Indians and the miners at the mouth of the Stewart River. The result of the affair, he alleged, was that four Indians and two white men had been killed, and that the Indians had come up the river as far as the canyon to lie in wait for any white men who might be going into the country. I did not have an opportunity of questioning him as he had gone to Juneau City the day before I arrived. The rumour seemed to me to be somewhat improbable; but true or false, it was an unpleasant one to hear, and the only way to verify it was to go and see whether the Indians were hostile or not. Happily, the whole story proved to be untrue, as I subsequently learned from the miners in the interior that he had difficulties with them, in consequence of which he was ordered in mid-winter to leave the region, which the miners consider equivalent to a sentence of death.[43]

Regardless of any risks ahead, Ogilvie's immediate problem was to get his equipment and supplies, a total of six tons including an eighteen- and a nineteen-foot canoe over the Chilkoot Pass and into the waters of the Yukon River system. The Chilkoot Indians, who still controlled trade to the Interior, showed little interest in helping out, demanding an exorbitant $20 a hundred pounds in place of the usual $9. The second chief, in sole control of the packing, had recollections of an old quarrel with the English in which his uncle had been killed, and this was his way of settling the score.[44] Ogilvie requested help from Captain Newell of the USS *Pinta,* whose ship was in the area, and the two met at Healey's store at Dyea to discuss the problem. Newell refused to compel the Indians to work for Ogilvie at the usual price, and he also refused to extend protection to the Interior or "Stick" Indians that Ogilvie hoped to use, claiming they were aliens with no rights in the area. Finally, a compromise was struck, and the Chilkoots agreed to pack to the summit for $10 a hundred while beyond it the Interior Indians would be used to take the gear to Lake Lindeman at $3 a hundred.

On the 6th of June 120 Indians, men, women and children, started for the summit. I sent two of my party with them to see the goods delivered at the place agreed upon. Each carrier when given a pack also got a ticket, on which was inscribed the contents of the pack, its weight, and the amount the individual was to get for carrying it. They were made to understand that they had to produce these tickets on delivering their packs, but were not told for what reason. As each pack was delivered one of my men receipted the ticket and returned it. The Indians did not seem to understand the import of this; a few of them pretended to have lost their tickets; and as they could not get paid without them, my assistant, who had duplicates of every ticket furnished them with receipted copies, after examining their packs.

While they were packing to the summit I was producing the survey, and I met them on their return at the foot of the canyon, about eight miles from the coast, where I paid them. They came to the camp in the early morning before I was up, and for about two hours there was quite a hubbub. When paying them I tried to get their names, but very few of them would give any Indian name, nearly all, after a little reflection, giving some common English name. My list contained little else than Jack, Tom, Joe, Charley, &c., some of which were duplicated three and four times. I then found out why some of them had pretended to lose their tickets at the summit. Three or four who had thus acted presented themselves twice for payment, producing first the receipted ticket, afterwards the one they claimed to have lost, demanding pay for both. They were much taken aback when they found that their duplicity had been discovered. . . .

While paying them I was a little apprehensive of trouble, for they insisted on crowding into my tent, and for myself and the four men who were with me to have attempted to eject them would have been to invite trouble. I am strongly of the opinion that these Indians would have been much more difficult to deal with if they had not known that Commander Newell remained in the inlet to see that I got through without accident.[45]

The problems of packing the supplies were incidental to Ogilvie's main project of completing a reconnaissance map from a known point on tidewater through to the boundary area on the Yukon River. In 1869, Dr. George Davidson, of the

U.S. Coast and Geodetic Survey, had made an astronomical determination of longitude on Pyramid Island, a pimple of sand and clay in the middle of Chilkat Inlet. Unable to locate Davidson's station mark, Ogilvie assumed it must have been the highest point on the tiny island. From there, Ogilvie carried his rough survey up Taiya Inlet, over the Chilkoot Pass and on to the foot of Bennett Lake, a distance of about fifty miles. At the latter point, members of Ogilvie's crew were building a boat of whipsawn lumber needed to carry part of their outfit.

Finally, on 12 July 1887, the party began their trip downriver. Ogilvie employed a system of rapid mapping using two canoes for transport. Two men in the lead canoe would chose a survey point, set up a survey rod, and wait until the bearing to it from the preceding station had been determined by Ogilvie or his assistant using a small transit. Also, the angle subtended by two targets on the rod, twenty links of a Gunter's chain or 13.2 feet apart, was carefully measured by micrometer. This done, the men were signalled to move ahead to the next station. Distances between stations were calculated by trigonometry, and despite the narrow base of the triangle, Ogilvie found that distances not exceeding a mile could be determined within a few feet of the true distance. Working in this manner, Ogilvie carried his survey ahead, and, later, after determination of the 141st meridian, he found the error in the seven hundred-odd miles from Pyramid Island was about three miles.[46]

Ogilvie and his party arrived at the site of Fort Selkirk on 13 August 1887 where they met Dawson's group, which had travelled via the Stikine River, Dease Lake, and the Liard and Pelly Rivers. Originally, the rendezvous had been planned for 20 July but Dawson too had been delayed and had arrived only two days earlier. Unable to find any evidence that Ogilvie had passed the point, Dawson's party began building a new boat, hoping that they could make the trip upstream without going to Forty Mile for additional provisions.[47] The parties stayed together for about five days, Ogilvie spending three of them on "a correspondence designed to satisfy my friends and acquaintances for the ensuing twelve months." This done, the Dawson party started upstream, their work easier now that they had Ogilvie's map and extra provisions. Ogilvie watched them go with "a feeling of loneliness that only those who have experienced it can realize."[48] Then, on the morning of the 19th, after a day spent taking magnetic and astronomic observations, Ogilvie resumed his survey downstream.

After stops at the mouths of White and Stewart Rivers, the party reached Forty Mile on 7 September. Here, Harper and McQuesten, pioneer traders, were building a new post following exciting gold discoveries on the Fortymile River the preceding summer. Ogilvie ran a short survey up that river and then continued downstream on the Yukon, reaching the boundary area on 14 September. Next came the search for an observatory site. Two things were needed, the best possible view of the horizon and, more difficult to find, a twenty-two-inch diameter stump to serve as the base for his portable astronomical transit.[49] The precision instrument, essential for the longitude determination, weighed about four hundred pounds. By replacing the awkward stand with brass plates that could be screwed to a stump, Ogilvie had cut its weight in half. After two days of searching, covering four miles on both sides of the river, the only tree that came close was a mere eighteen inches at the required height of five feet, and, even worse, it was on a steep hillside. There was nothing for it but to secure blocks on the sides of the stump to bring it up to the required diameter and build their winter quarters on the hillside, close to the observatory. Later, Ogilvie would find that the stump swayed alarmingly in the cold weather, probably owing to the heaving of the frozen soil it was rooted in. A small, open-roofed, transit house was built around the stump, and while Ogilvie set up and adjusted his transit, the rest of the party set to work on their winter quarters:

> After clearing away the top soil and excavating some distance into the side of the hill for a foundation, the bottom round of the house was laid and imbedded in the place so cleared; the next round of logs was then put up and fitted into place; it was then rolled off, and on top of the first round was laid a thick layer of moss; the second round of logs was then put back in its place on top of the moss which was so thick that the second round did not lie on the saddles at the corners, but rode on the moss. This was done with each succeeding round until the requisite height was reached, when the ordinary kind of shanty roof, consisting of poles, was put on. On these was laid a layer of moss about one foot thick, and on this about one foot of clay. In the roof were two ventilators, which could be closed altogether if necessary.
>
> To heat the building, a large stone furnace was built, in size about 3 by 8 feet; the front end of this was fashioned into a fireplace, with an oven on top for cooking; the other end was formed into a chimney. The structure was a large mass of stones bound together by a tough, white clay, which we found in the vicinity, and which baked hard and white and did not crack with the heat. When this mass was once heated, which took two days to do, it retained the heat for a long time.
>
> With the weight of the roof and walls the moss between the logs was so pressed that it filled every crevice, and almost made a solid wall. During the winter the ventilators were kept open all the time; yet the lowest temperature observed in the house during our stay was 48° Fahrenheit; the average in the morning before the fire was lighted was about 60° Fahrenheit.[50]

Their winter quarters nearing completion, Ogilvie began the observations needed to determine latitude and longitude. Readings were taken as selected stars or the moon transited or crossed the meridian of his station. From his star observations, Ogilvie could determine both latitude and local time directly. Longitude was more difficult since it represents the difference between local time at the observer's meridian and that at the Reference or Zero Meridian in Greenwich, England. But, by making lunar observations, the corresponding Greenwich time could be derived from lunar tables published in the Ephemeris covering the period of his observations. Two types of observations were made. In moon culminations, the local time at which the moon transited the meridian was obtained through a series of readings. In an occultation, the moon passes between the observer and a star, eclipsing the latter, and the local time of disappearance and emergence was recorded. The computations involved in both methods are labourious.[51]

For Ogilvie, there was no simpler, more direct method. The chronometers available at the time would suffice for approximate determinations of longitude, such as Raymond's at Fort Yukon, but instruments capable of keeping accurate time over long periods and during extreme temperature variations were still unknown. Even in 1877, observing stations were being linked by telegraph, permitting the transmission of time signals and more accurate measurement of time differences. But this was no help to Ogilvie with the nearest telegraph line more than a thousand miles away in southern British Columbia.

Ogilvie completed his first set of observations in late September, soon after he adjusted his instruments, but then, as a result of clouds and storms, it was late November before he completed a second. He had planned to observe about sixty occultations during this period, but none were seen. By the time he abandoned his camp in late February 1888, Ogilvie had observed twenty-two moon culminations and three occultations. Preliminary calculations of the longitude of the observatory had been completed, Ogilvie putting the probable error in longitude at about three seconds of time or three-eights of a mile on the ground.[52]

Early in February, Ogilvie and two of his men set out to mark the boundary on the Fortymile River, at the time the centre of the placer mining activity in the area. There was deep, soft snow along the Yukon River, and it took three days of heavy going to reach the settlement of Forty Mile at the mouth of the river. After two days of resting and preparation, the survey of the Fortymile River was picked up and continued through to the boundary, about twenty-three miles upstream from the settlement. The line was marked by blazing trees on both sides of the river and marking a few with "A" for Alaska on the west side and "C" for Canada on the east.[53] Luckily, on the north bank, there was a natural marker in the form of a narrow, rocky spur about 150 feet high separating the channels of two tributary creeks. For the miners, Ogilvie's blazes were the first warning that their complete freedom from control by either government would soon be over. For the moment, most of the placer workings were on the Alaska side, while the miners themselves were wintering around the post at Forty Mile. On his return there, Ogilvie spent several days explaining the strict Canadian placer laws to a group of independent men, mostly United States citizens, accustomed to setting the mining laws at a miners' meeting. Both sides would benefit, and later, when the rush came, a new, more practical set of placer regulations were in force in Canada, thanks mainly to Ogilvie's efforts.

His work on the boundary completed, Ogilvie began preparations to travel northeast to the Mackenzie River system. By mid-March 1888, Ogilvie and the four men of his party fit to make the trip had moved most of their outfit down the Yukon River to the mouth of the Tatonduk River, a total distance of about twenty-five miles in a straight line. They had some help from miners wintering nearby, but though they asked all winter, there were still no signs of help from the local Indians. Growing anxious, Ogilvie made an offer of $2.50 a day for each team and driver, double the going rate, to a lone Indian who visited his camp to size up the situation. It did the trick, and three days later, nine men and thirty-six dogs appeared at the camp. After a day spent cooking food and arranging loads, the party began the journey up the Tatonduk River. En route, Ogilvie made a rough survey by taking compass bearings and estimating distances by time and rate of travel. In addition, "as no member of the Geological Survey staff was likely to pass here for generations, I paid more attention to the geology as I went along than I had heretofore done, and collected specimens of the different rocks I saw."[54]

When they left the Yukon River valley, the nature of the country began to change. After three or four miles, the valley of the Tatonduk closed in around them, and about twelve miles upstream they passed through a canyon about fifty feet wide and half a mile long where the river had cut a vertical slot, more than five hundred feet deep, through cream-coloured limestone. At a total of eighteen miles up on the main branch, or North Fork, the valley began to open out again, but by now it was carpeted by a heavy moss with a few widely spaced, stunted spruce trees. Many of the surrounding mountains, up to two thousand feet above them, were capped by buff-weathering cliffs of limestone resembling the ruins of a giant wall. At times, Ogilvie caught glimpses of the smooth upland surface behind it through slots or, in one case, a spectacular hole eroded through the wall.

After about fifty miles, Ogilvie looked out on the headwaters of the Tatonduk and the country beyond from a pass between two mountains they had taken to avoid a canyon on the river. "From this point up the valley is wide, with low sloping sides which end some twelve or fourteen miles up in a large plateau, and beyond this, some twenty miles, the peaks of the Nahoni range break the view to the north. This is one of the grandest views I have ever seen, and profound stillness and vast solitude impress one as perhaps few other scenes in the world would."[55]

Leaving the Tatonduk River at a point where it turns north towards the mountains, the party followed a side stream to a low ridge separating it from tributaries of another river that could be seen running east for thirty miles or more. The Indians assured him that the new river was a tributary of the Peel River, but Ogilvie could hardly believe that it could head so close to the Yukon drainage, and

> it was not until they had drawn many maps of the district in the snow, and after much argument with them, that I gave credit to their statements. I then

proposed to go down this stream to the Peel, and to reach the Mackenzie in that way, but at this they were horrified, assuring me as well as they could by word and sign that we would all be killed if we attempted it, as there were terrible canyons on it, which would destroy us and everything we had; in fact, we would never be heard of again, and they might be blamed for our disappearance. . . .[56]

At this point the Indians turned back. Nothing that I could say or offer to them would induce them to go any farther with their dogs, and it was with much difficulty that I persuaded two of them to go ahead with one of my men, and make a track as far as the head of the Porcupine. I paid off the men with the dog teams on the morning of 22nd of March, when they returned to their families. The other two, with my man, started for the head of the Porcupine, a distance of about fifteen miles. They returned on the 25th, and took their departure for home.

These people have a great dread of a tribe who, they suppose, dwelt at one time in the hills at the head of these streams and still exist somewhere in the vicinity, though exactly where they do not know. While on this plateau they spoke of them in a low tone, as though fearful that they would be heard and punished for their remarks, which were not at all complimentary. They called this tribe Na-hone; I have generally heard the word pronounced Na-haune by the whites. It appears that they inhabited the headwaters of the Liard and Pelly, and were much fiercer than the neighboring Indians. Probably rumors of their aggressiveness have reached these simple and peaceful people, and created this dread, for they do not appear to have ever seen anything to justify their fears, and when questioned they could not tell anything more definite than that some old man among them had seen some indescribable thing on the mountains when he was a boy, or at some other remote date. They described them as cannibals, and living altogether outside, without shelter from the cold, and believed them to be such terrible creatures that they required no cover, but could lie down anywhere to rest, and did not need a fire to cook their food, but ate it raw. They seemed to ascribe to them supernatural powers, for, when I was trying to induce them to go on farther with me, and showed them my rifle, and told them I would shoot any Na-hone who attempted to molest me, they gave their heads an incredulous shake, as if that was too much to expect them to believe. To whatever it is due, this dread appears to be lively, so much so, that I believed only some pressing necessity, such as hunger, would induce them to remain in this locality for any length of time, and then only if they were in strong force.[57]

Left on their own, Ogilvie and his four men manhandled their equipment, including the two canoes, the 16.5 miles to the Porcupine River and another 18 miles along its valley. It was heavy going and finally, on 10 April 1888, Ogilvie decided to camp and wait for breakup. A small hut with a canvas roof was put up in the wooded flat beside the river. Despite the elevation of about two thousand feet and the proximity of the Arctic Circle, the vegetation resembled that along part of the Yukon River about 350 miles to the south. Many of the spruce trees were over a foot in diameter, and there were scattered clumps of good-sized cottonwoods. The area had not been hunted for many years, and the abundant game paid little attention to the new arrivals. During the wait, Ogilvie plotted his survey from the Yukon River, and, in May, made rough determinations for latitude and longitude, despite the difficulties in observing in the now-continuous twilight of the north. On 29 April, the snow showed the first signs of melting, and the next day the first insect life appeared in the form of a small fly that seemed to come out of the river. Houseflies and mosquitoes followed over the next two weeks.[58]

Finally on 28 May, the party set out by canoe even though the river was still not completely free of ice. Aside from occasional waits for the ice to move, the first ten miles was relatively easy. At that point a large jam blocked the river and the party portaged three-quarters of a mile around it only to have the jam burst and the river clear, leaving them little better off for all their effort. About thirty miles from their starting point, the river left the mountains and meandered through a wooded undulating plain. By now they were in the area hunted by the Indians from Lapierre House on the Bell River, a tributary of the Porcupine. They reached that post on 6 June after a false start up the Eagle River and problems with the ice on the Bell River. To get through, the party would run their canoes straight into the sheets of ice which, if rotten or candled, would break into tiny, tinkling fragments on impact. If the sheets were still solid, the crew would jump onto them and drag their canoes across. Working through moving ice, they would have to haul out the canoes the instant the grinding ice threatened to trap and crush them. The wood and canvas canoes were a great novelty to the local Indians, and they were astonished as the apparent ease with which the Ogilvie party travelled.[59]

The Hudson's Bay Company post at Lapierre House was a small one, kept mainly to supply meat to some of their other posts. Hunting had been good with some thirteen hundred moose and caribou tongues shipped during the year. From Lapierre House, Ogilvie followed the summer route to Fort McPherson via the Bell River, McDougall Pass, and the Rat and Peel Rivers. Once again there were problems with ice, including a four-mile portage through the pass, but the party were on their way home and nothing could hold them back now. They arrived at Fort McPherson just before noon on 20 June 1888.

Three days later, travelling down the Peel River, Ogilvie rounded a bend and encountered R.G. McConnell and his party. As part of the Yukon Expedition, McConnell had ascended the Stikine River with G.M. Dawson, crossed to the Liard drainage, and followed that river to the Mackenzie, wintering at Fort Providence. Now, he was planning to cross the divide to the Porcupine River and descend it to the Yukon. The pair spent the next day together, Ogilvie jubilant that the hardest part of his journey was over and McConnell disturbed by Ogilvie's description of the rapid current he would have to battle in ascending the Yukon River.[60]

For Ogilvie's party, the canoe voyage ended when they reached Fort Chipewyan on Lake Athabasca in late summer. By now, he estimated the party had used the canoes for about 2,500 miles of river work and had portaged them for about 170 miles. He left them there, still in fairly good condition, noting that "with a little painting, they would go through the same ordeal again."[61]

The Yukon Expedition had been remarkably successful. As his part, Ogilvie had marked the International Boundary at the point where it was most likely to be questioned by the miners, and, together with Dawson and McConnell, he had mapped and described what would later become the main routes to the Klondike.[62] Considering the reconnaissance methods used, their work proved to be uncannily accurate when new maps, compiled from field work and aerial photographs, were finally published about seventy years later!

UNITED STATES COAST AND GEODETIC SURVEY 1889–91

In 1889, after a lapse of twenty years, United States field parties returned to make an independent determination of the 141st Meridian on the Yukon and Porcupine Rivers. Their methods would be the same as Ogilvie's and the latter was asked by the Canadian minister of the interior to prepare a report and supply information to them.[63] There were two ten-man parties, with J.E. McGrath in charge of the Yukon River work and J.H. Turner, the Porcupine. In addition, I.C. Russell of the U.S. Geological Survey accompanied the McGrath party.

The group arrived at St. Michael in early July 1889. The settlement, now a post of the Alaska Commercial Company, still showed signs of the earlier Russian ownership, including two of the old blockhouses and the red octagonal church surmounted by the double-barred cross of the Russian Orthodox Church. The spring rush was on, and the town was crowded with a cosmopolitan group including local Eskimos, Indians from the Porcupine River area, missionaries of several denominations, agents of the A. C. Co., miners from the interior, officers and sailors from the U.S.S. *Thetis* anchored in the roadstead, a number of mechanics brought in to assemble a new steamer, and the men of the survey parties.[64]

Only one steamer, a second *Yukon,* was available, and her boiler was condemned. A new boiler had been brought in, but in their rush to get away, they decided to attempt one more trip using the old one. Finally on 14 July 1889, the party left for the Yukon River, the men and equipment crowded aboard the *Yukon* and the two ten-ton barges and a whaleboat she had in tow. Even so, there was not room for everything, and the bulk of the provisions for McGrath's Yukon party were to follow once the new "knock-down" steamer was assembled.

Luckily, the weather was calm, and aside from dense fog, there were no incidents on the risky trip through the open waters of Norton Sound to the protected water of the Yukon River delta. Now, it became a steady battle against the current of the river as the *Yukon* struggled to make her way upstream. By now, the passengers were becoming more familiar with their crew which, according to Russell, "consisted of a captain of Scandinavian birth, an engineer from Finland, and a dozen or more Eskimos. The natives acted as pilots, assistant engineers, firemen, wood choppers etc., and did their work with remarkable efficiency. Even when the rough captain was too drunk to manage affairs, the crew navigated the dangerous rapids, and made landings for wood, in a way that spoke volumes for their intelligence and faithfulness."[65]

With frequent stops for "wooding-up," emergency boiler repairs, or at the native villages, the *Yukon* made her way to above the mouth of the Tanana River where

> we awoke one morning and found our little steamer struggling with the strong current where the river passes between bold bluffs known as the Lower Ramparts. For an hour or more no perceptible advance was made, and at times the little boat was carried slowly down stream in spite of its quick puffing and the cloud of spray thrown up by the paddle-wheel at the stern. As a last resort, a heavy wrench was hung on the safety valve, in disregard of all regulations of steamboat inspectors, and sufficient steam pressure obtained to enable the brave little craft to ascend the swift water and gain the broad quiet reach of the river above.[66]

Unexpectedly, when the boat crossed the Arctic Circle near Fort Yukon, the passengers suffered from the intense summer heat filling the river bottom. "The temperature in the shade was at times above a hundred degrees of the Fahrenheit scale. There was scarcely any relief from the heat at night, but only a prolonged twilight connecting the discomforts of one day with those of the succeeding day."[67]

Turner's Party on the Porcupine River

At the site of old Fort Yukon, now marked by a broken chimney, several mounds of ashes, and a few graves, the *Yukon* dropped off the McGrath party and then ascended the Porcupine River with Turner's. It was the first time a steamer had attempted the translucent green water of the Porcupine, and after three days of following countless meanders and struggling against the current, Captain Petersen had had enough. The river was falling the whole time, and now the soundings showed that it was impossible to go ahead. In fact, there had been so many shallow places on the way up that if he waited longer, it might not even be possible to return to Fort Yukon. There was only one thing to be done, and on 6 August 1889, Turner and his party were hurriedly dropped off and the *Yukon* turned downstream. Turner's calculations indicated that the point lay some thirty-seven miles west of the boundary, and it was certain to be much farther than that following the windings of the river. There was nothing for it; the party would have to make their way upstream as best they could. Rampart House, the Hudson's Bay Company post opposite the mouth of the Salmon Trout River, lay somewhere ahead, and for the moment at least, there could be no help from there. To their chagrin, the river now began to rise, gaining two feet in the next ten days, and if the *Yukon* had only waited they could have steamed right to the boundary!

On New Year's Day 1890, Turner, still upset, wrote his superintendent in Washington about the struggle that followed:

That the steamer had reached the head of navigation for August 6th is beyond dispute. A change of one week one way or the other in the date of the steamer's arrival would have saved the party three fourths of the hardships which they have undergone since that date. The whaleboat *Lottie* brought from San Francisco and one of the A.C. Co's lighters kindly placed at my service by Capt. Petersen were used for tracking our supplies up the river.

On August 8th the lighter with the whale boat in tow started on its way up the river. Besides the services of the members of the party, excepting [two] who were left at the lower camp, I had secured four Indians to assist in pulling the boats up the river. Difficulties were encountered at the outset — the lighter being of a heavy draught ran aground several times and the rapid current proved almost too much for the men on the line.

By dint of great perseverance we succeeded in making about three miles the first day, being thoroughly fagged out. The next day on rounding a bend the current caught the lighter and but for the opportune dropping of the anchor the whole force on the line would have been jerked over the bank into the current and several doubtless drowned. In fact one Indian hung suspended by the neck over the brink for several minutes, barely escaping being strangled by his harness. At this point Otto Polte twisted his ankle so badly as to render his left foot useless for many days.

Shortly after this mishap the lighter ran aground: the continued exertions of the whole party failing to even start her. The anchor was thrown well upstream, the whaleboat loaded to the water's edge, and Polte left on the lighter to remain until our return. An Indian boy was left with him to minister to his wants. On August 11th we reached Rampart House during a thunderstorm!!!

Observations at the Rampart House placed it . . . 20 miles west of the boundary line. Having borrowed Mr. Firth's boat [the Hudson's Bay Company trader] and stowed it with some provisions and axes on 12th August, I started up the river accompanied by [four others], for the purpose of locating the Boundary and selecting a camp site. The whale boat had been sent back to bring up another load. While in camp for the night up the river, an Indian paddled up in his canoe. He brought a note from . . . the cook enclosing another from Polte which stated that Andrew Codhead the lead Indian on the line had been drowned while attempting to take the tow-line across the river. This deplorable accident had frightened the other Indians. One of them at least, entertained murderous thoughts, as he borrowed Polte's rifle under pretense of going on a hunt. This Indian, Peter Brule by name, was discovered by Mr. Firth, who was on his way down to arrange matters, seated alongside the trail for the purpose it was subsequently ascertained of shooting Polte, as soon as the lighter approached. However, an Indian in the H.B. Co's employ spoke to him, and warned him of the serious consequences that would certainly follow such an act of foolishness. Some weeks afterwards another Indian fell overboard and narrowly escaped drowning. His death would have led to open warfare with the Indians, who notwithstanding the efforts of the missionaries still cling to their superstitions and are prone to lay all their misfortunes at the doors of strangers.[68]

On 18 August 1889, Turner selected a site for his Camp Colonna at the mouth of Sunaghun Hun (Old Wife's River) which, according to his preliminary observations, lay just to the east of the boundary line. Returning to Rampart House the same afternoon, Turner found that the lighter and the whaleboat *Lottie* had already been brought to that point.

The whale boat made several more trips to the lower camp often in charge of the Indians, whose honesty, (in such unlooked for quarters) surprised me. Four skins ($2) per day for each man together with a certain allowance of tobacco, tea, meat, crackers and molasses, was the tune to which they dispoiled the strangers. Before everything had been finally landed on the Bluff at Camp Colonna their wages reached a good figure. The American dollar, hitherto unknown, grew suddenly popular and many desired their pay in coin. This coin invariably flowed into the coffers of the H.B. Company from whence I borrowed it to pay it out again. By lowering prices on cotton drilling, thus bringing it much into demand, I was enabled to hedge considerably on the total expense, by avoiding payment in coin. . . .

By the 17th September the whole outfit (excepting some flour and meat stored at Rampart House) had been transported fully 50 miles upstream in the face of a rapid current and numerous mishaps: a space had been cleared in the forest and a house erected thereon fifty feet long and fifteen wide with a projecting T fifteen by twenty feet. Although great assistance was derived from the hiring of natives, yet it is to the members of the party that the praise is due. . . .

By the fourth of October the house was ready for occupation, doors, windows etc. having been fitted, stoves put in place etc., the astronomical observatory, a log structure ten feet square, was already finished and the meridian telescope in position.[69]

Everything was ready but now there were unexpected difficulties with cloudy weather and fog. It was 6 November before Turner could complete his first observation, and by New Year's only one occultation and eleven moon culminations had been obtained. In addition, the Arctic winter was closing in around the party: "The days rapidly shortened as the season progressed, and on November 16th the sun in his course southward disappeared beneath the horizon. During the shortest days lamps were extinguished at 11 A.M. and lighted at 1 P.M. By 2 P.M. observations upon the stars were perfectly practicable. This state of affairs continued until January 26, on which date the sun reappeared. As the first feeble rays of the luminary struggled through the frost-laden windows the spirits of the men brightened and, rushing forth from the cabin, they capered about like mad men in an excess of joy."[70]

On 27 March 1890, Turner together with two members of his crew, John Firth, the trader, and three Indians started north on an expedition to follow the boundary line to the Arctic Ocean. The party used four sleds each pulled by four dogs. But there were unexpected problems, and by the third day, both chronometers had failed, making quick determinations of longitude out of the question and "the exploration degenerated into sort of a rough reconnaissance." Surprisingly, there was little concern over the route as two of the Indians had already travelled it. At the time, there was occasional trade with the Eskimos. Wolverine skins were exchanged for Walrus hide, and the Eskimos, in turn, traded the skins, to passing whalers for whisky or breech-loading Winchester rifles. After crossing a divide between the Porcupine River and the Arctic Coast drainage, the party passed through a "bewildering mass of broken ranges" and followed a frozen river to the Arctic Coast. "On April 10th we reached the Arctic Ocean opposite Herschel Island. A gale blew in from the Southeast sweeping the fine snow in blinding clouds before it obscuring objects a half mile distant. The thermometer stood at 30 below Fahrenheit. There was no sign anywhere of a spring thaw. On the following day the wind abated somewhat and the air cleared, revealing frozen sea to the limit of vision. A line of white hummocky ice skirted the shore, not a living thing was visible on the landscape. At one P.M. after having made some observations and ascertained the meridian altitude of the sun we turned homeward arriving at Camp Colonna six days thereafter, having made the round trip of 400 miles (approximately) in 18 days."[71]

On their return, they completed the triangulation in the camp area and erected three large monuments on the approximate boundary line. Finally, on 15 July 1890, their work completed, the party started downstream aboard two lighters belonging to the A.C. Co.[72] The first lighter was the one left them by Captain Petersen, and the second was transferred to them by Mr. Wallis, an Anglican missionary, on the condition that they deliver it to an agent of the company. They were still mapping; Turner's assistant took sextant observations for latitude, and Turner himself completed a plane table survey of the 210 miles of river to Fort Yukon. His method was much the same as Ogilvie's on the Yukon River. A man travelling in a skiff preceded the main party and set poles for azimuth or bearing lines. Distances were measured by micrometer and the topography of the surrounding country sketched in as much as possible. They reached the mouth of the Porcupine River on 6 August 1890 but had to wait until 13 August when the steamer *Arctic* arrived. They set off the next morning but, delayed by storms and poor weather, the party did not reach St. Michael until August 30. Once again their luck failed them; the Revenue Cutter, *Bear,* had sailed for San Francisco eight days earlier, and no other ships were expected. Instead of a quick trip to San Francisco and home, they faced another winter in the north. Bitterly disappointed, they tried to make the best of it. A new observatory was soon built and observations made for time, latitude, longitude, and azimuth. In addition, they produced three topographic maps and recorded meteorological, magnetic, and tidal observations. Finally, on 9 July 1891, the party escaped from St. Michael aboard the steamer *St. Paul* and arrived in San Francisco in early August. Once the excitement of homecoming was over, all that remained was the office recalculation of Turner's observations and a nagging dispute with the A.C. Co. over their bill, $10,000 above what Turner considered reasonable.[73]

McGrath's Party on the Yukon River

McGrath and his party did survey work around Fort Yukon while waiting for the *Yukon* to return from the Porcupine River trip. On 12 August 1889, they started upstream on the Yukon River again, arriving at Ogilvie's observatory a week later. The buildings, quickly renamed Camp Davidson, were in good condition, and the new occupants set to work to clear them out and modify them to suit their needs.[74] No time was wasted and it took less than a week to get the heavy timbers of a new twenty-two by twenty-six foot building in place. Others in the crew were busy whipsawing lumber or cutting firewood and rafting it to camp. Their own preparations for winter were going well, but there was still no sign of the new steamer *Arctic* and the main supplies. On the last day of September, McGrath inventoried the provisions on hand, trying to decide what to do if their supplies failed to arrive. At the moment, they had enough for two full months with the exception of kerosene, which was nearly gone. If they had to leave, every day they hesitated lessened their chances of reaching food before ice jammed the river.

Early in October, there was word that no supplies could be expected that fall.[75] The *Arctic* had set out on her maiden voyage only to be lost within 10 miles of St. Michael.[76] Caught in a sudden storm while at anchor to wood up, she had tried to get underway but fouled her towline in the paddlewheel, drifted onto a rock, and sank a few minutes later. Much of the cargo had been salvaged and was at St. Michael, while one lot had been brought to a point about 150 miles below Fort Yukon. McGrath read the news to his party at Camp Davidson, then announced that he intended to stay but that the others were free to do as they wished. All agreed to stay, and, in turn, they were guaranteed an equal share of the remaining food.[77]

Miners in the Forty Mile area, about forty miles upriver from Camp Davidson, faced the same situation. Many chose to flee downriver in search of food and on 10 October half a dozen boatloads of miners, "the advance guard of the Hegira," arrived at the camp to prepare the lighter left by the *Yukon* for the trip downstream.[78] Later the same day the tiny steamer, *New Racket,* arrived jammed with miners and promptly set off downriver with the lighter. McGrath sent two of his men along with instructions to hire dog teams and bring up what supplies they could or, if unable to do that, to do everything they could to safeguard them for the winter.

For those remaining at Camp Davidson there were two unexpected sources of food; a plentiful supply of game in the area and a bumper crop of turnips from trader Jack McQuesten's garden at Forty Mile. By the following spring, they had eaten their way through some thirty-five hundred pounds of game, mostly caribou, and nearly a thousand pounds of turnips.[79] There was little else; many of the staple items were missing, and each man's bread ration worked out to about two ounces per day. Perhaps as depressing as the diet were the short winter days. December and January seemed almost endless. There was enough light to work outside from about 10 A.M. to 3 P.M., but it was always too dark to read inside, and there was barely enough kerosene to keep a lamp burning for four hours each day.

During October 1889, McGrath had an unexpected problem with Ogilvie's work of 1887–88. The latter reported that he had marked the boundary on both sides of the Yukon River, but McGrath, perhaps distracted by his other problems, had to search until late October to find the first mark, a blazed tree, and, even then, took another two days to find a similar mark on the opposite bank.[80] Everything was ready at the observatory, but the weather continued cloudy, and aside from two observations in November 1889 there were no more until the following March.

As the winter dragged on, the entries in McGrath's daily journal grew shorter. On 28 November he wrote: "Thanksgiving day — River froze across to the other shore today for the first time. First sled of the season arrived today, about 4 P.M., with 150 lbs. of flour, for us, from 40 Mile Creek."[81] But on 25 December the sole notation was "Christmas Day." By early January he was writing: "Party employed as on yesterday" opposite each day, and by late in the month even this was shortened to: "party employed as usual."

But by late March 1890, the men were at work digging ditches about the camp to carry off the snow water, and in mid-April, McGrath and five of his party set out to run a traverse to Forty Mile and on up the Fortymile River to the boundary. But, once again, their luck failed, and, caught in a spring blizzard, they were forced to abandon their chaining and push on to Forty Mile. From Forty Mile, where observations were made, the party travelled close to twenty miles up Fortymile River, reaching the boundary in a single day. The following day was spent at Ogilvie's line making observations for time and latitude, and over the next few days, they completed a traverse back to Forty Mile. Once again, chaining along the Yukon River had to be given up, this time as a result of soft snow, water on the ice, and two men down with painful cases of snow blindness.

On 2 May 1890, three days before the ice broke, the two men sent downriver for supplies in October 1889 arrived back at Camp Davidson.

> The two men ... set out for the main camp in February with a hand sled & a toboggan drawn by 3 dogs. These they loaded with flour and beans knowing how scant our lot was and after 70 days of a journey got into our camp on May 2nd, having traveled 350 miles and most of this gone over thrice, as they could not haul their load all at a time. They would go forward with half, cache it & then go back for the remainder. When they reached us they had only the clothes on their backs, one pair of blankets & no coats but on their sleds were 200 pounds of flour. For the last days, they cut off the tops of their boots to feed the dogs, gave them deer sinew and line from the toboggan & whatever they could spare; their own clothes they cached on the road. There were 32 miners at winter quarters where these men stopped; a half dozen started out with them ... and out of the whole number not one got more than 40 miles up the river. The names of the two men are James McLarty and Jas. A. French.[82]

Despite everything the party had gone through, McGrath was still not satisfied with the observations he had been able to complete. In mid-June, he sent word to Washington, D.C., via the first downriver steamer that he intended to spend another winter at Camp Davidson. The supply situation was still uncertain; some of the salvaged goods from St. Michael had arrived, but about a third of them were completely spoiled. By late August the situation improved with the arrival of the resurrected *Arctic*. Once again there had been a close call in the open water of Norton Sound:

> She encountered some rough weather and for a period of almost two hours every man on board thought she was lost. Her frame is still weak and in a moderately heavy choppy sea she seemed so pliable that all hands were momentarily expecting the steam pipe to snap; the boiler swayed to and fro, and the pipe carrying steam to the gauge broke. After the troubles of last year another week would be ruinous for the people in here. Even as it was, the steamboat did not get up one day to soon, at [Forty Mile] the man in charge of the store ... had cooked his last flour on the morning of the boat's arrival.

The goods remaining at St. Michael this Spring and a small surplus that Mr. Turner had were brought up on the *Arctic* and we now have an ample supply for the time we must remain; a big lot of our coal oil was also on board and there will be no lack of light in the camp this winter.[83]

On 20 June 1891, McGrath took time off from packing his equipment to write to Superintendent Mendenhall of the Coast and Geodetic Survey:

The autumn months last year proved very unfavorable for us: September being marked by almost continuous rain and October & November being very cloudy — still we were more fortunate in securing nights to observe moon culminating stars than we were last year, and, in addition, the occultations of two stars were observed; last year I secured none. . . .

This Spring the gap that remained between this camp and the traverse line from the Boundary Mark on [Fortymile River], was closed by the measurement, with a steel wire, of about 28 miles down the Yukon River on the ice. An expedition also was made to determine chronometrically the difference of longitude between this station and the Trading Post located at the mouth of [Fortymile River].

Plenty of provisions came up for the party last year as a great many of the articles that were wrecked in 1889 . . . were sent to this point together with some supplies from the Alaska Commercial Company's stock at St. Michael. . . . As it happened that the traders at [Forty Mile] did not receive much of a supply, the extra quantity that came to us was a welcome addition to the stock in the country and has been a material benefit to White and Indians. Everything we could spare, almost, was eagerly picked up, the white men paying for their goods in gold dust and the Indians trading meat, moccasins, etc. for their share. Game was very scarce and a good many white men had to depend to a far greater extent than they liked upon flour and turnips.[84]

Starting downriver soon after, McGrath and his party did a running survey of the river from Camp Davidson to Holy Cross Mission on the Lower Yukon. By now, worried by upstream winds that reduced the speed of their barge to about a mile an hour and the possibility of missing the Revenue Cutter *Bear* at St. Michael, McGrath accepted a tow from the mission steamboat and abandoned his survey. The party reached St. Michael on 28 July well before the arrival of the *Bear* on 1 September. Finally, on 2 October 1891, they were back in San Francisco.[85]

Later, office computations of McGrath's observations gave a result very close to Ogilvie's determination, and for the moment at least, both countries accepted Ogilvie's lines at the Yukon and Fortymile Rivers as their temporary boundary.[86]

WILLIAM OGILVIE RETURNS TO THE BOUNDARY, 1895-1896

In the summer of 1895 Ogilvie returned with a party of six men to mark the Alaska Boundary from the Yukon River south to Sixtymile River, a distance of about fifty-five miles.[87] Once again he travelled by way of Dyea and the Chilkoot Pass, but this time it was an easier journey with pack-horses available to take the loads from tidewater to Sheep Camp at the base of the steep climb into the pass itself. From there his old friend Skookum Jim and the latter's cousin, Tagish Charlie, were on hand to help pack the loads to Lindeman Lake. This time there were three canoes, and the trip down the Yukon River was more leisurely, in part owing to bad weather. It was the last day of August when the party reached Forty Mile.

There were many changes since Ogilvie's last visit early in 1888. The town had grown and McQuesten and Company, agents for Alaska Commercial Company, had put up a large warehouse. A new trading post, Fort Cudahy of the rival North American Transportation and Trading Company, had been built across the Fortymile River and about a mile downstream along the Yukon River. In addition, Inspector Constantine of the North-West Mounted Police had brought in a nineteen-man detachment in late July, and his men were at work building their post, Fort Constantine, about five hundred feet south of Fort Cudahy. In addition to his police duties, Constantine had been appointed Canadian government agent, acting initially as magistrate, gold commissioner, land agent and collector of customs.

Ogilvie spent several days with Constantine. It must have been awkward; the two had met previously in Ottawa after Ogilvie turned down the agent's job, and they had differed on the number of police required. Maintaining there had never been trouble in the area, Ogilvie insisted that twenty would be enough, and he had finally carried the day. On a personal level there was mutual dislike. Ogilvie was still furious over an abortive winter trip to the Taku River area he had been ordered to make as a result of the wondrous stories the citizens of Juneau fed to the gullible Constantine on the latter's reconnaissance trip north in June 1894. The Taku trip had taken over three months, and when Ogilvie, half-starved, returned to Juneau on 1 March 1895 he was met with the news that his second son, sick when he left Ottawa, had died almost six weeks earlier.[88]

Ogilvie must have been glad to escape the police post and head downriver, even if it was to find his old quarters "pretty well wrecked" and the observatory itself burned.[89] It was quickly rebuilt and everything readied for winter. This time there was no problem with fresh meat, the caribou migration came right through their camp, and there were literally thousands of the animals milling around the camp for more than a week. "Our houses were objects of great curiosity to them, and numbers would swim over, approach the buildings cautiously, whistling and snorting as they did so. They often came so close and were so noisy that they became a nuisance, and we would go out and chase them away."[90]

When Ogilvie checked his transit, he found that dampness on the trip in had changed a system of thirteen vertical and horizontal cross-hairs in the instrument into

> a useless mass of lines, some in, some out of focus. . . . I repeatedly dried them, thinking I might make them serve, but after a few hours in the cool, damp atmosphere, they were as bad as ever. Finally one of them became detached at one end, fell across the others, and rendered them completely useless, there being a lump of glue attached to the loose end.
>
> A diligent search for several days discovered no spider lines that could be used to replace them, and I was hopeless of doing anything with the transit this winter until one day I discovered that a solution of India-rubber I had might with careful manipulation furnish what I wanted. I tried it, and after several attempts succeeded in getting five fair threads on in the place of the original five, ten seconds apart. These [vertical] wires posses the virtue of always being taut by reason of the elasticity of the rubber, so temperature does not affect their positions, but they stick together like gum if they touch, so that I could not use a [horizontal] micrometer wire, and consequently cannot get latitudes with the zenith telescope bubble.[91]

Using the longitude determined in his 1887–88 work, Ogilvie ran a careful triangulation and traverse survey from his observatory to the boundary line at the Yukon River, a distance of about three miles. His original mark, found by micrometer methods, proved to be 109 feet too far to the east, and from his new mark he moved the line 42.5 feet farther west to have the line cross the Yukon River at the mouth of a small creek, forming a natural landmark.[92] Before the cold weather set in, the line had been run five miles to the north of the river and seven miles to the south. Nothing more could be done for the moment, and Ogilvie paid a brief visit to the Forty Mile community. On this and other winter trips, the party used hand-drawn toboggans to carry their outfit.

> After sending my last report I left Cudahy on the 12th January [1896], reaching the boundary on the 13th, when I immediately set to work reducing the observations I had taken of lunar culminations up to that date, six in number, on one of which both limbs of the moon were observed, making seven determinations of the longitude.
>
> After my return there was some fine clear weather in January, but it was exceedingly cold, more than 60° below zero, one night 68.5°; and as I had both my ears pretty badly frozen and could not go out in such cold without having them covered, so that I could not hear the chronometer beat, I could not observe until the end of the month when we had two fine nights — 29th and 30th — mild enough for me to work. On the 29th I again observed both

limbs, the moon on both these occasions being suitable full at transit here. This makes in all ten different determinations of the longitude to be summed, with my work of 1887–88, and as most of my observations then were on the first limb, and most of these on the second, the total result is better balanced.

Having reduced all my observations, and the days having attained a reasonable length, I went into camp on the line on the 20th February, resuming work on the 22nd. But as the hill tops are all bare and from two to three thousand feet above the river we lost many days through the fierce winds.

Our progress was necessarily slow for this reason and also from the fact that I photographed from several stations, which took some time. As there were no important creeks between the Yukon and Fortymile Rivers I did not cut the line out continuously, but left it so that any one wishing to can place himself on or very near to the line. The distance from the Yukon to Fortymile River is a little over twenty-five miles. In the valleys along the line the timber was thick, with much underbrush, but very little of it is of much value. Curiously enough the line kept generally in the valleys or on the sides of them and very little of it was in the open. Going from point to point we had to follow as much as possible the hill tops and ridges. I reached Fortymile River with this survey on the 13th March. From this point southwards there are many streams cut by the line, all of which are more or less gold-bearing and all have been more or less prospected. This necessitated my cutting the line out continuously from Fortymile River onwards, which increased our work very much. The valleys traversed are generally upwards of 1,000 feet deep and often very steep, so that the work was exceedingly laborious.

Transporting our outfit from camp to camp was often a very hard task as the hills were so steep every thing had to be packed up them, which in the deep soft snow was anything but easy. I reached a point within two miles of Sixtymile River on the 14th April, and as I had passed all the creeks of any note, and many of them were already running water and our way lay down them, I thought it well to quit work on the line and return to Forty Mile and Cudahy, and attend to the local surveys there. The weather was fine and warm and so much water ran in the creeks by which we had to return that we could only travel a few hours in the early morning and forenoon. Had the season been more favorable I would have visited Glacier and Miller Creeks which were generally supposed to be in Alaska but are found to run in Canada for some distance. They are the two richest creeks yet found in the Yukon and both tributaries of Sixtymile River. Both creeks are fully located and worked, each claim being 500 feet along the creek and the width of the valley or creek bed. There are nearly 100 claims, all of which pay well. One on Miller Creek I understand will yield 75 to 80 thousand dollars this season and the owner will net, it is said, between 40 and 50 thousand dollars. He took out, it is reported, nearly half that sum last year off the same claim and expects to do equally well next year. This is much the richest claim yet found, but all on these creeks do well. There are many other creeks in this vicinity yet to be prospected and some will, I have no doubt, pay well. Gold is found all along the valley of Sixtymile River and under more favourable conditions, both mercantile and climatic, it would yield good results to large enterprises. The mercantile conditions will improve: the climate is a serious difficulty but will be surmounted in time I believe. Along the last 10 or 12 miles of the line I ran, the mountains consist principally of quartz and schists, which no doubt originally held the gold found in the valleys and doubtless hold some yet. Several men have taken to quartz prospecting, and from indications . . . I believe we are on the eve of some magnificant discoveries.

The miners on all the creeks referred to have quietly accepted my line as the boundary *pro tem,* and as far as I can learn at present the general feeling is satisfaction that one can now know where he is. Even if the line is not final, no one doubts its being very near the final position. The line as far as run is marked by cairns of stones wherever it was possible to procure them with reasonable time and labour, and is cut through the woods and blazed so that no one who wants to find it can mistake it. Another source of satisfaction to all is that they now know distances and directions. Many miners remark to me "we now know how we are going, and can see where south is." In this high latitude in the summer months it is impossible to tell when the sun is near the meridian because its change in altitude is so little for 8 or 9 hours, consequently any point between east and west was called somewhere near south. This helps to explain much of the variance in the direction of points as given by miners and others who have no compass or are unacquainted with the use of one and the application of the declination.[93]

On returning to Fort Cudahy with his party, Ogilvie rented two cabins from the trading company, carefully explaining the added expense "because there are no convenient camping places in the vicinity and in the spring all the flats are like lakes along the river until well into the month of June."[94] After a few days of well deserved rest, Ogilvie began preparations to make other local surveys. On 15 May 1896, he sent official notice of his boundary survey to Inspector Constantine, adding a qualification that the line as he had marked it was not binding on either Canada or United States since it was approximate, made solely to enable Canada to exercise authority until such time as a joint commission should fix the final location.[95] Constantine, as government agent, would have to deal with the miners in the Sixtymile gold field who, quite unexpectedly, found their claims lay in Canada.

Accompanied by two policemen, Constantine arrived at Miller Creek on the afternoon of Sunday, 31 May 1896. The trip from Fort Constantine had taken four days, two to ascend the Fortymile River to the mouth of Moose Creek, just upstream from the boundary, and two to back-pack the twenty-five-odd miles along the ridge line and over the divide into the Sixtymile River drainage. Constantine spent three days at Miller Creek and two at Glacier Creek explaining the Canadian mining regulations to the miners and making entries for their claims. A few miners protested Constantine's authority, pending a joint survey of the line, but after making their point, all recorded their claims and paid the $15 entry fee.[96] Most paid in gold dust, accepted at $17 an ounce, Constantine collecting $1,000 in that form and a mere $20 in coin. Fortunately, the claim size of five hundred feet measured along the course of the creek coincided with that set by miners' meetings when the creek was first staked. Of more immediate concern was the miners' worry that the Canadian government would demand a royalty on the gold produced.[97] Completing their work on Glacier Creek in the evening, the party walked all night, arriving at the mouth of Moose Creek after fourteen hours on the trail. After a few hours rest, they set off down the Fortymile River by boat, arriving back at Fort Constantine early in the evening. All in all, it had been a hard ten days for Constantine, who was more accustomed to directing operations from his base at the Fort.

Less than a month later, Constantine's authority was challenged by a miners' meeting held on Glacier Creek. Such meetings had been the only form of government when neither country cared about the remote area and they were destined to continue for a few more years on the Alaska side.[98] The meetings, called by the miners themselves, fixed mining regulations for the camp and dealt with both civil and criminal matters. The general procedure was to elect a chairman and secretary, then the disputants were asked to state their case, other evidence was heard, and after an open discussion, the vote was taken. The verdict, determined by majority vote, was carried out promptly. Since imprisonment was out of the question, the most common punishments were fines or banishment from the camp, the latter a virtual death sentence in midwinter.

The meeting in question was called on 28 June 1896 by labourers employed on Claim No. 19 Above Discovery on Glacier Creek. The claim was owned by Messrs. Van Wagener and Hestwood, and it had been recorded and entry fees paid when Constantine visited the creek early in June. However, since late August 1895, it had been leased to another miner, who had employed the labourers and had now skipped the country without paying $800 in wages. The miners' meeting had ordered Van Wagener and Hestwood to pay the $800. If they failed to do so within a given time, the claim would be sold to satisfy their judgment. A committee had been appointed to carry out the orders of the meeting. The owners had appealed to Constantine for protection, and he had sent a notice to the camp warning the miners not to proceed. The notice arrived about three hours after the forced sale, and when he read it, the highest bidder had backed out and another miner, Jerry Baker, had taken the claim for $1,075. Baker had offered the balance of $275 to Hestwood, but the latter had refused it and sent word to Constantine by special messenger.

Forewarned, Constantine was ready when Baker appeared at Fort Constantine on 4 July and attempted to register a bill of sale prepared by the committee and signed by twenty-three miners. He refused to accept it and dispatched Inspector Strickland, his second-in-command, and eleven other ranks to take possession of the claim. Constantine and the few men remaining at the fort would stand by, prepared to support the party if necessary. The part was well armed; each man carried a Lee-Metford carbine and forty rounds of ammunition in addition to their regulation service revolvers and twelve rounds for that. Baker, meanwhile, had left for the creek "breathing defiance and saying that the miners would see him through."[99]

In reporting to Constantine, soon after his return to the Fort, Strickland wrote:

> After a very hard walk over a villainously mountainous country we reached Glacier Creek and went to Messrs. Van Wagoner and Hestwood Claim No. 19 Above Discovery, the seat of the trouble. Mr. Hestwood informed me that Jerry Baker had put a man in possession of the claim. I ejected this man and warned Jerry Baker to attempt no further occupation of the place. I saw the Chairman of the committee appointed by the miners and gave him a similar warning. I think they saw the force of our argument as one of the committee took to the brush immediately on our arrival at the creek. The better class of miners on the creeks are in favor of law and order and seem to be glad that the so-called laws made by miners' meetings are null and void. Several of the miners of the worst class indulged in some big talking and were very anxious that I should call a meeting of the miners to explain the law to them. I gave a decided refusal to this proposition, stating, that on your previous visit to the creek, you had explained the law on the point at issue to them clearly — further that you had sent them a written notice which they have chosen to utterly ignore and that my present business on the creek was not to talk but to act. They had nothing further to say to this. I remained on the creek two days and finding that things had quieted down and receiving the assurance of the principal parties concerned that no further trouble would ensue I left Glacier Creek on the morning of Thursday the 10th July for Fort Constantine arriving there about 1 A.M. of Friday the 11th July.[100]

In the rush to get to Glacier Creek, the armed police party had cut a corner too by deliberately trespassing in Alaska. Ignoring Ogilvie's newly cut line, they had continued up the Fortymile River to the mouth of Moose Creek and then followed the established trail along the ridge. With no prisoners to bring back, the party had taken the same route on the return trip, saving themselves several miles of struggling through the muskeg along Ogilvie's line. The miners were talking about it but, other than that, there was little they could do aside from some who might "write all kinds of stuff to the American papers."[101]

Ogilvie, anxious to return to Ottawa and not involved in the Glacier Creek incident, waited at Fort Cudahy for the Yukon River to drop enough for him to make reasonable time on the upstream journey to the passes. During the period, he surveyed some mining claims and then the Fort Cudahy and Forty Mile townsites, the latter "the worst jumble I ever saw."[102] Early in the summer there was word from Ottawa that negotiations were underway with the United States for a Joint Commission to mark the International Boundary and Ogilvie, who would be the Canadian commissioner, was ordered to stay in the area and await further instructions.

He was still waiting early in September, and as yet, there was no sign of another Canadian mail. Uncertain what to do, he wrote to the surveyor general on 6 September 1896, sending the letter downriver with the A.C. Co's steamer *Alice*. His tentative plan was to go out with Jack Dalton and map the latter's trail from Fort Selkirk to Chilkat Inlet. In addition, there was another piece of news:

> I am very pleased to be able to inform you that a most important discovery of gold has been made on a creek called Bonanza Creek, an affluent of the river known here as the Klondike. It is marked on the maps extant as Deer River and joins the Yukon a few miles above the site of Fort Reliance.
>
> The discovery was made by G.W. Carmack, who worked with me in 1887 on the coast range. The indications are that it is very rich, indeed the richest yet found, and as far as the work has been carried on it realizes expectations. It is only two weeks since it was known, and already about 200 claims have been staked on it and the creek is not yet exhausted: it and its branches are considered good for 300 or 400 claims. Besides there are two other creeks above it which it is confidently expected will yield good pay, and if they do so we have from 800 to 1,000 claims on this river which will require over 2,000 men for their proper working. . . .
>
> News has just arrived from Bonanza Creek that 3 men worked out $75 in four hours the other day, and a $12.00 nugget has been found, which assures the character of the ground, namely, coarse gold and plenty of it, as three times this can be done with sluice boxes. You can fancy the excitement here. It is claimed that from $100 to $500 per day can be made off the ground that has been prospected so far.[103]

Less than a week later, the Canadian mail arrived bringing Ogilvie word that negotiations with the United States for a Joint Commission to survey the 141st meridian had collapsed and that he should return to Ottawa for the winter. Ogilvie's work on the boundary was over. There was no need to do anything more on it at the moment; it was already marked where mining was underway, and there could be no question that the newly discovered Klondike lay in Canada. After waiting two weeks for the A.C. Co.'s *Arctic,* expected hourly on her way to Fort Selkirk, Ogilvie prepared to start upriver by canoe. On 25 September, two days before he planned to leave, a tremendous snowstorm swept in, and when it ended the river was choked with ice, both up- and downriver. Feeling that the $1,000 it would cost him to travel by dog-team could be better spent making a survey of the Klondike, Ogilvie decided to stay in for another winter. It was a momentous decision; without his presence the history of the Klondike might well have been different.

Over the winter Ogilvie undertook a number of surveys including the Dawson townsite and an adjacent forty-acre government reserve. But the most serious problem he had to deal with involved the staking on Bonanza Creek. Once again, most of the trouble arose from a miners' meeting, this one held on the creek on 22 August 1896 with twenty-five men present.[104] At it, they decided that a "survey" of the claims already staked on Bonanza Creek should be made using a fifty-foot length of rope as their measure. The adjusters had worked down the creek, covering more than fifty claims in an afternoon and making changes as they went along. One claim staked near 12 Below was arbitrarily moved to 50 Below, while others were shortened or lengthened and, in a few cases, simply struck out. Constantine, as government agent, had compounded the mess by accepting the results of the "survey." Soon after, Constantine had second thoughts and requested Ogilvie to make an accurate survey of the claims.[105] Ogilvie refused, stating that there was nothing he could do until the original parties involved agreed to accept the results of his survey. Meanwhile, mining some of the claims was out of the question until it was certain who owned them and where the boundaries of the claims lay.

Finally, after a delegation of miners called on Ogilvie and a petition drafted by him was circulated, Ogilvie agreed to undertake the survey. As nearly as possible, the original staking was retained and the miners' "survey" done away with where it conflicted with earlier staking. There was some "wild and woolly" talk but nothing came of it; one of the most belligerent miners meekly accepting a one-hundred-foot fraction instead of a full claim.[106] By mid-April, when melting snow made further work out of the question, Ogilvie had completed surveying 120 claims on Bonanza Creek and an additional 50 on Eldorado Creek.

Through the winter, Ogilvie and others in the camp had tried to send word of the Klondike discovery to the Outside, the miners term for the world beyond the Yukon basin. The news was beginning to spread, and Ogilvie was in Dawson on 16 May 1897 when the ice on the Yukon River went out and two hundred boatloads of stampeders arrived in Dawson.[107] By mid-July 1897, when Ogilvie left for St. Michael aboard the *John J. Healy,* a gold commissioner and police reinforcements had already arrived. Aware of developments through Ogilvie's reports, Clifford Sifton, Canada's new minister of the interior, would soon begin preparations to send a large party of government officials to the Yukon. Unfortunately for the Yukon and its miners, many of the new appointees, unlike Ogilvie, took more interest in the spoils system and their personal fortunes than in good government.[108]

Despite their intense personal dislike, Ogilvie and Inspector Constantine of the Mounted Police complemented one another.[109] It was Ogilvie, friend to all the miners, who could travel quickly in the district and settle disputes on the ground while "the agent," as Ogilvie referred to him, spent most of his time at Fort Constantine, complaining that he needed more men and, most of all, a steamer or steam launch of his own in order to carry out his duties. He would never understand, let alone appreciate, the independent spirit of the restless miners who had made their way into the god-forsaken country in the search for gold. To him, they were riffraff and he worried constantly that they would hoist the American flag and ask for protection. Still, the police were fair, and in the rush to follow, it would be respect for them and a few dedicated government officials like Ogilvie that made a confrontation out of the question.

3

Staking a Claim to the Panhandle
(1876–96)

THE PETER MARTIN INCIDENT AND A TEMPORARY BOUNDARY ON THE STIKINE RIVER,
1876–77

After 1840, when the Hudson's Bay Company leased the mainland portion of the Panhandle, the actual location of the boundary line meant very little. There was no need for company men to travel the country; its fur trade was bottled up between coastal stations and inland posts reached from the Mackenzie River. But the isolation was ending, especially after 1862 when Captain Moore took his sternwheeler, the *Flying Dutchman*, up the Stikine River. The first gold rush had been short-lived, but other miners were still searching. The Hudson's Bay Company had followed them, building a temporary post about 135 miles up the Stikine River in the summer of 1867.[1] A year earlier the river steamer *Mumford* had landed thirty-three thousand pounds of telegraph wire at the site of Telegraph Creek, part of the Western Union scheme to build a land line to Europe via Alaska and Siberia.[2] The scheme collapsed the same year with the successful laying of the first trans-Atlantic cable, and the wire was hauled away. But, like the phoenix, it would return in 1901 when a land line from Dawson to Ashcroft, B.C., was laid over a long section of the original route.

In 1867, the United States had purchased Alaska on an "as is, where is" basis with the boundary description with British territory copied word for word from the Anglo-Russian Treaty of 1825. In 1872, the government of British Columbia had asked the government of Canada to discuss a joint survey of the boundary line with the United States government. President Grant recommended it in his message to Congress of December 1872, but aside from cost estimates, nothing further was done.[3]

Then in 1873, the placer creeks of the Cassiar gold field were discovered.[4] They lay about seventy-five miles northeast of Telegraph Creek, and the Stikine River was the only practical route to the new camp. By 1874, about fifteen hundred men had joined the rush, and Canadian and United States customs officials were squabbling over the collection of duties. At one stage, a Canadian insisted that all goods for the Stikine should be declared at Victoria or Esquimalt, in effect prohibiting direct sailings from Wrangell.[5] Later that summer a Canadian customs post was established on the Stikine, and before long the Americans were complaining that it lay in their territory. There were more discussions about a joint survey of the boundary, but nothing was done. Things drifted for another year, when, unexpectedly, the boundary question was brought to a head by the actions of one man, Peter Martin, sometimes known as "Bricktop."

Martin claimed to be a United States citizen despite doubts raised by "a fresh Irish accent," and according to one observer, he "came to the Cassiar mines with a bad reputation and . . . his constant study and endeavour was to sustain it."[6] At a court held at Laketon, B.C., in early September 1876, he had been sentenced to three months for escaping custody to be followed by an additional twelve months at hard labour for assaulting a police officer. Serving the sentence in the Cassiar was out of the question, and the local authorities dispatched him to Victoria, via the Stikine route and under escort by two special constables.

On 21 September 1876 at a lunch stop on the lower Stikine, Martin, restrained by handcuffs, had grabbed a shotgun loaded with buckshot and pointed it at Frank Beegan, one of his guards, calling out: "Now, you son of a bitch, I've got you."[7] It became a contest between the two with Beegan, now armed with a small five-shot revolver handed him by the other guard, and Martin glaring at one another from behind trees about forty feet apart. Neither the other guard nor others travelling with the party came to Beegan's assistance. Beegan fired twice, missing both times, and then Martin dropped to his knees and took aim. He missed in turn, and then Beegan's revolver misfired. Beegan rushed Martin but stumbled just as he reached him, and Martin broke the stock of the shotgun over Beegan's head and shoulder. During the ensuing struggle the revolver went off, the bullet ploughing a furrow through Beegan's cheek and coming out just under his eye. Finally, the other constable and an Indian travelling with the party came to Beegan's aid and subdued Martin. The constables were not taking any more chances, and Martin was put in leg irons in addition to handcuffs before the party set out again in the canoe. At the mouth of the Stikine, Martin was put directly aboard the British steamer *Grappler* while Beegan went into Wrangell for medical attention.

Martin insisted that the incident had taken place in Alaska and that he, an American citizen, had been held illegally by the Canadian constables. Six weeks after the fracas, Hamilton Fish, United States secretary of state, made the initial protest to the British ambassador in Washington.[8] Canada was not fully independent at the time, and the formal chain of communication between Washington and Ottawa ran from the British ambassador, to the foreign Office in London across to the Colonial Office, from there to the governor general, the Queen's representative resident in Ottawa, and from him to the Canadian government. It was hopelessly slow and all too easy for notes to cross along the route or be misunderstood. In dealing with less important matters one or more of the steps were often bypassed, and, at times, there was direct, but unofficial, communication between the American and Canadian governments.

Martin was something of a celebrity when his trial began in Victoria in mid-December 1876. He asked that the American counsul be present at the trial, and this was agreed to, although the consul took no part in the trial itself.[9] Martin, conducting his own defence, questioned the two special constables and an American citizen who had been travelling with the party at the time of the incident. None were certain of the exact location on the Stikine, let alone what country the incident occurred in. The judge preferred the opinion of the American witness, who placed it at between ten and twenty miles from the mouth of the river. In his address to the jury, the judge stated that, in his opinion, the lunch stop had been in Canada or, failing that, in territory that was in dispute. If the latter, Canadian law would still apply since each country would handle its own affairs.[10] The jury found Martin guilty of assaulting a constable, and he was sentenced to an additional twenty-one months at hard labour to be served on completion of the Laketon sentence.

Martin joined the Victoria chain gang, but the diplomatic correspondence over the incident continued. Finally, in March 1877, the surveyor general of Canada instructed Joseph Hunter, a civil engineer from Victoria, B.C., to proceed to the Stikine and mark his interpretation of the boundary on the ground.[11]

Hunter and his party travelled north on the Hudson's Bay Company steamer *Otter* and were in camp near the mouth of the Stikine River on 2 April 1877. Point Rothsay, starting point of the survey, was identified and monumented by an eight-foot post banked up with a pyramid of earth. From there, the survey was carried upstream for almost fifty-four miles with the angles turned off by transit and distances measured by chaining. The river was still frozen, and most of the work was done on the river ice.

Hunter monumented two points on the river, one 53.99 miles upstream at the point he considered ten marine leagues distant from the general line of the coast and the second 24.74 miles upstream where his interpretation of the line "following the summit of the mountains situated parallel to the coast" crossed the Stikine River.[12] The latter was no easy matter to determine from the river bottom, and a study of present-day topographic maps suggests a number of lines, almost all west of Hunter's choice. North of the Stikine, Hunter chose Elbow Mountain lying in the Great Bend of the Stikine where the river changes course from south to northwest. South of the river he chose Mount Whipple, about thirteen miles southeast of Elbow Mountain and the highest peak visible from the river bottom. From Mount Whipple, he ran his line westerly to Mount Cote and from that peak north across the Stikine to Elbow Mountain. On both sides of the river, Hunter marked his line by large posts set twenty to thirty feet above high water mark and protected by cribbing six feet high.

In addition to marking the line, Hunter had been ordered to fix the location of the Peter Martin incident of the year before. Frank Beegan, one of the special constables involved, was with the party. He was unable to recognize the exact spot since the ground was still covered with snow and some of the trees in the locality had been cut in the interim. However, a spot believed to be within one hundred yards had been pointed out by Beegan. It lay about thirteen miles from the mouth of the river or about eight and a half miles within Alaska from Hunter's line.[13] Their work completed, the party was back at Wrangell by early May 1877 and in Victoria about two weeks later.

More diplomatic correspondence followed, and, finally, in mid-September 1877, Canada's minister of justice recommended that Martin be released. In official communications no mention was made either of the lunch stop incident and Hunter's line or of Martin's discredited claim to American citizenship. Instead, the reason given was that the unauthorized conveyance of Martin through the Panhandle was an infraction of United States' sovereignty, and, as such, that country could demand his release.[14] By early March 1878, both the United States and Canada had accepted Hunter's line as their temporary boundary, pending a final decision and a survey. By this time, Peter Martin, set free on the first anniversary of the lunch stop incident, had gone on to other things and was in a Washington State jail, sentenced to a year at hard labour for attempting to smuggle a case of brandy from Canada.[15]

CANADA FUSSES OVER THE PANHANDLE, 1884-92

For the moment, Hunter's 1877 line at the Great Bend of the Stikine River was the only boundary on the Panhandle. Neither country was satisfied with it, each certain that a correct interpretation of the 1825 Treaty would see the line shifted in their favour. Things drifted until April 1884 when William H. Dall of the U.S. Coast and Geodetic Survey raised the boundary question in replying to a note on another matter from George M. Dawson of the Geological Survey of Canada.

The matter of the boundary should be stirred up. The language of the treaty of 1825 is so indefinite that were the region included for any cause to become suddenly of evident value, or if any serious international question were to arise regarding jurisdiction, there would be no means of settling it by the treaty. There being no natural boundary and the continuous range of mountains parallel to the coast shown on Vancouver's charts like a long caterpillar, having no existence as such, the United States would undoubtedly wish to fall back on the "line parallel to the windings of the coast and which shall never exceed the distance of ten marine leagues therefrom" of the treaty. It would of course be impracticable to trace any such winding line over that "sea of mountains." I should think that the bottom of the nearest valley parallel to the coast might perhaps be traced and its stream form a natural boundary; even then it would be difficult to determine the line between one valley and the next. Before the question has attained any importance, it should be referred to a committee of geographers, a survey should be made and a new treaty should be made stating determinable boundaries. Perhaps at some time you may be able to set the ball in motion on your side, and it would be only a matter of time when it would follow here.[16]

Dall's suggestion was not followed up, but it served as a warning that the boundary question could not be put off indefinitely.

By now, the British Columbia government was worrying the text of the 1825 treaty. Their interpretation was that the words "along the channel called Portland Channel" in Article III should be ignored since: "From all the information that [this] Government can obtain it has reason to believe that those words will not be found in the original, or if there, the term has been misapplied—not as to where the Portland Channel really is, but as to its being the channel contemplated by the Treaty."[17]

By dropping the reference, they ran the boundary north through Clarence Strait, Behm Canal, and Burroughs Bay to the 56th parallel of latitude, putting Revillagigedo Island and a number of smaller islands in Canada. The concept was the brainchild of Mr. Justice J. H. Gray of the British Columbia Supreme Court, who had been interested in the boundary question since he conducted the assizes at Laketon in 1876. The Canadian government never took British Columbia's interpretation too seriously, and, in 1880, one expert summed it up when he wrote: "As the Provincial Government has officially asked the Dominion Government to maintain this contention, and as some defence of it may be undertaken as an 'outwork,' if nothing more, I would suggest that its criticism may be left to the United States authorities."[18]

In 1886, another interpretation that was taken more seriously was put forward by Colonel D. R. Cameron in memos and reports to Britain's Colonial Office.[19] Cameron, living in England at the time, had been the British boundary commissioner when the 49th parallel was surveyed from Lake of the Woods to the

Rocky Mountains between 1872 and 1876. He maintained that inlets less than six miles wide became territorial waters at the point where the three-mile limits met, and, as such, they were no different from fresh-water lakes or streams. From his study of the correspondence leading up to the signing of the 1825 treaty, he was certain that neither the British nor the Russians considered the inlets as forming part of the coast. With the inlets out of the way, a boundary line following the summits of the mountains parallel to Cameron's "coast" would lie close to the latter, cutting across the inlets near their mouths. Surveying it would be relatively simple as most points on it would lie within a few miles of tidewater. Cameron also pointed out that Captain Vancouver had given the name "Portland Canal" to the narrow body of water lying north of Kanagunut, Sitklan, Wales, and Pearse Islands rather than to the larger inlet to the south, the "Portland Inlet" of the current maps.

In 1887-88, during fisheries negotiations between Great Britain and the United States held in Washington, arrangements were made for Dall and Dawson to meet informally on the Alaska Boundary question.[20] They met several times in February 1888. Dawson, armed with Cameron's interpretations, hoped to obtain some concessions from Dall. Instead, he found that they disagreed on the meaning of the boundary description in the 1825 treaty and that Dall was unwilling to consider anything that might involve a loss or transfer of territory. Alternate schemes to mark the boundary at a number of points along the Panhandle were discussed, but fixing these required agreement on the boundary description. Failing all else, Dawson hoped that the two governments might come to some arrangement to allow the transport of prisoners and to waive customs duties for miners taking supplies into the Yukon.[21]

In December 1888, the superintendent of the U.S. Coast and Geodetic Survey wrote directly to Canada's minister of the interior and invited the Canadian government to send three or four parties to take part in surveys along the Panhandle during the coming summer. The purpose of the work would be to fix the position of a number of accessible points and make a topographic reconnaissance to obtain "the geographical information requisite to the proper negotiation of a Treaty establishing a boundary."[22] The Canadian government declined the invitation, maintaining that the boundary was already defined by the 1825 treaty.

In August 1889, the Canadian government attempted to learn what surveys, if any, the Americans were making along the Panhandle boundary. Their agent was Otto J. Klotz, assistant chief astronomer, acting on verbal orders from the deputy minister of the department of the interior.[23]

Klotz hurried to Victoria hoping to charter a steam schooner, but with one exception, all were away working at salmon canneries along the coast. The one, the *Saturna*, forty-six feet long and of sixteen tons burden, was offered for sale at $4,500. Buying it was out of the question, and Klotz decided to go north on the *Corona*, a commercial steamship on the Tacoma to Sitka run. In addition, he made arrangements with Canadian customs to land at Port Simpson in hopes of arranging a charter either from there or from a nearby point.

Travelling incognito, Klotz boarded the *Corona* on 15 September 1889. He was in luck; among his fellow passengers were the pilot of the U.S. Coast and Geodetic Survey vessel *Carlile Patterson* and a number of other American government officials. Klotz pumped the pilot for information about the ship and the survey work. Then, at Juneau, he succeeded in photographing the ship herself.

Klotz learned that the *Patterson* and her crew has been engaged in hydrographic work in Stephens Passage, south of Juneau, during the past season. In the work, they had measured base lines three to four miles long using a continuous length of piano wire supported by boats about a quarter to half a mile apart. A tension of thirty pounds per mile was applied to the wire to keep it taut, and the length of the wire was carefully measured while under tension. From stations at the ends of the base line other stations were sighted in by theodolite, and with the angles and the length of the base line known, distances to them could be calculated by trigonometry. The triangulation net thus developed was carried along the passage, and the location of lines of depth soundings was determined from triangulation stations along the shore. They had done no inland topographic work aside from sighting in some of the more prominent mountain peaks and occupying stations on the occasional hilltop easily reached from the shore.

Klotz saw a great deal of the Panhandle on his trip. The *Corona* called at most of the settlements, including the canneries at the head of Chilkat Inlet and the now-defunct Haines Mission on Chilkoot Inlet. There was even a tourist trip to Glacier Bay and an opportunity to walk along the eastern flank of the Muir Glacier for a few miles. From there the ship turned south again to call at a cannery in Bartlett Cove. Klotz was unimpressed by the settlements, with the exception of Juneau where the great Treadwell gold mine was operating on Douglas Island. Sitka was a "picturesque but dilapidated . . . capital, whose glory is buried in past generations" and Wrangell simply a "deserted village."

At every stop Klotz would question the inhabitants about survey work in the area, but as far as he could learn, nothing was being done other than the work from the *Patterson*. Surprisingly, one of his best sources of information was the Canadian customs officer at Port Simpson, less than twenty miles south of the tip of the Panhandle. It turned out that the port was the base station used for all the longitude determinations in the Panhandle. There were two reasons for this; British navigators had determined the longitude there before the American surveys got underway, and the settlement, with its Hudson's Bay Company post, was an excellent place to store the American launches for the winter. On the trip north from San Francisco, the *Patterson* would call at Port Townsend to check the ten chronometers aboard with a direct telegraph circuit from Washington, D.C., and then continue on to Port Simpson. At the latter, astronomic observations were made for local time and the chronometers checked once more before continuing on to the work in the Panhandle. The same procedure was repeated on the trip south in the fall.

After returning to Victoria, Klotz decided to visit the U.S. Coast and Geodetic Survey office in San Francisco. He was still asking questions, and his hosts must have guessed the reason for his visit. However, he did pick up two pieces of information. The first was that McGrath's and Turner's parties had been sent to Alaska to mark the 141st meridian on the Yukon and Porcupine Rivers, and the second, that a triangulation survey of Portland Canal had been done in the summer of 1888. Klotz was shown the plan of the latter, and noticing an astronomic station on the west side of the Bear River at the head of the Canal, he made a mental note of the latitude of 55° 56' marked beside it.

Following his trip, Klotz prepared a map showing his interpretation of the boundary line according to the 1825 treaty. He rejected Cameron's conclusion that it should cut across inlets less than six miles wide and instead ran it around the heads of all the inlets although seldom more than a few miles from tidewater.

In September 1891, W. F. King, Canada's chief astronomer, set out on a month's cruise along the Panhandle coastline aboard the *Vigilant*, a small steamboat belonging to the Indian department.[24] Before starting out, King made his own interpretation of the 1825 treaty, and as he worked his way north, he marked his proposed boundary directly on the latest charts of the U.S. Coast and Geodetic Survey. To King, a "mountain" had a peak rising above timber line, the "summit of the mountains" referred to the summit ridge of individual mountains with lines joining adjacent ones being straight rather than following a watershed, and the "coast" referred to the general line of the coast, excluding inlets less than six miles across as territorial waters.

Near the southern tip of the Panhandle, King viewed Tongass Island where the United States Army had built their Fort Tongass in 1867. A company of artillery had been stationed there in 1869, but the fort had been abandoned soon after.[25] Some of the old barracks were still standing and King learned that there was now one man living there, engaged in salting salmon. From there, the *Vigilant* steamed through Sitklan Passage and Pearse Canal of present-day maps, which, by King's interpretation, were the "Portland Channel" of the 1825 treaty. King wrote of them:

> The channel called Portland Channel, or Canal, by Vancouver, which begins south of old Fort Tongass and runs inland between the mainland and Kanagunut, Sitklan, Wales and Pearse Islands is not the intricate and tortuous passage it is sometimes represented to be. It is deep and straight, though narrow, from its mouth to the southern point of Fillmore Island.
>
> Between Fillmore and Wales Islands are the only obstructions in the passage—a group of rocks and rocky islands which make caution necessary (in navigating an uncharted passage) for a mile or two only.

After this the channel widens out, and a few miles past the south-western end of Pearse Island becomes of the same width as the upper part of Portland Canal with which it is continuous in direction.[26]

From the tip of the Panhandle, the *Vigilant* worked her way north to Lynn Canal, poking into many of the larger inlets and, at times, moving out into some of the straits between the islands to allow King to catch a glimpse of the mountains on the mainland. King's proposed boundary line, seldom more than ten miles from the coast, cut across many of the inlets near their mouths. It crossed Lynn Canal at the first point the waterway appeared to be less than six miles across, roughly fifty-five miles south of present-day Skagway. King also disagreed with Hunter's line on the Stikine River, placing his own about fifteen miles farther downstream.

King concluded that the survey of his line "ought not to be a very difficult or expensive task, the mountains being so readily reached from the sea." But, in the next paragraph, he went on to express a nagging doubt: "If any of the interior ranges are taken as the dividing line the labour and cost will be incalculably increased."[27]

Following King's trip, there was increasing awareness among Canadian officials that time was on the side of the United States. The American survey parties had the coastal area to themselves, and it was the only practical starting place for carrying surveys inland to the contested area. Interest in the north was growing, and it was probably only a matter of time until the United States would be marking its boundary claim on the ground. With monuments in place, it would be difficult for Canada to hold out for an alternate line.

The break came early in 1892 when Canada accepted a counter-proposal put forward by James Blaine, United States secretary of state, calling for a joint survey of the contested portion of the Panhandle. On completion, the two countries would have the data necessary to establish the boundary "in accordance with the spirit and intent of the existing Treaties."[28]

THE ALASKA BOUNDARY COMMISSION MAPS THE PANHANDLE, 1893-95

On 28 November 1892, the two commissioners chosen under the Convention of 22 July 1892 met in Ottawa to begin planning the field work. The United States commissioner was T. C. Mendenhall, superintendent of the U.S. Coast and Geodetic Survey, and Her Majesty's commissioner, acting on behalf of Canada, W. F. King, chief astronomer of Canada's Department of the Interior.[29]

Faced with a two-year deadline, the commissioners decided to make the survey a joint one. Each country would provide its own field parties and carry the expenses involved. Initially, each party in the field was accompanied by an attaché representing the other country, but with one exception, this practice was discontinued after the first season. The work was divided: United States parties would work mainly along the larger river channels, while the Canadians mapped the topography of the intervening areas. In addition, the United States parties would improve the triangulation along the coastline and make additional astronomical determinations of latitude and longitude, all essential to providing a suitable base for plotting the new mapping. Temporary observatories would be built for the astronomic work, and the U.S. Coast and Geodetic Survey's *Hassler*, carrying nine chronometers, would spend the summers shuttling between them and the Sitka observatory to provide the accurate time checks needed in the longitude determinations.

Each country had its own interests very much in mind. The United States parties planned to erect markers ten marine leagues from the ocean, the boundary specified in the 1825 Treaty if no "summit of the mountains" lay inside this limit, while the Canadians were intent on proving that such a summit did exist and that it lay very close to tidewater. Opinion played a part, and at times as the work went on, surveyors who could agree on the location of their station above timberline would differ totally in their interpretation of the panorama of mountains and glaciers spread out before them.[30]

Eleven parties, four American and seven Canadian, were sent out in the 1893 season, their field areas strung out along the Panhandle from the Unuk River in the south to the Lynn Canal area in the north. Initially, the field men met in Victoria, B.C., in April 1893 when the *Patterson* put into port with the American crews aboard. Then, in early May, they met again in Wrangell, Alaska, when the Canadian parties arrived aboard the *Quadra*. The latter vessel, belonging to Canada's Department of Marine and Fisheries, was a last-minute substitute for the *Sir James Douglas* of the same department whose boiler had just been condemned. At the second meeting, final plans for the season were worked out between the party chiefs and W. F. King, the Canadian commissioner. Then, at five in the morning on 9 May 1893, the flotilla set out for the field areas north of Wrangell with the *Patterson* in the lead, followed by the *Quadra*, with the *Hassler* bringing up the rear.[31]

The United States parties built observatories near the mouths of the Unuk, Stikine, and Taku Rivers and attempted to mark the ten-marine-league limit on these rivers.[32] They were only partially successful. On the Unuk River, E. F. Dickens' party, working together with a Canadian one, was turned back by the raging torrent in the Second Canyon, about twelve miles short of their objective. In the Taku area, some two hundred miles to the north, the parties had better luck. One, led by J. E. McGrath, mapped Taku Inlet, while the second, led by H. G. Ogden, carried the survey up the Taku River, where the ten-marine-league line was marked by a brick pier resting on a cement base. By late July, all three parties had moved to the Stikine area to help out there.

The United States party in the Stikine area was led by O. H. Tittmann. Initially, the work had gone smoothly. An observatory had been built near

Wrangell and a base line measured on the river flats near Farm Island. Then, on 23 May, the party started upriver aboard the *Alaskan*, a small river steamer that made between three and seven trips a summer between Wrangell and Telegraph Creek, the number depending on business available and river levels. The party set off in high spirits, Tittmann and the Canadian attaché joking that they would put the boundary line at the first point the captain would sell them whiskey, a nominally illegal commodity on the Alaska side.[33] Half an hour later, a leaking joint in a steam line forced the *Alaskan* to anchor until repairs were completed at noon the next day.

Camp was set up on a sand bar near the upper mouth of the Porcupine River, about fifty-four miles upstream, and somewhere near the ten-marine-league marker left by Joseph Hunter in April 1877. Next morning, Tittmann and the Canadian attaché walked to the top of a small knoll overlooking the river.[34] Nothing seemed to match the maps and sketches they had with them, and they had no idea where to start looking for Hunter's marker, a big cottonwood tree cut off nine feet from the ground, squared for three feet, and protected by a crib of logs. Quite possibly it had been washed away as the braided channels shifted over the years.

That afternoon, Tittmann and some of his party made an exploratory trip down a side channel, the main river being too swift for their whaleboat. On landing about a mile below, they found themselves cut off from shore in a maze of sloughs and small channels. Even worse, with every oar manned, it took them three hours to row back to their starting point.

Next morning, Tittmann sent his crew out to cut a trail to below a difficult point on the side channel, but they came back without accomplishing anything after Tittmann's assistant cut his foot with an axe. Tittmann was in a "fit of discouragement" with his boats, an old whaleboat and two dories unsuited to river work, and with his crew, "all salt water sailors that did not know anything about poling, paddling or tracking and all too clever to learn river work in a short time."[35]

Stymied where they were, the party caught a ride on the *Alaskan* about five miles downriver to the lower mouth of the Porcupine River where the current was not so swift. From there, Tittmann planned to carry his triangulation downstream along the main river channel using stations about fifteen hundred feet apart. Problems continued; the river stayed unseasonably high, flooding the gravel bars that would have made the work easy and forcing the party to cut line through the tangle of alder and cottonwood along the shore.

Tittmann was in Wrangell when McGrath and his party arrived there on 3 July 1893. After listening to Tittmann's problems, McGrath decided that his dories would be useless on the river and arranged to have river boats made locally.[36] Less than a week later, McGrath's party, complete with their new boats, were dropped off by the *Alaskan* near Hunter's line at the Great Bend of the Stikine to carry the survey downriver. Tittmann returned to his camp upstream, by now convinced of the merits of river boats and canoes, preferably with Indians to man them.

On 8 August, Tittmann joined his triangulation to McGrath's at the Great Bend of the Stikine. From there, the party returned upstream to complete the additional three miles needed to reach the ten-marine-league line. Hunter's mark was never found, but Tittmann put in his own, a spruce post eight inches square referenced by a cross drilled on one nearby granite outcrop and a triangle on another and also by three bearing trees, suitably blazed and marked with copper tacks.[37]

Their work completed, Tittmann's party struck camp on 22 August 1893 and set off downriver to assist the other parties. On finding that McGrath had almost competed his work and that Ogden and Dickens who had filled in the lower ten miles of the river had already left, Tittmann continued on into Wrangell. Working from there, he spent the last few days of the season joining his triangulation in the area to earlier work by hydrographic parties. At last his party were back on salt water, working under conditions they were accustomed to. Field work was over by early September, and all the United States crews sailed for the south aboard the *Patterson* and the *Hassler*.

The Canadian parties, using photo-topographic methods, were involved in a different type of field work. For them, the main task was to establish camera stations located high enough in the coastal mountains to afford a clear view of the mountains and valleys farther inland.

The photo-topographic method, developed for mountain work, had been in use for about five years. Much of the initial work had been done by E. Deville, Canada's surveyor general.[38] From a camera station, accurately located by triangulation, a series of photographs were taken covering the full 360 degrees visible from that point. The specially designed camera was carefully levelled for each photograph and the centre line of each established by transit observations on known points. Later, in the office, the centre line and horizon line in each photograph were shown by reference marks on the edge of the glass plate negatives. With these, and knowing the focal length of the lens, the location and elevation of any prominent feature identified in photographs from two camera stations could be calculated. Next, using a framework of known points, the intervening topography could be sketched from the photographs. The new method replaced plane-table methods in which the surveyor sketched his interpretation of the topography directly onto a carefully oriented work sheet. The old method was final; little could be added or revised once the surveyor packed up his equipment and left the station. Now the photographs contained a wealth of information that could be used later to revise or extend the mapping.

Seven Canadian parties were sent out in the 1893 season. From south to north they were: A. Saint Cyr in the Unuk River area, O. J. Klotz to the north and northwest, A. C. Talbot south of the Stikine River, J. L. Gibbons north of the Stikine River, A. J. Brabazon on the east side of Stephens Passage, J. J.

McArthur north towards Juneau and William Ogilvie in the Juneau-Taku area. Klotz was assigned the steamer *Thistle*, chartered for the summer, with instructions to provide transportation wherever needed and to fill in any gaps in the work. In addition, he was to collect the glass plate negatives and develop some aboard the *Thistle* to make certain that all equipment was working properly.

Weather was poor throughout the Panhandle that season with less than one day in four clear. The Canadian parties spent much of their time simply waiting, in contrast to the Americans, who could do some work, albeit not too efficient, in the dripping river bottoms. On the very few clear days, the Canadians rushed to reach their camera stations, struggling through matted undergrowth and over rocks with a treacherous moss cover prone to slide off underfoot. Lower slopes were seldom dry; on bright sunny days a heavy dew kept the bush wet until close to noon. Long climbs were involved with some of the stations as much as seven thousand feet above sea level. Near the summits there were often large patches of soft snow to struggle through and all too frequently clouds of mosquitos and other biting insects would appear from nowhere to harass the surveyors. Where the pests came from and how they survived in the climate of the Panhandle was a mystery.

For Brabazon and the seven other men in his party, field work began on 10 May 1893 when the *Quadra* landed them at Holkham Bay, about one hundred miles northwest of Wrangell.[39] Within hours, beginnings of their first tent camp appeared on shore. During the season, the party could expect supply visits from the steamer *Thistle* about every three weeks, but aside from this, their transportation depended on a sailboat, about thirty feet long with a seven-foot beam, and a fifteen-foot canoe.[40]

Over the next few days, Brabazon and H. P. Ritter, the United States attaché, occupied stations at the ends of their base line, measured angles to prominent topographic features, and did photo- and plane-table-topography. Others in the crew were involved in chores such as camp improvements, getting in the wood supply, and readying the sailboat. Once these were done, the men had little to do but wait until the persistent rain and fog lifted and mountain stations could be occupied. In this slack time, one would-be hunter managed to get lost in the heavy brush on the lower slopes. He was in sorry shape when the others sent out to look for him found him on a beach about four miles from camp. Somewhere in his wanderings, he had fallen over a cliff, injuring himself and smashing the government rifle.[41] Brabazon's order not to go alone in future probably confirmed a decision already made!

Finally, early on the morning of 23 May, the party occupied their first mountain station, a peak on the east side of Endicott Arm. The peak was about sixty-two hundred feet above sea level, and the climb that morning was from a temporary camp at the fifteen-hundred-foot level. Looking inland, the surveyors could see portions of the high snowfields and the jagged peaks that towered above them. The party occupied a second mountain station a few days later. Early in June, they moved to a new camp on the south side of Endicott Arm, across from the entrance to Fords Terror. The weather had turned worse, and they could not occupy the camera station behind the camp to complete the needed photography before 8 July. It was the eighth try for the observing party, the first seven climbs all ending in failure when anticipated breaks in the clouds failed to materialize.[42] On the evening of 20 July, the weather cleared again, and the party, now camped at the head of Endicott Arm, occupied another camera station the next day. Then, on 5 August, Brabazon completed this portion of his work by reoccupying the initial camera station.

Next day, the crew embarked with their gear in the sailboat and started for the head of Port Houghton, a water distance of about fifty-four miles. The trip took four days, most of it spent battling strong headwinds. There was nothing for it but to row most of the day and seek shelter in small bays along the coast at night.[43] By the evening of 10 August a rough camp had been set up about a mile up the stream at the head of the bay. By midnight, the camp had been flooded out with two feet of water everywhere and still rising. One unfortunate, busy salvaging gear, fell in the creek over his head and was forced to wait out the rest of the night in his underclothes. A new, higher camp was set up and on 19 and 20 August the party's efforts were rewarded by two good days of observations. Part of the price paid included a crushed foot, countless bruises and scrapes, and faces swollen from fly bites. There were no more clear days, and on 2 September 1893, the party left for Wrangell aboard the *Thistle*.

The season was over. All told there had been ten clear days since the first of June. Brabazon and his party had made the most of them despite minor injuries, the dangers of working the sailboat and canoe close to moving icebergs, and, worst of all, the long depressing waits for a real break in the coastal weather.

The 1894 season was a better one for the surveyors of both countries. This year there were five American and seven Canadian parties in the field.[44] In addition, an observatory was built at Pyramid Harbor, near the head of Chilkat Inlet, and the *Hassler* shuttled the chronometers between there and Sitka.

For the United States, E. F. Dickens and his party returned to the Unuk River.[45] Starting upriver on 13 May, the party made good time walking on top of the frozen snow and towing their canoes. They passed the First, or Waterfall, Canyon in a few hours though it had taken two days in 1893, and they passed the Second Canyon just as the weather turned warm and the river began to rise. However the Third proved too swift, but by now the party was close to their objective, and the survey line was run along the top of the cliff overlooking the canyon. They finally reached their goal, the ten-marine league line, and marked the station using four large hemlock trees all suitably blazed and marked with copper tacks as references. By now the Unuk was rising at an alarming rate, and the party set off downriver as quickly as possible. Rounding a sharp bend, one of the canoes struck a sunken log and capsized, throwing Dickens and two of his men into the icy water. It was a close shave; the men were saved, though some of the instruments and equipment were lost. Soon after there was another close call when one of the boats was smashed and additional equipment lost. This year there was no steamer waiting for them at the mouth of the river, and the party had to sail a whaleboat through about fifty miles of inland passages to Loring, a small settlement north of Ketchikan. Finally, on 7 June, the *Hassler* appeared to take them north to the Lynn Canal area where parties lead by J. A. Flemer, J. F. Pratt, and H. P. Ritter were already at work.

For J. E. McGrath of the U.S. Coast and Geodetic Survey the summer of 1894 meant a return to the Malaspina Glacier area along the outer coast. In the 1892 season he had measured a base line near the mouth of the Osar Stream and later observed Mount St. Elias from triangulation stations on Mount Hoorts and Ocean Cape on the opposite side of Yakutat Bay. This season his instructions were to run a survey around the toe of the Malaspina Glacier and make new observations of Mount St. Elias from a base line in the Yahtse River area, just to the west of the 141st meridian.

On 22 May 1894, when the party landed near the mouth of the Osar Stream it was still midwinter.[46] The landing had been easy; the *Patterson* was protected from the surf by a great mass of ice lying about half a mile offshore. On land there was snow everywhere with the exception of a narrow band along the beach between high and low tides and that was bounded by an ice wall about four feet high where the salt spray had coated the snow. Their camp, such as it was, was located about 250 yards from the beach on an exposed ridge where the snow was not quite as deep. The men dragged firewood from a nearby spruce forest, and when the party returned in July they found that trees cut at the snowline had stumps six to twelve feet high!

From a reconnaissance along the open beach, McGrath realized that a survey could be run along it but that progress would be slow until the snow melted and the party could obtain the driftwood needed for fuel. On experimenting, McGrath concluded that chaining along the beach would be preferable to the optical methods originally planned. A fifty-metre steel tape was used with empty tin cans buried in the sand as improvised station markers. Pieces of paper were secured to the tops of the cans, and after the chain was brought to a uniform tension using a spring balance, one of the men would scribe the fifty metre mark on the paper.

Despite continuing bad weather, their survey reached the Sitkagi Bluffs on 13 June. Here, the rock-strewn Malaspina Glacier reaches the sea, and for about eight miles the survey had to be carried across the jumble of rock at the toe of it, accessible only at half to low tide at times when the surf was down. Moving camp by the same route was out of the question, and McGrath ordered his crew to move it by boat while he and three others took the instruments and notes across the glacier for safety. It was a wise precaution. The first boat trip went smoothly, but by the second the surf had come up and as McGrath described the landing:

On a signal from the shore the boat was headed in on top of a long roller but unexpectedly it broke some distance out, the bow of the boat touched the sand & almost quick as thought another high comber broke almost on top of them and in an instant the boat was lying keel up & the crew & outfit were buried entirely out of sight. It seemed almost before the men on shore could cry out, the boat was righted by another fast following wave & seized by the crew & the men on shore who dashed out through the surf to their assistance, to their great astonishment in another minute they all found themselves safe on the beach without injury to anyone. What their risk had been one glance at the boat showed to all — one of the largest oars had been twisted entirely around & parted in two & one jagged end had been driven through the side just under the gunwhale — smashing three of the planks in a manner which suggested what would be the consequence if it was a man's body & not a good oak plank that had been its sheath. It was a great relief to find that the upset had resulted so favorably, as far as injury to life & limb was concerned, to everyone but sudden & prompt action was at once necessary to retrieve the clothing, blankets, tents & provisions which the resultant waves were rapidly distributing up & down the coast or sending to the bottom according as their varying specific gravities made it more suitable. Most of our provisions, that were not canned, were badly damaged by the water, but I believe our most serious loss (that is so far as our immediate interests were concerned) was the disappearance in the waves of our two frying pans. This reduced the "batterie de cuisine" to a coffee pot, an old dish pan, a saucepan & a miner's sampling pan. For nearly three weeks all frying, stewing, baking & bread-making for the party was done with this simple outfit but where there is little to cook one does not need an extensive line of kitchen utensils. "The Lord tempers the wind to the shorn lamb" and we had some mercies shown to as the day after our accident was one of the two really fine days we had in seven weeks and thanks to the salutary warmth that nearly an entire day of sunshine brought, we were able to save ourselves from what might have been a very serious loss of provisions and enable us to dry our hardtack, flour, coffee etc.[47]

By late June, McGrath had completed his survey and was ready to observe Mount St. Elias from a new base line. The weather was still against them and as food was running low, "we had to turn to the Indians' delicacy and after we had eaten five seals we thought they were not bad."[48] They had to wait until the evening of 9 July for the clouds to lift from the peak. Observations were made from the station at the west end of the base line that evening and at 5 A.M. the following morning from the east end. Before 8 A.M. the mountain was obscured again and by afternoon the entire sky was cloud covered. McGrath's preliminary computation gave a distance of 33.3 statute miles from the west Yahtse base to Mount St. Elias, putting the peak just within the ten marine league limit of the 1825 Treaty.

Their work completed, the party were only too happy to leave when Indians from Yakutat kept their word and arrived in the largest canoe available after the peak had been clear for the required two days. There was more field work to be done from their first camp and, later, from Lituya Bay, but by early September the crew had been paid off and McGrath and most of his party were back in San Francisco.

In the 1894 season, the Canadian parties were anxious to make up for the time lost owing to weather in the 1893 season. Once again, they were strung out all along the Panhandle. From the south the parties were A. Saint Cyr in the Portland Canal-Chickamin River area; O.J. Klotz in the Bradfield Canal area; J. L. Gibbons along about fifty miles of coastline beginning just north of the mouth of the Stikine River; William Ogilvie on the east side of Lynn Canal and later on the outer coast beyond Cape Spencer; J. J. McArthur at the north end of Lynn Canal and later on the outer coast at Lituya Bay; A. C. Talbot on the west side of Lynn Canal towards Glacier Bay, and, finally, A. J. Brabazon in the Glacier Bay, Cross Sound region. Despite difficulties in moving the widely scattered parties, the season was highly successful, and the group returned with about seventeen hundred glass plate negatives, almost triple the number obtained the season before.[49] Then, in the winter of 1894–95, William Ogilvie was ordered to the Taku River in a futile search for a practical route to the interior. Battered by fierce storms, the party accomplished nothing beyond a traverse survey of part of the Taku River.

The 1895 season was a "cleaning-up" one for both the American and Canadian surveyors.[50] United States parties made new determinations of latitude and longitude at Port Simpson, B.C., Mary Island in the southern part of the Panhandle, and Lion Point near the head of Portland Canal. This season, the *City of Topeka*, a commercial steamer on the Puget Sound to Alaska run, carried the chronometers from Seattle to Port Simpson and Mary Island, while a government launch was used between Port Simpson and Lion Point. In addition, one Canadian party led by A. J. Brabazon did photo-topography between Alsek River and Yakutat on the outer coast.

As the mapping went on, both sides had been exchanging their technical information. Now, both set to work to produce a set of maps of the mainland portion of the Panhandle at a scale of 1:160,000 or about 2.5 miles to the inch. The end results were very different. The Canadian maps were preliminary topographic maps with contour lines at elevations 250 feet apart, while the American maps simply indicated some of the larger peaks and gave their elevations. To some extent, the maps reflected each country's interpretation of the 1825 Treaty; the Canadian ones suggesting a range of mountains parallel to the coast, and the American, a random distribution of mountains, resembling an attack of measles. Regardless, the value of photography had been proven; without it, it would have been impossible to produce either set of maps in the time available.

As required by the revised convention, the two commissioners, W. W. Duffield, now representing the United States, and W. F. King, representing Her Majesty on behalf of Canada, signed their final report at Albany, New York, on 31 December 1895.[51] Subterfuge was involved; the accompanying maps referred to in their text were still incomplete and would not be turned over until early May 1896.[52]

It made no difference. Unfortunately, the United States and Great Britain were involved in a bitter dispute over the Venezuela-British Guiana boundary, and it was no time to raise a new boundary issue. On 17 December 1895, President Cleveland had sent a special message to Congress denouncing Britain's refusal to submit the Venezuelan dispute to arbitration and threatening direct intervention.[53] Eventually, Britain agreed to arbitration and, to T. C. Mendenhall for one, this represented a new threat to U.S. claims in Alaska. In April 1896, Mendenhall, who had resigned as superintendent of the U.S. Coast and Geodetic Survey in September 1894, wrote: "Having driven [Britain] to accept arbitration in this case [Venezuela] it will be impossible for us to refuse it in Alaska, and we shall find ourselves again badly worsted by the diplomatic skill of a people who, as individuals, have developed intellectual activity, manliness, courage, unselfish devotion to duty, and general nobility of character, elsewhere unequalled in the world's history, but whose diplomatic policy as a nation is and long has been characterized by aggressiveness, greed, absolute indifference to the rights of others, and a splendid facility in ignoring every principle of justice or international law whenever commercial interests are at stake."[54]

The surveyors of both countries had done their part. Their maps were complete, and for the moment, they could be filed away ready to be brought out once the bitterness subsided and the politicans were ready to make the next move.

UNITED STATES ARMY STOREHOUSES IN THE PORTLAND CANAL AREA, 1896

In late summer 1896, Captain D. D. Gaillard, U.S. Corps of Engineers, was ordered north to oversee construction of four stone storehouses in the Portland Canal area. His party, fifty in all, including the ship's crew, left Seattle crammed aboard the lighthouse tender, *Manzanita*, their conditions made worse by five hundred sacks of extra coal piled in the stern and along the gangways.

The project was conducted as a military operation.[55] At each of the four sites, the *Manzanita* landed a crew consisting of a mason, carpenter, cook, mason's helper and two labourers together with a tent camp and tools. Flagpoles were erected and the flag hoisted in ceremonies that involved a salute, three cheers, and uncovered heads. The stone storehouses were identical; each ten by fifteen feet inside and about eight feet high·with a door in front, a window in the back wall, a floor of one-inch planks, and a roof of cedar shingles. Each had a dressed stone near the door bearing the words "U.S. Property Do Not Injure." Only nature defied regimentation; for Storehouses No. 1 and 2 the required sand had to be sacked and brought from near No. 3, and only at No. 4 could stone be quarried on site; elsewhere boulders had to be broken up and the stone rafted in.

The task completed, the work crews were picked up one by one while their camp gear, except for eating utensils needed on the voyage south, was locked in the storehouses. The *Manzanita* arrived back in Seattle on 4 October 1896 and the crews were paid off. As for the storehouses, one set of keys was left with a brother officer in Seattle, and Gaillard took the other set to Washington in the unlikely event that someone might wish to use the buildings in the future.

In building the storehouses, the United States had staked out her territorial claim in the Portland Canal area. Two of them, No. 1 on Wales Island and No. 2 on Pearse Island, were on territory claimed by Canada and the subject of discussions in 1888. Canada did not receive official notification either before or after the event.[56] Now, together with the ten-marine league markers on the Unuk, Stikine, and Taku Rivers and reconnaissance work around the head of Lynn Canal, everything was ready when the time came for the final settlement.

4

The Klondike Rush and Temporary Boundaries
(1896-1903)

The Klondike Gold Rush started in late July 1897, close to a year after Carmack and his party made their discovery on Bonanza Creek on 16 August 1896. It took time for the word to spread, and, initially, there was Carmack's reputation to overcome. William Ogilvie wrote of the reaction to the news at Forty Mile:

> Carmack proclaimed the discovery but very little attention was paid to him for some time. I am glad to be able to say I helped to establish his credit in this case. He told me the story of the find . . . showed me the dust and described the country to me too circumstantially to be purely imaginary which many around Forty Mile thought it all was, and maybe but for the presence of the Mounted Police in the town he would have been ordered out of town, back to his Indian wife in so little respect was he held.
>
> A few days after he came down and when he was getting ready to return I met two old-timers in the country one of them a Canadian from New Brunswick, the other a Swede. Knowing them both intimately I laughingly asked them what they thought of the new discovery? Both of them having made previous attempts in the Throndy as they called it then laughed and said they thought it was a d———d fraud and countered by asking me what I thought of it! I said I thought there was something in it. At which they laughed and said Siwash George is the greatest liar this side of hell and who would believe him. I said that may be so but even the greatest liar can tell the truth if he wants to and in this case I think he wants to. He has twelve dollars in gold dust, that is fact number 1, we know he has been at the mouth of the

Trondy for some time fact number 2, we also know he left here dead broke, strapped, fact number 3 and we know he has not been near any of the diggings since he left here fact number 4, now where did he get that twelve dollars? I believe he got it where he says he did. They reflected a moment or two and then said well that looks d———d likely when you view it that way. I said it is the only way I can see to look at it. Then the excitement began.[1]

Many claims were staked in late 1896, but actual mining had to wait until surface waters had frozen and shafts could be sunk through the permanently frozen black muck and gravel to the bedrock surface where most of the gold lay. Once the paystreak was located underground, about four feet of gravel and broken bedrock, thawed by fires set at the working face, would be hoisted to the surface for washing in the spring as soon as water was available. Test-panning could give the miners some idea of the values in their frozen dumps, but it would be May 1897 before their gold was actually recovered.

By late 1896 and early 1897, some word of the new strike had reached the Outside. Little attention was paid to it until 17 July 1897 when a special edition of *Seattle Post-Intelligencer* carried the story of the steamer *Portland,* inbound from St. Michael with a ton of Yukon gold aboard.[2] With that the rush was on, and would-be miners scrambled to collect an outfit and get through the passes at the head of Lynn Canal before the Yukon River closed for the season. Every ship available was pressed into service, many of questionable seaworthiness and all crowded to the gunwales with stampeders.

There was no boundary question in the Klondike. Ogilvie had already marked the line itself, almost fifty miles west of the new town of Dawson, and Constantine and his North-West Mounted Police were there to maintain order. It was different at the head of Lynn Canal. On paper, both the United States and Canada claimed the boom towns of Skagway and Dyea, starting points on the routes to the passes. But not on the ground. By August 1897 there were deputy collectors for United States Customs in both towns, while Canadian Customs were setting up at Tagish, about seventy miles inland.[3] Each country collected customs duties from stampeders unfortunate enough to have outfitted in the other. Such duties, levies, and other harrassments were all part of the struggle over which country would control the Klondike trade. Both governments might talk of making things simpler, but behind the scenes, they were under pressure from commercial lobbies. The stampeders, lacking political clout, were the victims of it all.

Forewarned by Ogilvie's reports, Clifford Sifton, Canada's minister of the interior, moved quickly to deal with the rush. On 17 August 1897, J.M. Walsh, a retired Mounted Police officer, was appointed commissioner of the Yukon, and on 2 October, the Walsh party sailed from Vancouver aboard the *Quadra.*[4] Numbering thirty-four in all, it consisted of Walsh and six other government officials, ten mounted police, nine dog-drivers, six Ontario Indians skilled in swift water work, Walsh's brother, who was in charge of transport, and a servant. Their outfit included four months' rations for sixty men, seventy-eight dogs, twenty-five dogsleds, carbines and revolvers for everyone, and two machine guns. Determined to see for himself, Sifton accompanied the party to Dyea with an entourage of seven others. The latter included W.F. King, former boundary commissioner, and William Ogilvie, back from the north a few weeks before.

On reaching Skagway, they learned that the advance party had let them down. Worried over escalating costs and sick and discouraged, the assistant commissioner of the Mounted Police who was in charge had done very little in the way of preparation. By now, it was raining incessantly, and the cost of packing had risen to a high point as the stampeders attempted to reach the Yukon River before it closed for the winter. No reliable information was available on conditions ahead, and, after consultation, it was decided that Sifton, Walsh, and Ogilvie would make a quick inspection trip over the passes and beyond to Bennett and Tagish. In their absence, other party members would start moving the outfit over the passes.

The inspection party set out on 10 October accompanied by two policemen and the Ontario Indians. The trip in over the Chilkoot Pass was not too difficult except for the steep climb from The Scales to the summit. Reaching Tagish on 13 October, they found Inspector D'A. E. Strickland of the North-West Mounted Police and his men making rapid progress on building a barracks and an officers' quarters on a site selected just a week before.[5] Nearby, the Canadian customs had been collecting duties since September.

On their return to Bennett, a police escort failed to meet them as arranged, and the party was forced to purchase horses and feed. It was a bargain typical of the scramble going on around them, $50 total for six selected pack-horses and another $30 for half a sack of oats. Walsh wrote of their trip over the White Pass:

> The Skagway trail is all that it has been described to be, such a scene of havoc and destruction as we encountered through the whole length of the White Pass can scarcely be imagined. Thousands of pack horses lay dead along the way, sometimes in bunches under the cliff with pack saddles and packs where they had fallen from the rocks above, sometimes in a tangled mass, filling the mudholes and furnishing the only footing for our poor pack animals on the march — often, I regret to say, exhausted but still alive, a fact that we were unaware of until after the miserable wretches turned beneath the hoofs of our cavalcade. The eyeless sockets of the pack animals everywhere accounted for the myriad of ravens all along the road. The inhumanity which this trail has been witness to, the heart-breaking sufferings which so many have undergone, cannot be imagined. They certainly cannot be described.[6]

The party reached Skagway on the afternoon of 19 October, and on 22 October, the *Quadra* sailed for Vancouver with Clifford Sifton and his entourage aboard. Over the next few days, the Walsh party and the remainder of their outfit cleared the Chilkoot Pass. From his trip, Sifton, sceptical at first, realized the import of the Klondike rush and gained the background needed to deal with it. In his public statements he maintained that Canada had a legitimate claim to Skagway and Dyea, but one of his first moves was to try to establish an all-Canadian route to the Klondike via the Stikine River and a railroad to Teslin Lake.[7]

Over the next few months, a contract was negotiated with railroad contractors William Mackenzie and Donald Mann to build a narrow gauge railway from a point near Telegraph Creek to Teslin Lake, an estimated distance of 150 miles. The contract was signed on 25 January 1898, and the bill authorizing it was introduced in the House of Commons on 8 February 1898 by A.G. Blair, minister of railways and canals.[8] It was to be built in a hurry; the contract called for completion of a sleigh road within six weeks of signing and of the railway before 1 September 1898. Blair went through the twenty-five clauses of the contract in some detail. Contentious ones included: Clause 4, protecting the contractors for five years against the building of a railway from Lynn Canal over Chilkat Pass and on to Fort Selkirk; Clause 11, authorizing a land grant of twenty-five thousand acres per mile of completed railroad and Clause 17, fixing a royalty of 1 per cent on any placer gold mined from the land grant.

There were stormy sessions over the bill in the House of Commons. When questions were raised about the American granting bonding privileges for the transhipment of goods at Wrangell, Prime Minister Laurier, for one, was prepared to extend the railway to a Canadian port south of the Panhandle failing an acceptable agreement.[9] The House of Commons approved the bill, but the scheme collapsed on 31 March 1898 when the Conservative majority in the Senate voted fity-two to fourteen to delay consideration of the bill for six months. Later, the government of British Columbia tried to keep the project alive by offering a subsidy of $4,000 a mile, but by early 1899, this offer too had been rescinded.[10]

It was all for the best. The Stikine route was impractical. One correspondent summed it up in the description of his visit to Wrangell in late May 1898:

> Wrangell has been booming itself lately as a point of departure for the Yukon. This spring has shown that it cannot be such except in the few summer months when the Stikine is navigable. The winter trail up the Stikine is too difficult for use. Thus the Teslin route involves a continuation of the projected railroad southward from Glenora to some accessible point on the coast or in the interior of British Columbia if it is to be of any real use all the year around.
>
> I looked in vain for the many wharves promised as gold mines by prospectuses issued in London during the last winter. The very few new wharves are quite sufficient for all the traffic to Wrangell. There are plenty of little stores and Indians and low-class saloons. . . . I saw one clever thing

there: — A wag had set up on two iron tram-rails a stove with its stove-pipe for a locomotive and behind it two boxes for cars; over the whole he had fixed up a sign board on which he had written in fine contempt "Yukon Railway." This was the chief ornament of the main street! Messrs. Mackenzie and Mann ought to conduct the Canadian law-makers on a pilgrimage to this quaint shrine? But they must go in gum-boots and oilskins, for there is real rain at Wrangell. Wrangell is picturesque and not much more. I liked it best from the boat, — on leaving it.[11]

There was another surprise move in February 1898. Questioned in the House of Commons about press reports of United States troop movements to Skagway and Dyea, Laurier acknowledged that the Canadian government had not been informed of the move.[12] He went on to add that although this was disputed territory that, as far as he was aware, American occupation of it had never been protested. What Laurier chose not to disclose was that the Mounted Police had been ordered to take possession of the Chilkoot and White Passes and that their advance parties should be in the passes already.

MOUNTED POLICE OCCUPY THE PASSES, 1898

The move had been made in great secrecy. On 29 January 1898, Superintendent S.B. Steele, in charge of the Fort McLeod District on the Canadian prairies, was ordered to turn over his command to another officer and leave for Vancouver on the first train. In Vancouver, two days later, he opened a letter from Superintendent A.B. Perry, then on duty in Victoria, and learned of the scheme. Instructions came from Clifford Sifton, minister of the interior. The commissioner of the Yukon, J.M. Walsh, in charge of the police and wintering somewhere in the Yukon, had been bypassed and would not learn of the order until it had been carried out. Perry, who was in charge of the first stages, left Vancouver for Skagway on 2 February, and Steele followed on the sixth, aboard the *Thistle*. The latter, formerly in the Alaska fur seal trade, was crowded with stampeders. Steele's berth was one of three "situated above the screw, in a little cabin which had a strong odour of ancient cheese."[13] At least he ate with the captain and the pilot rather than at one of the six servings that crowded the dining tables all day.

It was 30 below Fahrenheit when the *Thistle* docked at Skagway on 14 February 1898. Steele's party struggled along the dock, facing into a biting blast roaring down at them from the White Pass. Perry was somewhere ahead, and if all was going according to plan, the police parties should be moving into their new posts in the Chilkoot and White Passes. Steele's orders were to remain on the Skagway side of the passes until the new posts were in operation and the command turned over to him.

The post in Chilkoot Pass was established by a party led by Inspector R. Belcher.[14] He had been in the Mounted Police office in Skagway for about a month when Superintendent Perry arrived and ordered him to the summit immediately. By the next evening, 10 February, Belcher and two constables had reached Sheep Camp on the Chilkoot Trail together with a small amount of lumber freighted from Dyea. As they arrived, a vigilance committee was trying two men for theft. One, sentenced to hang but somehow left with his revolver, escaped and began firing at his captors. The fire was returned with interest, and later his body, with a bullet wound in the forehead, was found close to Belcher's tent. The second man, sentenced to fifty lashes of the cat, was punished next morning and turned loose with a large placard reading "THIEF" tied to his back.

Belcher's party pitched their tent on the summit of Chilkoot Pass on the evening of 11 February 1898. The last of the lumber for their shack was delivered next morning after Belcher greased a few palms, considering it "wiser, under the circumstances, to expend a few dollars judiciously and prevent delays."[15] At 3 A.M. on the morning of the thirteenth, the moonlight was bright enough for all hands to set to work on the building. By dark, the four walls were up. It was a tiny structure, twelve feet by twelve feet, with a door, a single window, and a canvas tarpaulin for the roof. Worse, it was built of green planks, all that was available, and as the wood dried, cracks opened and fine snow drifted in. On the fourteenth, a party consisting of a sergeant and fourteen constables together with six horses arrived from Bennett on the Canadian side of the pass. For the moment, it was out of the question for them to remain at the summit, and the party camped at Crater Lake, about four hundred feet below the level of the pass. On 18 February, after three days of stormy weather, the water in the lake rose, covering the ice and flooding the tents to a depth of six inches. Most of the mens' blankets and bedding were soaked, but moving the tents during the storm was impossible. The best the men could do was to drag sleighs into the tents and perch their beds on them. Finally on the twenty-first, the storm slackened enough for them to move the tents and join Belcher on the summit, a cold spot but much preferable to the water below.

On 26 February 1898, the party hoisted the Union Jack and began collecting customs duties. Belcher and a corporal sharing the shack found another defect in their structure. A thick coating of frost would collect on the canvas roof overnight, and after the stove was lighted in the morning, the place was like a shower bath until noon. Belcher was quick to order lumber for a roof, but in the midst of the rush, it was six weeks before it was delivered. Despite weather, a near-critical shortage of firewood, and loose talk of an assault by volunteers, the police clung to the summit, checking through some twenty-five to thirty thousand people. At times, a small box or kitbag in the shack, watched constantly by Belcher or the corporal, held close to $90,000, most of it in gold coin.[16] For the moment, keeping it at the summit was preferable to risking a shipment through territory controlled by Soapy Smith and his gang.

Conditions in the White Pass were similar for Inspector D'A.E. Strickland and his party of twenty non-commissioned officers and men.[17] Strickland, who had been in and out of the north since 1895, was ordered to the summit on 9 February on his return to Skagway after a six-week trip to the south. Reaching the summit on the thirteenth, the party pitched their tents on the ice. The nearest timber for building and firewood lay twelve miles away, and Strickland left two men cutting while the remainder used horses to haul it to the summit. Blizzards raged for ten days, and Strickland worried about losing his men. Luckily, there were no serious mishaps, and on 27 February the party hoisted the Union Jack and began collecting customs duties.

With posts in both passes, the Mounted Police were now in full control of the two main routes to the Klondike. No serious opposition to their *fait accompli* was anticipated, but just in case, each post was equipped with a Maxim machine gun, an ample supply of ammunition, and supplies for six months.[18] Of more immediate concern to the stampeders toiling up the passes was the order, originally given by the commissioner of the Yukon, that each man entering Canadian territory must bring a year's supply of food, totalling about eleven hundred pounds at the specified three pounds per day.[19]

For Sifton, writing to Walsh to explain the swift move, it was a "case of possession being ten points in the law, and we intend to hold possession." If United States troops had arrived first and reached Bennett Lake, "it would have taken twenty years of negotiating to get them out, in fact I doubt if we would ever have got them out."[20]

The United States troops, four companies of the 14th Infantry, landed near the end of February 1898. Colonel T. M. Anderson was their commanding officer, and each consisted of 4 officers and 108 men. Two companies, B and H, were posted to Dyea and the other two, A and G, to Skagway. Their instructions from the president, relayed through the acting secretary of war, stated they were sent "in the interest of good order and of the safety of persons and property there . . . which the troops are expected to conserve. The force should be used with kindness and consideration and within the measure of the strict necessity of the occasions as may arise."[21] There was no mention of a boundary dispute.

While he was busy getting his men settled in, Colonel Anderson was besieged with conflicting reports about the boundary and the new Mounted Police posts in the passes. American citizens who had laid out a townsite at Lindeman complained that they had been told they were subject to Canadian law, and other stampeders, lacking proper outfits, were bitter over being turned back from the passes. On 15 March 1898, Anderson wrote to Superintendent Steele, who was still in Skagway, asking him to explain "why you find it necessary to exercise civil and military authority over American Territory, or on Territory at least in question."[22] Steele forwarded the letter to J. M. Walsh, commissioner of the Yukon, who replied that, in his understanding, "the disputed territory commences at the summit of the Chilkoot Pass and extends some distance south of Skagway, and over that district we have not exercised our authority."[23]

Then, on 20 March 1898, Governor John G. Brady of Alaska and J.W. Ivey, U.S. collector of customs, appeared at Anderson's headquarters asking if he would provide military assistance to station a deputy customs collector at Bennett Lake. At Chilkoot Pass the day before, the pair had been told that a deputy would be turned back at the police post. Colonel Anderson refused to involve his troops, citing Walsh's statement on the disputed ground.[24] Uncertain what to do, he kept his own counsel and referred the problem to the Army's Department of the Columbia at Vancouver Barracks, Washington.

Brigadier H. C. Merriam, officer commanding, dealt with the issue 1 April 1898, the day after Anderson's letter arrived. He had already made his own interpretation of the 1825 Treaty and to him "it appears plain that the summit or divide between the waters of the Yukon and tidewater at Dyea, being less than ten marine leagues from tidewater, was, beyond a doubt, the limit of our jurisdiction." Anderson, although supplied with a text of the treaty defining the boundary, had "continued to entertain the subject, perhaps needlessly" by his letter to Superintendent Steele of the Mounted Police. However, in view of the instructions given to the U.S. customs collector as well as the complaints of citizens "it would now seem that this subject calls for official attention by the Departments concerned, in order that possible friction may be avoided on that border."[25] Merriam's interpretation was accepted, and, with that, the possibility of a confrontation in the passes ended. There was remarkably little protest in the American press, probably because the sinking of the *U.S.S. Maine* on 15 February 1898 and preparations for war with Spain had driven reports on the gold rush from the front pages.

By late May 1898, close to thirty thousand stampeders waited along the shores of Lindeman and Bennett Lakes ready to push off in their boats and barges as soon as the ice went out. Sam Steele and his Mounted Police had good reason to be proud of their accomplishments in dealing with the Rush: "We had seen the sick were cared for, had buried the dead, administered their estates to the satisfaction of their kin, had brought on our own supplies and means of transport, had built our own quarters and administered the laws of Canada without one well-founded complaint against us. Only three homicides had taken place, none of them preventable."[26] In addition, police supervision had done much to avert famine at Dawson, and now fifty thousand pounds of food had been freighted to the foot of Lake Laberge ready to ship in specially built boats as soon as the river opened.

In May 1898, a new North-West Mounted Police post was established on the Dalton Trail, an overland route that ran from the head of Chilkat Inlet over Chilkat Pass, reaching the Yukon River near present-day Carmacks. The police party, consisting of Inspector A. M. Jarvis and eighteen other ranks, left Calgary in early April and landed at Haines, Alaska, on 14 April 1898.[27] The proposed site at Rainy Hollow lay about ten miles south of the Chilkat Pass at the beginning of the steep climb out of the Klehini River valley, a point well beyond the ten-marine league limit of the 1825 Treaty.

Next morning, in pouring rain, the men set to work to assemble their carts and wagons only to find that most of their twenty-eight horses, brought from Calgary, were Indian ponies and total strangers to both carts and harness. After breaking a few pairs of shafts and replacing several axles, the ponies were harnessed in tandem, and the first loads were moved to an Indian village about five miles along the route. The trail was in horrible condition, much of the snow had melted, and in several places the carts sank to their axles in the mud. At least it reduced the risk of runaways. From their new camp the outfit was ferried across the Chilkat River by canoe. Aside from a social visit by three officers while this was underway, United States troops in the area took little notice of the new arrivals.

Once across the river, the party relayed their outfit upriver, travelling partly by trail and partly over river ice. On 4 May 1898, Jarvis and a small advance party had reached a point about seven miles up the Klehini River where they hoisted the Union Jack and began collecting customs duties. From this camp, Jarvis and two constables snowshoed about ten miles ahead to the Rainy Hollow site only to find that the snow was still very deep and so soft that they sank almost to their hips on every step. Certain that it would be late June before his outfit could be moved ahead, Jarvis decided to build the post near Dalton Cache, about a mile and a half above the camp they had set out from. The scouting trip had taken thirty-six hours with the men on the go continuously except for a single meal break.[28]

The police had unusual company along the Dalton trail, a herd of reindeer originally part of the the United States Relief Expedition. Five hundred and twenty-six reindeer and their fifty-seven Lapp herders had been landed at Haines, Alaska on 30 March 1898, just over three weeks after the relief expedition had been abandoned.[29] There was a delay at Haines until arrangements were completed to turn most of them over from the war department to Dr. Sheldon Jackson of the department of the interior. Jackson had promoted the scheme of using reindeer pulling sleighs to rush supplies to the miners in Dawson before the rivers opened in the spring of 1898. Once there, the animals themselves would be used as food.

The delay was a catastrophe. The reindeer moss brought from Norway was used up, and none could be found on the hills around Haines. While waiting, the reindeer were fed dried alfalfa, and they were soon dying at the rate of three or four a day. There was a desperate search to find suitable moss, and only 164 were still alive when some was found on the hillside behind Dalton Post in early May.[30] Later, as the snow melted, the reindeer were driven up into the Chilkat Pass area where there was abundant feed, and in late January 1899, the remaining reindeer were driven past Dawson on their way to Circle, Alaska.[31]

The Dalton Trail Post was built on sloping ground with natural drainage into the Klehini River. Clear brooks flowed nearby, and there was abundant timber close at hand. Three large buildings, floored with whipsawn lumber and roofed with hand-made shingles, were put up. Good limestone outcropped nearby, and the party built a lime kiln, using the product to plaster the chinks between the logs. Even more of a luxury for a police post were the two milk cows and fifty yellow leghorn hens Jarvis had purchased with government funds. The party had a plentiful supply of milk and eggs all summer, saving enough from their rations to repay the extra cost.[32] The post soon had a new name, Pleasant Camp, used everywhere except in the official correspondence.[33] Even the police duties were not too arduous. Much of the expected travel over the Dalton Trail failed to materialize after steamboats began plying the upper lakes of the Yukon River system. The trail was used mainly for livestock, and perhaps two thousand head of cattle and an equal number of horses were landed at Haines and driven in over the route in the summer of 1898.

MODUS VIVENDI AND A PROVISIONAL BOUNDARY, 1899-1900

In February 1899, a Joint High Commission dealing with a number of issues between United States and Canada had foundered on the Alaska Boundary question. Differences were over ports at the head of Lynn Canal and control of Yukon trade. The United States considered Canada's "new" claim to the upper end of Lynn Canal unreasonable and was unwilling to include it in any arbitration.[34] Both sides offered proposals for a Canadian-controlled port at Pyramid Harbor and a corridor through the Panhandle, but they were unable to reach a final agreement.[35]

Mining activity was growing around the head of Lynn Canal, and something had to be done before there was an incident. The alternative chosen was the *modus vivendi* fixing a provisional boundary concluded by an exchange of notes between John Hay, U.S. secretary of state, and Sir Reginald Tower, British chargé in Washington on 20 October 1899.[36] In the negotiations there was quick agreement on the White and Chilkoot Passes, but there were problems along the Chilkat River. Canada suggested that the line should cross the Chilkat near the mouth of the Klehini River, about nineteen miles from the head of Chilkat Inlet. This recommendation was agreed to, but then, on Hay's insistence, the line was run along the south bank of the Klehini for about twelve miles, leaving most of the newly discovered Porcupine mining camp in Alaska.[37] Perhaps it was just as well. Most of the miners there were American citizens, and few had any use for British Columbia or its government. Too many had taken part in the rush to the Atlin area that began in late July 1898 only to learn a few days later that the new camp was in British Columbia.[38] Under provincial laws, the length of a placer claim was a mere one hundred feet along the creek,

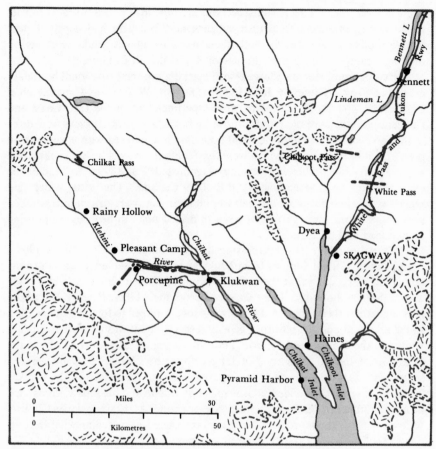

Map 2: Provisional boundary, **modus vivendi** of 20 October 1899

and there had been a recent unsuccessful attempt in the legislature to restrict claim-staking privileges to British subjects or those who had declared their intention of becoming one.[39] Surely their own government would never permit their new camp to be dropped holus-bolus into British Columbia!

The two commissioners charged with marking out the provisional boundary arrived at Skagway in early June 1900.[40] The pair, W. F. King, Canada's chief astronomer, and O. H. Tittmann, now superintendent of the U.S. Coast and Geodetic Survey, were old hands on Alaska boundary work. Surveys were done in the three areas and the provisional boundary line marked with wrought-iron posts. Each of these posts, which were five feet long and 1¾ inches square, had a special cap painted blue on one side and embossed "P.B. 1899 U.S.," and on the other painted red and embossed "P.B. 1899 Canada." The posts, which had ragged tips to make it more difficult to pull them out, were driven into wooden posts sunk in the river gravels or fixed in drilled holes in bedrock by pouring molten lead around them.

The new boundary had repercussions in the Chilkat area. On 20 June 1900 a delegation of Chilkat Indians from Klukwan village presented a petition to the commissioners asking that they be allowed to continue to hunt, fish, and trade across the new boundary line that sliced cross the Chilkat River valley about a mile north of their village.[41] The commissioners agreed to forward the petition to the president and the governor general respectively. It was no mere formality; whites in the Haines and Dalton Trail area were already worried about the threat of an Indian uprising. Not long before, the Chilkats had murdered a settler and his pregnant wife following their custom that deaths in the Chilkat Tribe, in this case the accidental drowing of an Indian and his squaw, demanded an equal number of deaths in another tribe or nation. At the time, eleven Chilkats were on trial for the murders in Skagway, and there was no telling what the outcome might be if they were convicted and punished.[42]

Miners in the outlying portion of the Porcupine district that had been turned over to British Columbia thought so little of their new government that they boycotted a commission sent to record their claims and settle disputes.[43] Some 164 claims were involved, just over half of them having been staked prior to the *modus vivendi* of 20 October 1899. Their owners preferred to wait it out, believing that once the 1900 presidential election was out of the way they would find their ground shifted back to Alaska.

"RUSSIAN BOUNDARY MONUMENTS" IN THE CHILKAT AREA, 1902–1903

On 3 April 1902, the *Seattle Post-Intelligencer* carried a sensational special dispatch from Washington, D.C., claiming that a surveyor employed by the Canadian government had destroyed Russian boundary markers. It continued that the State Department considered the information authentic and that the president had appointed a committee to investigate. Its members were to be Captain Wilds P. Richardson, U.S. Army, and Lieutenant G. T. Emmons, U.S. Navy, retired, both old Alaska hands. The offending surveyor's name was given as Richard Frasier, reasonably close to George R. White-Fraser, who had worked in the Chilkat area in the fall of 1900.

Lt. Emmons was in the Chilkat area in the summer of 1902, watched by the Mounted Police, who tried to learn what, if anything, he had been able to find. W. F. King learned more in direct correspondence with White-Fraser. In December 1902, the latter wrote that he had seen the "monuments" but considered them simply stone shelters. More to the point, his cook had met Emmons in Skagway and reported back that he had given Emmons "a good spiel" about destroying monuments. The damage was done, and White-Fraser was certain that the United States was determined to find a Russian boundary marker "and therefore will find one; if they have to manufacture one; but Mr. Emmons must be hard pressed for evidence."[44]

King had decided to forget the incident when, unexpectedly, it became one more thing to check as Canada prepared her case for the final boundary settlement. It would have to be done quickly and, if possible, without the Americans' knowledge. King's choice for the assignment was A. O. Wheeler, a senior government surveyor who had never worked in Alaska. On receiving two urgent telegrams from the surveyor general and King at his home in Calgary, Wheeler caught the train for Ottawa the same evening. Briefed by King and the comptroller of the Mounted Police, Wheeler, accompanied by a young English assistant, landed at Skagway on 7 April 1903.[45]

Posing as tourists interested in glaciers, the pair carried cameras and field glasses and were outfitted in Norfolk jackets, knickerbockers, golf stockings, and tweed caps. There were anxious moments after the customs officer going through Wheeler's trunk came across his instruments and photographic plates. Wheeler told the officer of his interest in glaciers, and the latter insisted that Wheeler meet his chief who was also interested in glaciers. There was no escape; the chief, enthusiastic about meeting someone with the same hobby, showed Wheeler his albums of photographs and ended up by promising to arrange a boat trip to Glacier Bay on Wheeler's return. Wheeler feeling horribly mean about it all, reminded himself that "orders is orders."

Free of the customs, Wheeler went to a hotel to wait for a contact with the Mounted Police. It came when a man wearing a Stetson hat strolled up to the table where Wheeler was sitting, picked up a paper and stood looking at it, finally asking in a low voice: "Is your name Wheeler?" From there he was sent by boat to Haines and then on to Dalton Trail post, always met by policemen who would appear from nowhere with the now familiar: "Is your name Wheeler?"

From the police post at Pleasant Camp, a party of seven travelled by dogteam to Rainy Hollow, where a small shack about ten feet square served as their base for almost two weeks. Outside it, a crowd of snarling, yapping sled dogs waited for their next meal of dried salmon or the chance to take a piece out of anyone who came too close.

The "Russian monuments," on the uplands about five miles to the north, proved to be slivers of granite set in the ground for a few inches and held upright by small stones.[46] There were half a dozen in all, several fallen over and buried by snow, plus a "stone house" consisting of a few slabs of rock that appeared to have been dragged together as a temporary shelter. Wheeler concluded that it was absurd to consider them Russian markers and later speculated that they may have been placed by the Chilkat Indians to mark the limit they would permit the Stick or Interior Indians to approach in trade. Wheeler completed a survey of the monuments, made astronomical observations for two nights, and connected his surveys to the Provisional Boundary marker close to the Porcupine mining camp.

On his return trip south Wheeler lay low in Skagway, hoping to slip aboard the boat unnoticed. He thought he had succeeded when he felt a hand on his shoulder and a voice said: "You are just the man we want."[47] It was the customs officer, full of plans for a boat trip to Glacier Bay starting the next day. Wheeler, a poor liar, mumbled something about an urgent summons from home and hurried aboard, leaving the perplexed officer standing on the dock.

Wheeler should have gone to Glacier Bay when he had the chance. The whole affair was a tempest in a teapot, and the question of "Russian boundary monuments" was never raised at the Boundary Tribunal.

Plate 1.   Schwatka's raft at the end of its 1,300 mile journey, August 1883.

Plate 2.   William Ogilvie's party on the Yukon River en route to the boundary area, 1887. The two canoes were portaged to the Mackenzie River the following spring.

Plate 3. The Forty Mile area, looking upstream on the Yukon River, 1895. The *P.B. Weare* is unloading at Fort Cudahy and the settlement of Forty Mile lies in the background across the Fortymile River. Fort Constantine is under construction at the end of the short road running south from Fort Cudahy.

Plate 4. William Ogilvie's party at their observatory, October 1895. Ogilvie is seated, second from the right, and the building is almost hidden behind the woodpile.

Plate 5. One of the Canadian photographs used in photo-topographic mapping of the Panhandle by the Alaska Boundary Commission, 1893–95. Taken from camera station B210, south of Lituya Bay, it shows Mount Fairweather and Mount Quincy Adams (both indicated and later B.P.s 164 and 163, respectively). Notched reference marks on the margin indicate the centre line and horizon line of the photo.

Plate 6. The observatory and part of the American camp at Pyramid Harbor, 1894. The slot through the former permitted telescope observations along the meridian of the station.

Plate 7. J.F. Pratt's party leaving Pyramid Harbor to survey the Chilkat River, 1894.

Plate 8. Canadian government party en route to Skagway aboard the *Quadra*, September 1897. J.M. Walsh, commissioner the Yukon, second from the left in the front row followed by Clifford Sifton, minister of the interior, and Dr. W.F. King, ch astronomer and boundary commissioner. T.D. Patullo, secretary to Walsh and later premier of British Columbia, is on t right end of the second row.

Plate 9.　The summit of the Chilkoot Pass during a snowstorm in the spring of 1898. Part of the roof of the mounted police building is visible to the right of the flag.

Plate 10.　The alleged "Russian boundary monuments," photographed by A.O. Wheeler in April 1903.

Plate 11.   United States Army storehouse No. 4 in the Portland Canal area, photographed in 1905. The bronze obelisk is B.P. 1 of the 1903 Award, and the boundary runs up the slope behind leaving the front of the building in Canada.

Plate 12.   The Alaska Boundary Tribunal at the close of their first meeting on 3 September 1903. The six tribunal members seated in front of the maps are, from the left, George Turner, Sir Louis Jetté, Elihu Root, Lord Alverstone, Henry Cabot Lodge, and Allen B. Aylesworth.

BREAKING THE NEWS

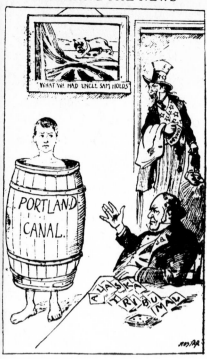

"WHAT WE HAD UNCLE SAM HOLDS"
PORTLAND CANAL.
J.B.
ALASKA TRIBUNAL

JOHN BULL :—"I regret to report that the **award** gives yer h'uncle h'all yer clothes."

UNCLE SAM:—"Yes, but I kalkilate he kin **keep the** barrel."

Plate 13. From the Toronto *Evening Telegram*, 19 October 1903.

DEPARTMENT OF STATE.

WASHINGTON.

Oct. 21. 1903

The newspapers do not seem to get the rights of the Portland Channel. There are two entrances to it like this, with two little islands in it. We

alaska

Canada

Boundary

agree that the Boundary shall be by the North Channel instead of the South, which gives them those two little Islands — worth nothing to us. That is all poor Canada gets by the decision, and I do not wonder they are furious. But as Will Thomson used to say "Serves 'em right, if they cant take a joke".

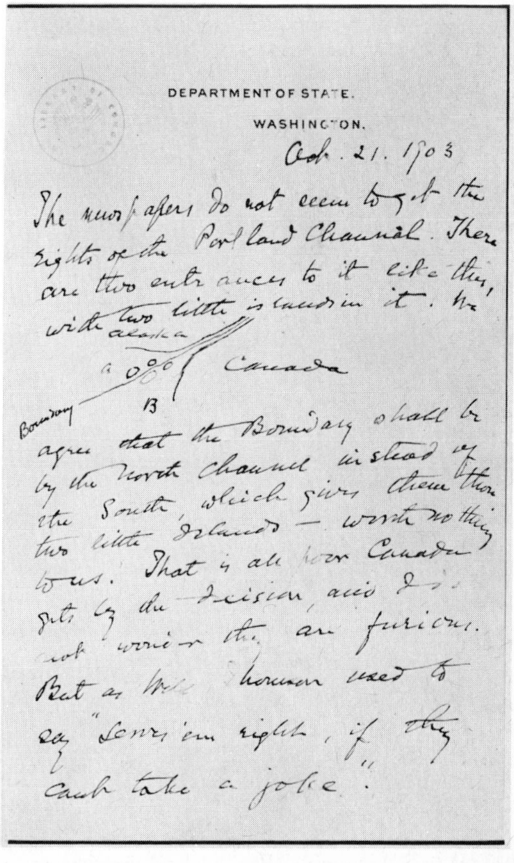

Plate 14. Secretary of State Hay's comment on the award in a letter to Mrs. Hay.

The newspapers do not seem to get the rights of the Portland Channel. There are two entrances to it like this, with two little islands in it. We agree the boundary shall be by the North Channel instead of the South, which gives them those two little islands — worth nothing to us. That is all poor Canada gets by the decision, and I do not wonder they are furious. But as Will Thomson used to say "Serves 'em right, if they cant take a joke."

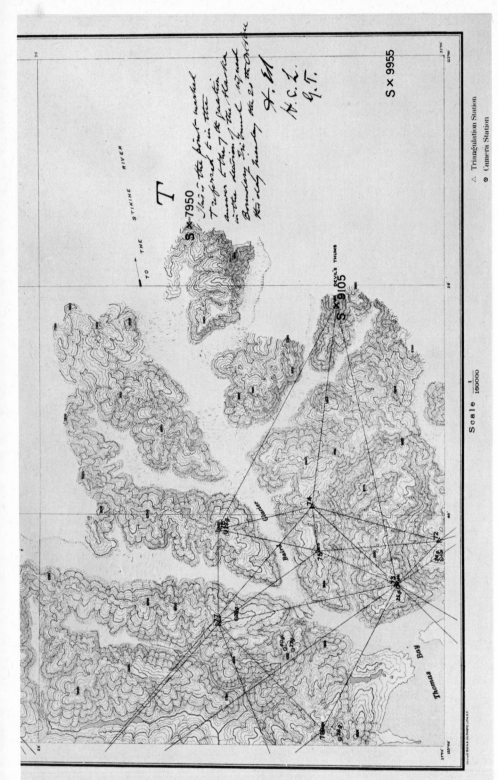

Plate 15.   A portion of an official copy of the 1903 Award map showing the boundary between Kates Needle (S 9955), Devils Thumb, and T Mountain (B.P.s 70–72, respectively). The base is the remarkably detailed Canadian map of 1895, which, as printed here, is reduced from the original scale of 1:160,000. The position of Kates Needle, not shown on the Canadian

5

Forced Settlement: The Alaska Boundary Tribunal (1903)

Following the *modus vivendi* of 20 October 1899 and the survey of the provisional boundary the following summer, there had been fitful negotiations over the type of tribunal, or similar body, that would fix the Alaska Boundary. For the moment there was no need to hurry. The excitement of the Klondike Gold Rush was over, and interest had turned to events elsewhere. Gold production had peaked at just over 22 million in 1900, and individual miners, forced out by the growing consolidations, were leaving to prospect elsewhere or, more often, to return to the south. In addition, Britain and, to some extent, Canada had been involved in the South African War which dragged on until the final surrender in May 1902. By then, Theodore Roosevelt was growing impatient to settle the matter finally. On 24 January 1903, a treaty signed in Washington by John Hay, secretary of state of the United States, and Sir Michael Herbert, the British ambassador, set the stage for another attempt.

The Hay-Herbert Treaty, as it became known, called for a tribunal consisting of "six impartial jurists of repute, who shall consider judicially the questions submitted to them, each of whom shall first subscribe an oath that he will impartially consider the arguments and evidence presented to the Tribunal, and will decide thereupon according to his true judgment. Three members of the Tribunal shall be appointed by His Britannic Majesty and three by the President of the United States. All questions considered by the Tribunal, including the final award, shall be decided by a majority of the members thereof."[1] There were seven questions dealing with the Anglo-Russian Treaty of 1825:

1. What is intended as the point of commencement of the line?
2. What channel is the Portland Channel?
3. What course should the line take from the point of commencement to the entrance to Portland Channel?
4. To what point on the 56th parallel is the line to be drawn from the head of Portland Channel, and what course should it follow between these points?
5. In extending the line of demarcation northward from said point on the parallel of the 56th degree of north latitude, following the crest of mountains situated parallel to the coast until its intersection with the 141st degree of longitude west of Greenwich, subject to the condition that if such line should anywhere exceed the distance of 10 marine leagues from the ocean then the boundary between the British and Russian territory should be formed by a line parallel to the sinuosities of the coast and distant therefrom not more than 10 marine leagues, was it the intention and meaning of said Convention of 1825 that there should remain in the exclusive possession of Russia a continuous fringe or strip of coast on the mainland, not exceeding 10 marine leagues in width, separating the British possessions from the bays, ports, inlets, havens, and waters of the ocean, and extending from the said point on the 56th degree of latitude north to a point where such line of demarcation should intersect the 141st degree of longitude west of the meridian of Greenwich?
6. If the foregoing question should be answered in the negative, and in the event of the summit of such mountains proving to be in places more than 10 marine leagues from the coast, should the width of the *lisière* which was to belong to Russia be measured (1) from the mainland coast of the ocean, strictly so-called, along a line perpendicular thereto, or (2) was it the intention and meaning of the said Convention that where the mainland coast is indented by deep inlets forming part of the territorial waters of Russia, the width of the *lisière* was to be measured (a) from the line of the general direction of the mainland coast, or (b) from the line separating the waters of the ocean from the territorial waters of Russia, or (c) from the heads of the aforesaid inlets?
7. What, if any exist, are the mountains referred to as situated parallel to the coast, which mountains, when within 10 marine leagues from the coast, are declared to form the eastern boundary?[2]

The new treaty could have no real meaning until ratified by the United States Senate and the British government. Ratification was by no means certain; just as in 1895, relations between the two countries were at a low point over a new dispute in Venezuela. Senator Henry Cabot Lodge of Massachusetts masterminded the strategy in the Senate. On 11 February 1903 after Senator Chauncey Depew of New York had droned through two hours of what would prove a six-hour speech, Lodge rose to move that the Senate proceed to the consideration of executive business. In the secret session that followed, Lodge obtained the two-thirds majority required for ratification, and the following day an attempt by aroused opponents to have the treaty reconsidered was turned back by a simple majority.[3]

On the British side there were a multitude of interests, many of them conflicting. How much support should be given to the Canadian claim at a time-when there was an urgent need to restore good relations with the United States? Canada still dealt with the United States through Britain's Colonial and Foreign Offices. For Laurier's government, it sometimes meant frustrations and misunderstandings and, at other times, an opportunity to pass the blame for their own indecisiveness on "the system."

There was consternation in Ottawa and London when Roosevelt's three nominations for the Tribunal became known. The three, Senator Lodge, former Senator Turner of Washington, and Elihu Root, secretary of war, seemed anything but "impartial jurists of repute." Lodge was an outspoken opponent of the Canadian claim, Turner coming from Washington State, must be against it, and Root, as a member of Roosevelt's administration, had an obvious conflict of interest.[4] But what to do about it was another matter. In the end nothing was, aside from verbal protests to Secretary of State Hay. On 3 March 1903 the British Foreign Office ordered Ambassador Herbert to exchange ratifications. With that move, Canada, still hestitating over formal approval, was locked into the Tribunal unless she chose to break with Britain and face the United States on her own. Speaking in Canada's House of Commons, Prime Minister Laurier defended the treaty inasmuch as both parties had agreed to accept the decision regardless of any loss of territory that might result, something the United States had always refused to do in the past.[5] Now there was even a possibility that the Tribunal might award Skagway to Canada. Laurier, concerned about the impartiality of Roosevelt's three nominees, promised to table the correspondence with Great Britain on the treaty as quickly as possible.

A time clock began ticking the moment ratifications were exchanged. It was all spelled out in the treaty: up to two months for each side to supply a written case, another two months for a written counter-case, and a final two months for the written argument. Following this, the Tribunal would meet in London to hear the oral arguments, and a final decision was expected within three months of the conclusion of the latter "unless His Britannic Majesty and the President of the United States shall by common accord extend the time therefor." Given Roosevelt's impatience, it seemed certain that it would all be over before the year was out.

Working against the deadline, both sides set to work to prepare their cases. On the British side, the three members of the Tribunal were named: Lord Alverstone, Britain's Lord Chief Justice, and two Canadians, Sir Louis Jetté, lieutenant-governor of Quebec and former member of its Supreme Court, and

Allen B. Aylesworth, a Toronto lawyer. The British agent in charge of preparation of the case was Clifford Sifton, Canada's minister of the interior, and the United States agent was John W. Foster, a former secretary of state. Both staffs included old hands who had served on the Bering Sea Arbitration Tribunal (1892–93) or the Venezuela Boundary Arbitration (1899).

Important as the Tribunal may have seemed to those caught up in its activity, in reality it was little more than a cover for Roosevelt's pressure tactics. In late March 1903, he wrote the three United States delegates: "The word *lisière* used in the treaty means the strip of territory bordering all the naviagable water of that portion of the Alaskan coast affected by the treaty, and this strip of territory is American of course." On that principle there could be no compromise, although "there is entire room for discussion and judicial and impartial agreement as to the exact boundary in any given locality — that is as to whether in such locality the boundary is to be pushed back ten marine leagues, or whether there is in actual fact nearer the coast a mountain chain which can be considered as running parallel to it." Laurier's "claim" to Skagway was something that was not open to discussion.[6]

There was another form of pressure on the British; in late July 1903, Roosevelt wrote to Oliver Wendell Holmes, newly appointed to the Supreme Court, who was then in Europe:

There is one point on which I think I ought to give you full information, in view of Chamberlain's remark to you. This is about the Alaska Boundary matter and if you happen to meet Chamberlain [Britain's Colonial Secretary] again you are entirely at liberty to tell him what I say, although of course it must be privately and unofficially. Nothing but my very earnest desire to get on well with England and my reluctance to come to a break made me consent to the appointment of a Joint Commission in this case; for I regard the attitude of Canada, which England has backed, as having the scantest possible warrant in justice. However, there were but two alternatives. Either I could appoint a commission and give a chance for agreement; or I could do as I shall of course do in case this commission fails, and request Congress to make an appropriation which will enable me to run the boundary on my own hook. As regards most of Great Britain's claim, there is not, in my judgment, enough to warrant so much as a consideration by the United States; and if it were not that there are two or three lesser points on which there is doubt, I could not, even for the object I have mentioned, have consented to appoint a commission. The claim of the Canadians for access to deep water along any part of the Canadian coast is just exactly as indefensible as if they should now suddenly claim the island of Nantucket. There is not a man fit to go on the commission in all the United States who would treat this claim any more respectfully than he would treat a claim to Nantucket. In the same way the preposterous claim once advanced, but

I think now abandoned by the Canadians, that the Portland Channel was not the Portland Channel but something else unknown, is no more worth discussing than the claim that the 49th Parallel meant the 50th Parallel or else the 48th.

But there are points which the commission can genuinely consider. There is room for argument about the islands in the mouth of Portland Channel. I think on this the American case much the stronger of the two. Still, the British have a case. Again, it may well be that there are places in which there is room for doubt as to whether there actually is a chain of mountains parallel to the coast within the ten-league limit. Here again there is a chance for honest difference and honest final agreement. I believe that no three men in United States could be found who would be more anxious than our own delegates to do justice to the British claim on all points where there is even a color of right on the British side. But the objections raised by certain Canadian authorities to Lodge, Root and Turner, and especially to Lodge and Root, was that they had committed themselves on the general proposition. No man in public life in any position of prominence could have possibly avoided committing himself on the proposition, any more than Mr. Chamberlain could avoid committing himself on the question of the ownership of the Orkneys if some Scandinavian country suddenly claimed them . . . .

Let me add that I earnestly hope the English understand my purpose. I wish to make one last effort to bring about an agreement through the commission, which will enable the people of both countries to say that the result represents the feeling of the representatives of both countries. But if there is a disagreement I wish it distinctly understood, not only that there will be no arbitration of the matter, but that in my message to Congress I shall take a position which will prevent any possibility of arbitration hereafter; a position, I am inclined to believe, which will render it necessary for Congress to give me the authority to run the line as we claim it by our own people, without any further regard to the attitude of England and Canada. If I paid attention to mere abstract right, that is the position I ought to take anyhow. I have not taken it because I wish to exhaust every effort to have the affair settled peacefully and with due regard to England's dignity.[7]

Holmes set to work spreading Roosevelt's message throughout the British government. Others, including Senator Lodge, brought similar messages. There seemed no reason to suspect the president was bluffing, but his continued threatening was becoming tiresome.

Members of the Tribunal and their staffs were all in London by late August 1903. Their first meeting, a social one, was on 2 September 1903 at a dinner given by Joseph Choate, the United States ambassador. Each side sized up the other, and the Americans were curious about the relationship between the British and Canadians making up the British delegation. Possibly there were differences that could be exploited. Lodge, who had already met and befriended Lord Alverstone, found the two Canadian members of the Tribunal "were not imposing looking persons, as a matter of fact they were insignificant in appearance, especially Sir Louis Jetté, a little French Canadian of the *chetif* French type and speaking English with a marked accent. Aylesworth is a round faced, bald headed, rosy, short man, looking amiable and commonplace, but I am told that he is a good lawyer and stands at the head of the Canadian bar."[8]

The formal session began the following morning. The three American members of the Tribunal

> went through the court yard [of the Foreign Office] & were marched up-stairs by the attendants, portentous in their solemn respectability. At the head of the stairs we three commissioners were separated from our following & conducted to the room of Mr. Villiers, chief Permanent Under Secretary. He ushered us into a large & rather handsome salle hung with portraits of deceased sovereigns, where the British government is to give us daily lunches during the sittings of the commission, & thence into the "cabinet room," also a large room looking on the park and hung with portraits of Chancellors and Foreign Secretaries. This cabinet room is to be the private room of the Tribunal & in it the consultations will be held. There we found Lord Alverstone, and presently the Canadian Colleagues appeared & we went to work. The commissions were exhibited & verified, the oaths were taken. We chose Lord Alverstone President, Tower, who used to be in Washington, Secretary, & Jack Carter & Pope, a Canadian, associate Secretaries. Then we discussed the important matter of time, & Lord Alverstone was all that was most considerate, in all ways anxious to hasten action & consult our convenience. We decided that the recess should not be more than a fortnight & that the arrangements must not extend beyond Oct. 9th. This done we proceeded to what is known as the "conference room," large and fitted up as for a court. We took our seats on the bench in an order carefully pre-arranged, & Lord Alverstone declared the Tribunal in session. Sir Robert Finlay, the Atty. Gen'l, presented the names of all the counsel on both sides. The Canadians' assistant counsel looked like a set of small country lawyers from remote towns . . . . For this reason I apprehend all the more troubles with them.[9]

At the meeting it was agreed that the oral arguments would be presented alternately by three counsel from each side beginning with Sir Robert Finlay, K.C., M.P., Britain's attorney general. The Americans felt that a week would suffice for their argument, but the British, wary of being "hustled," refused to set a limit. A compromise was reached with the Tribunal adjourning until 15

September to allow more time for preparation and stating that they expected the arguments to be over by 9 October. This way, the counsel were not bound to a final date but as Lodge noted: "I do not believe . . . they will undertake to go on for a minute after the date indicated by the Tribunal, for no sensible lawyer wishes to keep on talking when he knows that his judges wish him to stop."[10]

From the outset, it seemed certain that the three United States members and the two Canadians would each act as a unit. Lord Alverstone was the enigma; his decision could mean either a majority for the United States or deadlock. In effect, both sides would be speaking directly to him in their arguments, gauging his reactions and pressing home any point that seemed to appeal to him. Already it was an open secret that Alverstone favoured the United States contention that the *lisière* should be a solid strip, cutting Canada off from the heads of the inlets throughout the Panhandle. Indeed, in a confidence that would later be betrayed, Alverstone had attempted to sound out Joseph Pope, a prominent Canadian civil servant, on Canada's aspirations. The two were old acquaintances, having served together on the Bering Sea Tribunal some ten years earlier. Pope described the incident in his diary:

12 SEPTEMBER 1903 I went down to Ld. Alverstone's country place to spend Sunday.

13 SEPTEMBER 1903 . . . I had a long private talk with Ld. A. about Alaska matters. His Lordship spoke very confidentially. He told me he thought we have a convincing case on the Portland Channel and also for a mountain boundary. Adding that he feared our case for the heads of inlets was correspondingly weak. All this agreed quite with my own opinion. He added that of course this last opinion might be modified on hearing the arguments of our Counsel. He asked me if he [*sic*] thought Canada would be satisfied if we could get Wales and Pearse Islands and a mountain line. I said that I feared not. He asked which they would prefer — that or an absolute draw — 3 and 3 all round. I said I thought the latter. Personally I would greatly prefer the former, which I thought was all we could expect, but I added people were as unreasonable in Canada as elsewhere and that the inlets were the question. He told me I could let Sir W. L. know that he was most indignant at recent press reports, that he was influenced by nothing but a desire to render a just decision and that nobody had remotely suggested conciliating the U.S. at the expense of Canada. Altogether, he intimated he was going for Portland Channel and a mountain line and against our claim to the heads of inlets, but this was absolutely confidential between us. I was greatly relieved at this for I feared from the opening day that he was going to be dead against us all through.[11]

Later, after learning Lord Alverstone had misrepresented this discussion in talking to Clifford Sifton, Pope commented in a personal memo: "I never sought his confidence. He thrust it on me, and nothing could have been more distasteful to me under the circumstances than to receive it, but having given my word, I was debarred (though sorely tempted) from making any use of the knowledge, he, my host, had imparted to me — under the seal of secrecy — in his own home."[12]

The oral argument began on 15 September with Sir Robert Finlay speaking from eleven to four each day with a half-hour break for lunch. Both he and the counsel to follow spent much time on Question 2 dealing with Portland Channel. When the treaty was signed in St. Petersburg in 1825, both sides were obviously familiar with Captain Vancouver's map of 1798 showing Portland Canal and Observatory Inlet, but the United States counsel argued that they might not have had Vancouver's narrative with a more detailed description of his explorations. Did Portland Canal join Observatory Inlet at Point Ramsden or continue its general trend to pass to the north of Pearse, Wales, and some smaller islands, reaching Dixon Entrance at a point almost due east of Cape Fox? From his narrative, it was certain that Vancouver had sailed down this back channel in a yawl, mapping as he went, and even circumnavigating what is now Fillmore Island:

> In the morning of the 2nd [August 1793] we set out early, and passed through a labyrinth of small islets and rocks, along the continental shore; this taking now a winding course to the south-west and west, showed the south-eastern side of the canal to be much broken, through which was a passage leading S.S.E. towards the ocean. We passed this in hope of finding a more northern and westerly communication, in which we were not disappointed, as the channel we were then pursuing was soon found to communicate also with the sea, making the land to the south of us one or more islands. From the north-west point of this land, situated in latitude 54° 45½′, longitude 229° 28′, [130° 32′W], the Pacific was evidently seen between N. 88W. and S. 81.W.[13]

The name was given on 15 August 1793, when Vancouver sailed his yawl from near Cape Fox back to Salmon Cove on Observatory Inlet where the expedition's ships were anchored: "In the forenoon we reached that arm of the sea whose examinations had occupied our time from the 27th of the preceding to the 2nd of this month. The distance from its entrance to its source is about 70 miles, which, in honour of the noble family of Bentinck, I named Portland Canal."[14]

None of the Tribunal members questioned that Vancouver had sailed through the narrow passage north of Sitklan and Kanagunut Islands; clearly the geographic co-ordinates he gave for "the north-west point of this land" confirmed that. However, there was a diversion when Turner suggested that Vancouver's Portland Canal might run through the deeper Tongass Passage lying between

Wales and Sitklan Island. After all, Vancouver had sighted through the passage on his trip behind the islands, and might not he be referring to this entrance on his return from Cape Fox? In discussing the matter with Finlay, the British counsel, he concluded: "I do not want you to understand that my mind is fixed upon this proposition [Tongass Passage]. The view merely occurred to me when I was reading Vancouver's narrative, and I desired to get your views on this subject."[15]

Throughout the arguments, much attention was paid to the *lisière* and whether it went around the head of the inlets. Correspondence between the British and the Russians beginning in February 1824 and leading to the treaty a year later was considered in great detail to learn if the width of the strip were spelled out in detail. The United States contended that a "line parallel to the windings of the coast, and which shall never exceed the distance of 10 marine leagues therefrom" could only be drawn from tidewater at the heads of the inlets, while the British argument contended that "the coast" could only refer to the general trend of the coastline and that inlets should be disregarded in drawing the line. Lynn Canal was the main point at issue, and if the British were correct, surely the ten marine leagues should be measured from the point where Lynn Canal first narrows to less than six miles wide and is, therefore, using the concept of a three-mile limit, no longer part of the ocean but simply territorial waters. Such a line would put the boundary about fifty miles south of Skagway!

Throughout the arguments, Lord Alverstone did his best to remain neutral and keep his distance from both sides. Increasingly, the Canadians worried that he had been suborned by the Americans. The formal sessions were one thing, but what about all the social functions and country weekends? Somehow, the Canadians were seldom included.[16] Things came to a head on 7 October when Clifford Sifton, the Canadian cabinet minister serving as British Agent, cabled Prime Minister Laurier: "I think that Chief Justice intends to join Americans deciding in such a way as to defeat us on every point. We all think that Chief Justice's intentions are unjustifiable, and due to predetermination to avoid trouble with United States. Jetté and Aylesworth are much exasperated, and considering withdrawing from Commission."[17]

Laurier replied: "Our Commissioners must not withdraw. If they cannot get our full rights let them put up a bitter fight for our contention on Portland Canal, which is beyond doubt: that point must be decided in Canada's favour. Shame Chief Justice and carry that point. If we are thrown over by Chief Justice, he will give the last blow to British diplomacy in Canada. He should be plainly told this by our Commissioners."[18]

Unknown to the Canadian members of the Tribunal, their American counterparts were equally worried over Lord Alverstone. By now, they knew he would support them on the inlets, but he was holding out for a narrow mountain strip, totally unacceptable to them. Somehow the Canadians must be influencing him.[19] Possibly the British government could force a compromise. On 9 October,

Senator Lodge discussed the Tribunal at a private meeting with Arthur Balfour, Britain's prime minister, and came away with the impression that Alverstone would be told of the need for a "complete decision."[20]

The oral arguments had ended on Thursday, 8 October and the next meeting was held on the following Monday. Senator Lodge described it in a letter to his daughter: "October 12th. A long day passed in conference at the Foreign Office. The commissioners and no one else present. We went over all the questions except the 7th. Lord Alverstone read an opinion against us on the Portland Canal and for us on the great question of the line going around the head of the inlets, intimating that we must carry it on selected summits south of the Lynn Canal watershed. I walked up with the Chief Justice and told him the situation practically, that this was the only chance of a settlement, that if Canada broke off here she would get nothing and that now she might get the Portland Channel but that we could not take his mountains. He is most anxious for a decision and sticks to his mountains, which we cannot yield, so I doubt if we get a complete decision."[21]

The deadlock continued all week. Alverstone refused to budge from his theory of "selected summits," and Aylesworth was quoted in the press to the effect that he would never yield an inch of British Territory.[22] Finally, on Thursday, 15 October, the three United States delegates sent a lengthy cable to Washington:

No vote yet on any question. Informal expression on third and fifth shows equal division on Portland Canal but with feeling that while a preponderance of evidence is in favor of Southern Channel, yet it furnishes reasonable ground to concede passage north of Pearse and Wales Island if final decision of whole matter could be secured thereby but not otherwise. On fifth question English member has read an opinion in favor of affirmative answer, from which it would be difficult although not absolutely impossible for him to retire. On seventh question he stands stiffly for a line following mountains nearest the shore around heads of inlets, and giving us a strip only a few miles wide along the shore. He claims that this follows necessarily from the grounds on which he holds with us on fifth question, and that any other view would require a decision of the fifth question in negative. To stand on the ten marine leagues line throughout would in all probability involve a disagreement on all but fifth question and possibly on that question. The survey of Convention of 1892 is incomplete and leaves strip for ten to twenty miles inside of ten marine leagues line wholly unknown. It is therefore impossible except perhaps on St. Elias Alps and along watershed above Lynn Canal to lay out any line by identification of mountains or otherwise which involves any concession whatever from ten marine leagues line or to establish with certainty the fact that there is no mountain crest within meaning of Treaty or to show by comparison the fact that proposed line near the coast cannot be true line.

What do you think of suggestion that Tribunal employ experts under Article One to complete survey up to ten marine leagues line, thus giving full material for judical decision under Question 7, and adjourn long enough to allow next summer and fall for their work, the time for decision being extended under Article 5 of Treaty to some time after November, 1904. It is proper to add it seems improbable from present expression that any additional information concerning topography can change view of English Member since he insists on the principle of running line along summits of mountains nearest sea, although does not insist on direct contiguity to water. Even if he should accede to a line which our Commissioners could accept as a compromise, they do not now see, without additional surveys, any tenable theory on which they could sustain such a line. Additional survey might or might not give material to sustain a compromise line or might or might not show mountain boundary to be in immediate neighborhood of ten marine leagues line. In view of these facts would an adjournment as suggested be preferable to an immediate vote which would result in disagreement on all but fifth question and possibly on that?[23]

The cable, addressed to Secretary of State Hay, had been sent in Ambassador Choate's name. In fact, it was a direct appeal by the Tribunal members for instructions from Roosevelt.[24] Senator Lodge, staying in the country, travelled to the Embassy each morning looking for the answer. It was waiting on Saturday, 17 October, and in it Hay stated that if it could be announced that:

the Tribunal has decided question five favorably to the American contention, and if there is no prospect of a satisfactory decision at present on question seven, the President would not object to an adjournment of the Tribunal for the purpose and for the time you mention: that is to allow experts chosen under Article one of the treaty to complete survey up to ten marine leagues line during next summer and fall, the Commission meeting in November following to decide the question, in view of the authoritative additional information, as to the topography of the region. Most confidential. If it necessary in order to secure above announcement and if American Commissioners deem it proper, the third question can be decided in favor of English contention as to North Channel of Portland Canal.[25]

Not mentioned in the cables was a final, almost desperate attempt to influence Lord Alverstone through pressure on the British government. On Wednesday, 14 October, Ambassador Choate had asked for a confidential meeting with Lord Lansdowne, Britain's foreign secretary. At it, the old threat was repeated over again: the United States would simply take over the territory in question if the Tribunal broke down. But there was a new approach too: "The upshot of our conversation was the Commissioners, or four of them, must agree on the drawing line, and that, if necessary, we [Choate and Lansdowne] might ourselves agree on what would be a satisfactory line, and perhaps, if necessary advise the Commissioners what we thought . . . . I left satisfied that he and Mr. Balfour would, if they had not already done so, tell Lord Alverstone what they thought as to the necessity of agreeing upon that line, and that the present chance of settling the controversy ought not to be lost."[26]

Everything came to a head on Saturday, 17 October. The Americans, now certain of what Washington would accept, had reached agreement with an increasingly anxious Lord Alverstone just before the six members of the Tribunal met together. Aylesworth and Jetté, the two Canadians, had watched suspiciously as a series of hurried conferences took place between Alverstone and one or the other of Lodge and Root. Obviously, something was going on.[27]

The session began by Lord Alverstone asking the other members their opinion on the four islands in Portland Canal. Root spoke for about an hour claiming all four for United States; Jetté, unprepared made only a few remarks from his chair; Lodge (or Turner) agreed with Root; and Aylesworth said he agreed with Alverstone's printed opinion, handed down a few days earlier. After the others finished, Lord Alverstone stated that his judgment was now in favour of Canada for Pearse and Wales Islands and in favour of United States for Sitklan and Kanagunut Islands. He said that it pained him to decide against his own country and his colleagues, but otherwise there could be no agreement and no decision.[28] Aylesworth rose to denounce him, claiming his decision was not a judgment but a mere compromise. Despite the agreement between Alverstone and the three Americans, there was too much bitterness to railroad everything through in one day. The meeting adjourned at half-past three after the Canadians made "a last dismal and useless stand on question five."[29] The Americans had produced a map showing the proposed boundary, but there was still no formal vote on question seven. Lodge, disappointed, left the meeting worried that Alverstone might change his mind again.

The Canadians serving on the staff of the British delegation were incensed over the splitting of the four islands in Portland Canal. Right to the last minute a win, or at worst a tie vote, had seemed certain on this issue. Politically, either would have helped to sell the Tribunal decision to a sceptical Canadian public. Now there was nothing. Furious at the turn of events, Clifford Sifton cabled Prime Minister Laurier: "Chief Justice has agreed with American Commissioners. Their decision will be to give us Wales and Pearse Islands, but give Americans two islands alongside, namely Kanagunut and Sitklan which command entrance to canal and destroy strategic value Wales and Pearse. Remainder of line substantially as contended for by Americans, except that it follows watershed at White Pass and Chilkoot. Our Commissioners strongly dissent. Decision likely to be Tuesday next. I regard it as wholly indefensible. What is your view? Course of discussion between Commissioners has greatly exasperated our Commissioners who consider matter as pre-arranged."[30]

Laurier replied: "Concession to Americans of Kanagunut and Sitklan cannot be justified on any consideration of treaty. It is one of those concessions which have made British diplomacy odious to Canadian people, and it will have most lamentable effect. Our Commissioners ought to protest in most vigorous terms."[31]

When the tribunal reconvened on Monday, 19 October, the experts had completed marking the American's proposed boundary line on the big contour maps. The latter, prepared by the Canadians for the Alaska Boundary Commission of 1893–95, were still the best available. The map did not go far enough inland on the east side of Lynn Canal, and here the topography had been sketched in, presumably by one of the surveyors with the Canadian delegation.[32] In fact, it was a compromise line; Lodge had shown it to Alverstone on Friday morning, and he had accepted it in general aside from the line at the Stikine River. The Americans had moved this inland on purpose, anticipating that Alverstone would insist on moving it back to the provisional boundary of 1877.[33]

In the final marking, Lord Alverstone did what he could with Root and Lodge while the others took little part.[34] The "selected summits" chosen were marked with crude crosses and the letter "S".[35] South of Lynn Canal between points marked "P" and "T", roughly 120 miles apart, the boundary was not marked since "the evidence is not sufficient to enable the Tribunal to say which are the mountains parallel to the coast within the meaning of the Treaty."[36] The provisional boundary lines at the Stikine River and the White and Chilkoot Passes were accepted, but in the Chilkat area the line was shifted to the north, giving the United States the entire Porcupine mining camp.

When they had finished, Aylesworth reminded them that the early correspondence had specifically mentioned Mount Fairweather and that the line lay too far to the interior.[37] Lord Alverstone agreed that this was so, and the line was brought down to include the peak. None of them could have suspected that by 1912 Grand Pacific Glacier would retreat across the revised line, breaching the *lisière* and, aside from one or two surges, giving Canada tidewater at the head of Tarr Inlet until a new advance brought it back across the line about 1950.[38]

The Tribunal met the following day to hand down their award. The ceremony was not open to the public, and after an unexpected delay of two hours, it consisted of little more than the president, Lord Alverstone, handing a copy of the award to the two agents in the presence of the official secretaries.[39] The award bore only four signatures: the two Canadians refused to sign.

In an unusual move the following day, Aylesworth and Jetté took their dissent to the public in a statement appearing in *The Times*. They deplored the splitting of the islands in Portland Canal and the loss of the inlets, stating in conclusion:

If the six members of the Tribunal had each given an individual judicial decision on each of the questions submitted, we should have conceived it our duty under the Treaty of 1903, however much we might have differed from

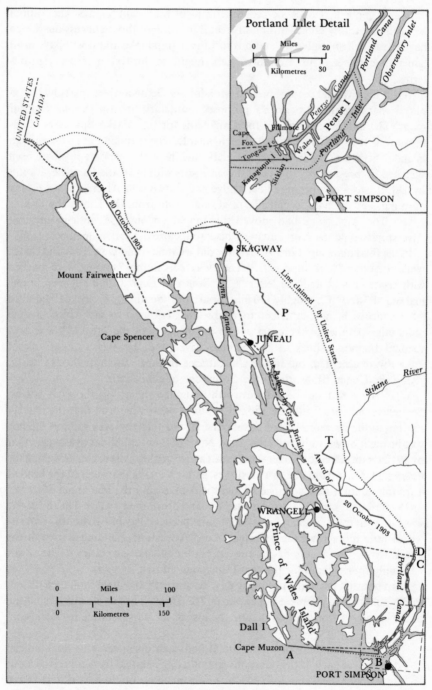

Map 3: Alaska Boundary Award of 20 October 1903

our colleagues, to have joined in signing the document which constituted the official record of the answers. We do not consider the finding of the Tribunal as to the islands at the entrance to Portland Channel, or as to the mountain line, a judicial one, and we have therefore declined to be parties to the award.

Our position during the conferences of the Tribunal has been an unfortunate one. We have been in entire accord between ourselves and have, severally and jointly, urged our views as strongly as we were able, but we have been compelled to witness the sacrifices of the interests of Canada, powerless to prevent it, though satisfied that the course the majority determined to pursue in respect to the matters above specially referred to ignored the just rights of Canada.

Over the next few days there were written opinions: a combined one by the three Americans and individual ones by Lord Alverstone, Sir Louis Jetté, and Allen Aylesworth. The latter's final paragraph went beyond the press release: "Finally, I have merely to say this further, that the course the majority of this Tribunal has decided to take in regard to the islands at the entrance of Portland Channel is, in my humble judgment, so opposed to the plain requirements of justice, and so absolutely irreconcilable with any disposition of that branch of this case upon principles of a judicial character, that I respectfully decline to affix my signature to their Award.[40]

It was a victory for United States and, in a way, for Britain since a cause of friction between the two countries had been removed. In Canada, the award left a legacy of bitterness. Even today, most Canadians believe that Britain is somehow to blame for the Alaska Panhandle cutting off almost half of British Columbia from the ocean. Yet, even if the British claim had been accepted in full, the Panhandle would be simply a slimmed-down version of its present form. The root cause is the splitting of the four islands in the Portland Canal area. The real loss there was not a mere six or so square miles of territory but rather Canada's only hope of saving face in the negotiations.

Lord Alverstone never discussed the reason for his about-face in voting to split the four islands.[41] Perhaps all he could say in public was his remark at the Lord Mayor's banquet in London in November 1903: "Discussions will arise between nations as they have arisen before. If you do not want a judicial decision, do not ask British Judges to be members of the Court."[42] Presumably he was under pressure from the British government to reach an agreement, and the Americans had refused to go along on the islands, even though they had Roosevelt's permission.

George Turner may have bluffed him.[43] Years later, Turner would write that a careful reading of Captain Vancouver's narrative had convinced him that the entrance to Vancouver's Portland Canal lay between Sitklan and Wales Island and that all but the two Canadian commissioners accepted this conclusion.[44]

Turner had made the suggestion on 16 September 1903 during the oral argument, but other accounts by fellow Tribunal members do not refer to a fuller discussion of it. Turner continues that at a dinner at the White House soon after his return from London, President Roosevelt, delighted over the Portland Canal decision and Canada's pique, remarked that he was going to name "those islands up there Turner's Twins." Later that evening, the president told Turner that he believed him "the only individual in all the history of the United States who, by his own unaided exertions, either secured or saved to this Country a single inch of territory" and that he appreciated his services accordingly.[45]

The Tribunal left one piece of unfinished business. Throughout its sittings, the owners of a newly built American cannery on Wales Island had been asking that their interests be safeguarded if the island was awarded to Canada. They had built in good faith, unaware of a boundary problem. Title to their land had been duly recorded in Ketchikan early in 1902, and the cannery was within a few miles of the United States Army storehouse on Wales Island. President Roosevelt, aware of the problem, had written to Senator Lodge on 5 October 1903, insisting that the owners rights be guaranteed.[46] Early in November 1903, after Lodge and Turner had returned to New York, the owners were still trying to learn what had happened.[47] The answer turned out to be nothing: the issue had never been raised. The cannery, which had packed thirty-five thousand cases of salmon in 1903, was now unable to obtain a suitable supply of Canadian fish and was shut out of the American market by tariffs. A claim against the United States government was made in January 1904, but it was 5 May 1936 before another President Roosevelt signed the bill granting the company $100,000 in compensation.[48]

6

Marking the Panhandle Boundary
(1904–1920)

Marking the Alaska Panhandle boundary on the maps in London was just the first step; now the surveyors were expected to risk their lives in attempting to identify and monument the peaks themselves. It was a near-impossible task, taking ten years to complete in a preliminary manner and involving between sixty and one hundred men each season in the first years. There must have been many times when a surveyor, struggling to reach a peak or shivering while waiting for the clouds to lift, wished that all six Tribunal members could be with him, sharing the discomfort!

Travel along much of the line was simply out of the question; nearly a third of it was perpetually covered by ice and snow. Instead, the surveys would have to be carried inland by triangulation from coastal stations already tied into the Southeast Alaska Datum.[1] This datum or network, established in 1901, would provide the underlying framework needed to produce accurate topographic maps of the boundary area. As new surveys were joined to it, the exact latitude and longitude of the added survey stations could be calculated. The datum incorporated nine different groups of triangulation, each built up around independent astronomic determinations of latitude and longitude, that had now been joined together. Most of the work had been done by the U.S. Coast and Geodetic Survey beginning with their initial work in the summer of 1867 and particularly between 1893 and 1895 when the Alaska Boundary Commission was active. As yet, there were no direct ties to the survey network extending across the mainland United States and southern Canada.

Despite objections to the award in Canada, preparations for a boundary survey went ahead quickly. Early in 1904, two commissioners were appointed: for the United States, O.H. Tittmann, superintendent of the Coast and Geodetic Survey, and for Canada, W.F. King, the chief astronomer. In April 1904, the new commissioners proposed that eight peaks be used as the boundary in the unmapped section of about 120 miles between the points designated "P" and "T" in the award and that, in the south, they be empowered to select additional peaks between peaks Nos. 7 and 8 and peak No. 8 and point T, on the condition that none of the new peaks should be more than twenty-five hundred metres from the straight line joining the respective points.[2] Almost a year later, on 25 March 1905, the recommendation was approved in an exchange of notes between the secretary of state and the British ambassador in Washington.[3] By then, field work was already underway. Points on the boundary would be monumented where possible, a vista twenty feet wide cut through timbered sections, and triangulation and topographic mapping completed along the entire boundary line. Later, the boundary points were numbered consecutively from the south, beginning with B.P. 1 at the head of Portland Canal.

Initially two types of boundary monument were used, a large obelisk sixty-three inches high at important points and a smaller cone thirty inches high for more general use.[4] Both were cast in aluminum-bronze and carried the words "Canada" and "United States" in raised letters on opposite sides. The approximate weight of the components of the obelisk was 253 pounds and of the single casting of the cone from 55 to 60 pounds. The former were set on concrete bases three feet square and from two to three feet high, and the latter on smaller bases or, on solid rock, grouted into holes drilled for the four fluted legs extending beneath the cone.

1904 FIELD SEASON

Chilkat Area[5]

Early in June 1904, two Canadian parties were under canvas at Pleasant Camp, about thirty-seven miles inland from Haines and a North-West Mounted Police post since the winter of 1897-98. The ten-man parties were under the overall leadership of C.A. Bigger.

There was an immediate problem; the "S" inked on the Award map lay somewhere in the gravel flat between Jarvis Creek and the Klehini River, a spot impossible to monument. There was already a tentative boundary line surveyed in February 1904 by Captain Wilds P. Richardson of the United States Army working with the officer in charge of the police post. Their line cut between Jack Dalton's roadhouse and the police post, leaving the latter in Canada as the tribunal intended. The commissioners, furnished with a blueprint of Richardson's survey, chose a slightly different line that also left the police post in Canada. Their line ran southwesterly from Surgeon Mountain (B.P. 144) to a turning point on the gravel flat, B.P. 147, where it swung northwesterly to Mount McDonnell (B.P. 150), passing through a point on Richardson's survey near the middle of the point of land between Klehini River and Jarvis Creek. The new line was surveyed and the turning point referenced by two monuments along each of the intersecting lines in order that it could be relocated quickly at times when the flat was free of water.

This done, the crews set to work cutting the vista in the timbered areas. The commissioners required that it be cut to give a clear skyline a full twenty feet wide, a difficult task in heavy timber. Later in the season, one party worked to the east towards Kelsall River while the other worked to the west and south. Members of the latter succeeded in reaching the boundary line on the Tsirku River on 17 September only to find that fresh snow had put an end to their season. However, camera stations were occupied, and some topographic mapping was done on the United States side.

Northeast of Pleasant Camp, an American party of fifteen men led by J.A. Flemer worked on the Chilkat and Kelsall Rivers. Until late July the party, assisted by Indians with their canoes, worked to get their outfit to the mouth of the Kelsall River, about fourteen miles up the Chilkat River from Wells, the point where the Dalton Trail left the Chilkat. Finally on 20 July with river conditions just right, the final load was brought up by Jack Dalton's small sternwheeler, *Chilkat*. It was the first time she had attempted this section of the river and, though she grounded three times, the Indian pilot made the fourteen-mile run in nine hours. From the mouth of the Kelsall River, the men cut twelve miles of trail to the boundary and bridged the river near it.

By the end of the 1904 season, the Canadian and United States parties had marked the boundary line and cut most of the vista between Mount Ashmun (B.P. 134) and Mount McDonnell (B.P. 150), about sixteen miles in a direct line. This section covered the Dalton Trail and most of the nearby area being prospected for placer gold and copper deposits.

White Pass[6]

A five-man United States party led by O.M. Leland pulled into the summit in late July 1904 aboard the White Pass train. After setting up camp, they began work on their assignment to identify B.P.s 114 and 119 and to locate a turning point in the pass itself. They climbed the peak designated B.P. 119, which is about four miles northwest and three thousand feet higher than the pass, on 4 August and marked the temporary station selected with a drill hole in the exposed rock. They did not climb B.P. 114, but the peak could be readily identified in photos taken by surveyors of the commission of 1893-95. The broad summit of the White Pass proved to be cut by a series of north-south ridges and valleys so that its limits were indefinite. The markers from 1900 were still there; four iron bars leaded into the rock and numbered 1 to 4 from west to east. No. 2, on the point assumed to be the summit, was considered unsuitable for a turning point, and an alternate turning point was selected subject to approval by the commissioners. In addition, a plane-table map was made of the pass and nearby surroundings. The commissioners arrived in late August, but they were unable to reach a final agreement, and the line was slightly modified during the following summer.

Stikine River[7]

Two parties of fifteen men each, an American one headed by Fremont Morse and a Canadian one by G.R. White-Fraser, met in Wrangell, Alaska, on 15 June 1904 and sailed the next day for the Stikine aboard the Hudson's Bay Company steamer, *Mount Royal.* It was raining when they landed at the abandoned North-West Mounted Police buildings near the boundary. As the Canadians had pack-horses and the Americans the better boats, it was decided that the former should work south of the river where the horses might be of some use. Later, when it became obvious that the horses were more trouble than they were worth, they were unloaded on a trader from Telegraph Creek.

The boundary line across the Stikine followed Hunter's line of 1877. While they soon made ascents on Elbow Mountain (B.P. 66) and Mount Cote (B.P. 62), to the north and south of the river, and established camps on their upper slopes, it was 9 July before the clouds lifted enough to locate a point on the south bank of the Stikine from which the line projection could begin. From then until the end of the summer, most of the men were kept busy clearing the vista unless they were needed for other duties. The work, as described by White-Fraser, was anything but easy:

> On the alluvial bottom is a dense jungle of willow and alder underbrush, springing up under a fairly close forest of cottonwoods, with occasional hemlock and spruce trees, attaining an average diameter of 5 to 6 feet with larger individuals not infrequently encountered running to 8 feet. This forest interspersed with patches of hay marsh, and intersected by larger or smaller side-streams of the Stikine and Katete Rivers. On the slope of Mount Cote the forest consists almost entirely of hemlock, with an occasional spruce; the cottonwoods practically disappearing and the place of the alder underbrush being taken by a close growth of berry bushes and that unpleasant member of the Fig family known as the "Devil's Club" whose malignant arms are ever stretched forth to assist the unwary climber, and whose poisoned bristles will make him wish he had never been born. The work of clearing the line up the slope of Mount Cote was of sufficiently arduous and gymnastic a

character to satisfy most of the innocents of whom my party consisted on leaving Vancouver.

A store bred youth balancing himself on a 10" chopping board, 18 feet above the ground, with no better support than the 9' saw which he is using on a 7' tree, is an object lesson in the control exercised by a steadfast mind over shrinking matter. But when on the 18th Aug. my line reached somewhat beyond a point where each tree as it fell, tobogganed down a slippery cliff face standing at an angle of probably 60° from the horizontal, and carried devastation in its course until it found a resting place 1,000 feet below — I decided to carry it no further, but move on to the Cote-Whipple line.[8]

But the weather was against both parties. The commissioners had visited the area at the first of September 1904 and as White-Fraser noted:

I returned to my Katete camp under a brilliant sky that gave favorable augury for the future. My camp was on the right bank about 10 feet above the then water level, near the mouth of what, at very high water was an island between the main stream and a highwater side channel. That night, September 3rd, it began to rain. It rained all that night, next day, next night, the following day, the river rising rapidly until we were on a true island, with roaring waters all around. Nightfall brought no abatement of the conditions, and a vibration of the earth, and a crashing sound in the air awakened me out of an apprehensive slumber — causing me to rush out of my tent — almost head over heels into the raging stream, which in a few hours of darkness had washed away the point of the island and sufficient of the frontage to leave my tent within 2 feet of the bank and the kitchen stove in the cook tent, actually overhanging the water. A few hours of working by candle light sufficed to remove the camp to a place of safety and to clear the point of the island of trees whose fall might have endangered it. But for three subsequent days, the state of the weather and of the river made it impossible to move.[9]

Both parties stuck it out waiting for better weather. It was a vain hope; the rain was almost continuous. The Americans left on 25 September, and the Canadians, delayed by the wreck of one of their boats, followed about a week later. For the Canadians, the season ended on a bright note. The townspeople of Wrangell had been good to them, and, in return, they chartered the Hudson's Bay steamer for the day to run all of them up to the Great Glacier for a picnic in Canada. Years later, Harper Reed, one of the crew, wrote down his recollection of the event:

The solid end of this glacier is about ½ mile inshore from the river bank and to get on the solid ice face a huge area of glacier quagmire had to be crossed. . . . Amongst the Wrangell visitors came the town's butcher and the town's laundry owner, a lady of heavy proportions and these two were not on speaking terms — both bad-tempered. However, they were the last to arrive at the quagmire safety crossing to the ice and the lady stepped into the quicksand, blue gummy stuff, and began to sink — screaming as loud as possible. It happened the butcher, also of heavy weight but strong, was following and he at once started to assist but the extra weight only added to the bad situation. The crowd ahead stopped and looked back to see the two of them sinking in the blue clay. The butcher had his arms around the lady, she was sinking and her summer clothing fast climbing over her shoulders with all her underwear showing, and both of them howling for help. The narrow gangway of safety would only allow passage of one person at a time but we all tried to get back to assist. By the time we could get near them to assist the butcher was holding the lady's wearing apparel and she had slipped through leaving her underclothes in the arms of the butcher. But with lots of assistance both were dragged to safety and took an icy-cold water splash bath in the small stream from the glacier. Yes they were talking and for foul language the laundry owner beat the butcher. The merriment caused lasted for nearly a week — a very successful picnic![10]

Portland Canal[11]

In late August 1904, Commissioners King and Tittmann arrived at the head of Portland Canal to fix the location of Point C of the Tribunal Award. It was a comfortable trip aboard the Canadian Pacific steamer, *Danube*, specially diverted from the Skagway run for the purpose. The site they chose lay just above high-tide level on Eagle Point, the tip of the ridge of granite separating the drainage of the Salmon and Bear Rivers. The stone storehouse built by United States Army Engineers in 1896 lay a few feet to the north. Members of the ship's crew were impressed to help set up the aluminum-bronze obelisk, B.P. No. 1, and with the task completed, the *Danube* continued on to Skagway.

1905-20 SEASONS

Things had moved swiftly; by the end of the 1904 season the boundary had been clearly marked at most of the points where there had been friction in the past. Finishing the work would obviously take many years, but the pressure was off, especially now that activity in the Klondike was waning and interest had turned to the Tanana gold field, well on the Alaska side.

A total of eighty-two "S" points had been marked on the award map, all but three of them on mountain peaks, and an additional eight peaks had been chosen by the boundary commissioners. In the new work, all would have to be identified, accurately located, and monumented when possible. The topographic mapping would have to be extended inland beyond the boundary line. Along the boundary line itself, boundary monuments were needed at river and stream crossings and in sections where there was mining activity. In addition, the vista, a full twenty feet wide, would have to be completed in the timbered areas, a total distance of fifty miles.

From 1905 on, the work was done on a piecemeal basis with the field parties strung out along the Panhandle. Most worked independently, having little or no contact with other survey parties. Party size varied with the assignment, most had between ten and twenty men. A few were smaller, and in one instance, thirty-five men were spread among four sub-parties that were working close together. Initially, parties from one country often included a representative from the other, but after the 1908 season even this became the exception. By then, much of the work involved surveying sections left incomplete in the earlier work or making minor revisions ordered by the commissioners.

The party chiefs received their assignments from the commissioners. Beyond that, it was up to them. They were responsible both for carrying out the field work and the accuracy of the surveys. When things went wrong, there was seldom any means of summoning help or asking for new instructions. The chief and party members were expected to deal with any emergency as best they could.

Most of the parties were self-contained units, equipped with boats, tents, and complete camping gear. Usually they were able to reach their base camps by boat and enjoy the luxury of at least some canned food. Even so, the staple items were bacon, flour, sugar, and beans. Since they were unable to keep fresh meat for more than a few days, any game or fish they could secure was a welcome addition to their diet. On back-packing trips and sledging glaciers and snow-fields, the weight of food carried was kept to a minimum by eliminating items with a high water content. The result was a simple diet, often little more than rice, bacon, sugar, pilot bread (hardtack), dried fruit, and tea. Above timberline, kerosene or alcohol stoves were used for cooking.

Conditions in the field changed very little over the years of the survey except that with more experience it became easier to cope with some of the transportation problems. As always, the work was at the mercy of the uncertain coastal weather. Even if the boundary line could be reached, triangulation and photography could only be done during the all too brief periods of clear weather.

Each of the parties, no matter how small or how minor their task, had their share of unexpected adventures. For many of the men involved, the work on the Alaska Boundary would be the highlight of their lives. Unfortunately, while all the survey notes and calculations were carefully recorded and preserved, too little of the human story has been saved. Rather than following the work from year to year, it seems preferable to follow it from south to north, just as the final Boundary Points are numbered.

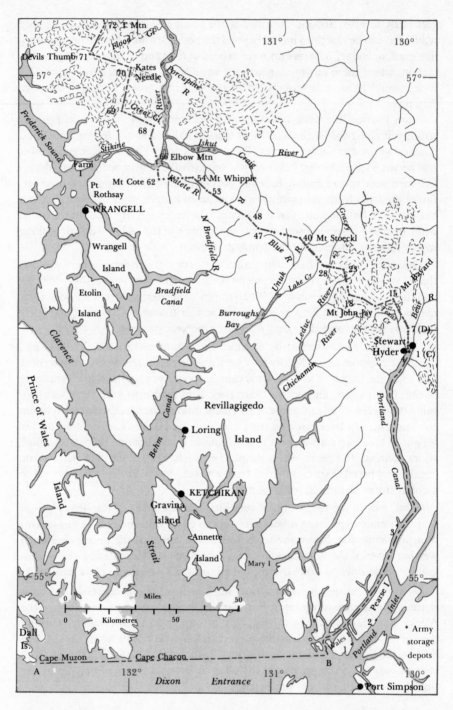

Map 4: Panhandle Boundary: Water boundary and Boundary Points 1
(Eagle Point) to 72 (T Mountain)

Dixon Entrance to the Head of Portland Canal (Points A to C of the 1903 Award[12]

1911: F.H. Mackie (Canada) with ten men, including Fremont Morse, United States representative.
1912: T.C. Dennis (Canada) with fifteen men, including Fremont Morse, United States representative.
1913: N.J. Ogilvie (Canada) with twenty men, including Fremont Morse, United States representative.
1914: N.J. Ogilvie (Canada) with twenty-nine men.

This portion of the boundary line lies over water and is referenced to monuments on shore. Point A, the initial point of the line, lies at Cape Muzon at the southern tip of Dall Island, which at the time of the 1825 Treaty was considered part of Prince of Wales Island. It is referenced by two concrete piers, one on the extreme south end of Dall Island and the other on the most southerly of three small rocky islands about five hundred feet offshore. From Point A the line runs directly to Point B at the entrance to Tongass Passage between Sitklan and Wales Island. This too is referenced by monuments on shore. Between Points B and C, the line threads through Tongass Passage, Pearse Canal, and Portland Canal as a series of straight lines with twenty-eight turning points, all referenced to monuments on shore.

One of the two fatal accidents of the entire project occurred on Cape Muzon on the night of 6 September 1913 when an immense slide buried the camp of C.H. Bode and G.R. Roberts, who were tending one of the signal lights used as a target in the triangulation across Dixon Entrance. The alarm was raised when two settlers living nearby became uneasy over not seeing the men and made their way to the camp. There had been heavy rain for several days, and about a dozen fresh slides had come down across the trail. At the site of the camp the only things visible in the mud and shattered trees were a sack of flour, a few tins of food, and a plate. Members of the party were brought in from other stations as quickly as possible, but the bodies were never located.

Stewart Area (B.P. 1 to B.P. 18)[13]

1904: Boundary Commissioners
1905: G.R. White-Fraser (Canada) with ten men, including Radcliffe Hordern, United States representative.
1910: F.H. Mackie (Canada) with eleven men, including Fremont Morse, United States representative.
1920: J.D. Craig (Canada) with fifteen men, including F.H. Brundage, United States representative.

This section of boundary line proved one of the more difficult to survey. In addition, there was considerable mining and prospecting activity in the district and a resulting need for the line to be clearly marked and monumented.

On 10 May 1905, G.R. White-Fraser and his party landed at Eagle Point from the Canadian Pacific Steamship's, *Tees,* which had made a special trip up Portland Canal. At the time, the town of Stewart boasted a mining recorder's office and a post office serving a small floating population of miners. The river flat at the present-day site of Hyder, Alaska, had been homesteaded, but as yet there was no road up the Salmon River Valley.

For the first two weeks the Salmon River afforded a good route towards the Boundary Peaks, the latter lying somewhere to the north amid the glaciers at elevations of over six thousand feet. The river was too swift to paddle against, but bars on either side gave good footing for tracking the boats and canoes. This ended when a heavy rainfall in late May followed by warm weather and melting snow filled the swollen river with uprooted trees and huge blocks of ice from the glaciers at the headwaters. There was nothing for it but to abandon the river route, cut trails, and resort to back-packing. Initially, the route followed the Salmon River to the mouth of Texas Creek, where they crossed the river using a rope stretched between two tripods, and after following Texas Creek, crossed it in turn, using a boat attached to an overhead rope.

The first duty of the party was to locate Point D of the 1903 Award, defined by the commissioners as: "the highest point on the 56th parallel of latitude between the waters flowing into the Bear River on one side and the Salmon River on the other."[14] But mining activity in the area posed a new problem for White-Fraser:

> Shortly after arriving I was referred to by Mr. Conway, the Mining Recorder, as to the exact boundary, as in consequence of the favorable appearance of the ore found, and the interest excited generally by the bonding of properties, many prospecting parties were starting out, who would have to be referred to their proper recording office, whether at [Stewart], B.C. or Ketchikan, Alaska.
>
> My instructions were to the effect that, the chopping of lines was to be considered of secondary importance to the triangulation, and only to be done if sufficient time was left after that work was completed. But it seemed to me that conditions had arisen subsequent to the formulation of those instructions, that raised the chopping of the line into higher relative importance. I therefore decided to expedite the other work as much as possible.[15]

Packing towards Texas Glacier continued. Early in July, the river rose again, flooding the trails and destroying the rope crossings, but they were rebuilt and, indeed, once more after the river rose a third time. It was not until 18 July that a base camp was finally established on Texas Creek. Next day, a small party set out to explore the glacier for a route to the west. There were problems:

> Although the main glaciers afforded obviously, the best route to the peaks I cannot say it was an easy one. Crevasses from six inches wide and deep to twenty feet . . . wide and apparently bottomless, hindered progress by the necessity of making often wide detours around them. Sometimes a crossing was effected over an ice bridge resembling a splinter that often joins the halves of a split log; but I took the precaution to never send men on such journeys without their being properly shod with spikes, provided with stout alpenstocks; and roped together. These precautions I am glad to say, on six different occasions proved their value. Near the far end of the line, the leader of a party of four, who were traversing the glacier with packs, disappeared entirely down a crevass which the snow that had been drifting for some days, had lightly bridged over. He fell as far as the rope would allow, and was pulled up without injury. These crevasses and broken ice hills, frequently are very confusing to a party travelling in a dense fog that often produces a semi-darkness. I had to provide two compasses for use at such times. And frequently a long wide crevasse would open with a roar reverberating along the mountain sides, between going and return, necessitating a new, unknown route.[16]

While Texas Creek was being explored, the main party determined the latitude of Mount Welker (B.P. 8) by triangulation, the calculated distance to the 56th parallel of latitude (766.3 metres) was measured down the ridge, and an aluminum-bronze monument was set at B.P. 7, Point D of the 1903 award. Following this, the main party took part in work from the advance camp, now located on a spur above Chickamin Glacier near Mount Jefferson Coolidge. They occupied a point believed to be B.P. 16 and erected targets on B.P. 17 and 18. By 15 September it became a race to complete the work as the weather closed.

On 19 September most of the party returned to the Texas Creek base camp, reaching it after trying experiences on the divide; several of them falling into snow-covered crevasses, from which they were pulled with difficulty. On 21 September, their provisions exhausted, the remaining party members were forced to abandon the work. Finding the return route by way of the divide between Chickamin and Texas Glaciers blocked by deep snow, they were forced to make their way through the canyons on the west fork of Texas Creek. They reached the base camp after thirty-six hours without food, leaving behind tents, blankets, and personal belongings. On 28 September some of the party made another attempt to occupy B.P. 15 but failed on account of the snow.

Retreating to their first camp near Eagle Point, the party began cutting the vista above B.P. 1 on 6 October. By 21 October 1905, when they left aboard the

Tees, the vista had been opened to timberline and B.P.'s 2 and 4 monumented with aluminum-bronze cones.

In the 1910 season, the area was booming when F.H. Mackie and his party arrived in mid-May. Fremont Morse, the American representative accompanying them, described it:

> This section . . . has begun to attract attention on account of the mineral discoveries up both the Bear and the Salmon River. At the mouth of the Bear River the Canadian town of Stewart has been located. Three large hotels have been built there. There are several stores with ample stock of merchandise. The town has a water supply piped through it, and also boasts an electric light plant and two banks. It is also provided with a Customs officer. During the season a very substantial railroad wharf was built out over the mud flats to deep water, and a railroad was graded part way up the valley. A locomotive and cars were on the way North when the party left. The road will furnish an outlet for the mines up the valley, and it is rumored that it will eventually form part of a trans-continental line, with Stewart for its western terminus. The fact that at a sale of the Canadian Government's portion of the townsite, held at Vancouver during the summer, lots sold at prices ranging from $2,000 to $20,000 each, and the total sum realized from the sales was $440,000, as reported by the papers, lends color to this report. There would be no justification of such prices in a mining town.
>
> On the American side, at the mouth of the Salmon River, a town was laid out on the tide flats, named Portland City. Half a dozen frame buildings were erected on pile foundations so as to be above the reach of the spring tides. Of these, one is a good sized hotel. But practically no traffic developed for it, and hopes for the future of the mining claims located up the Salmon River are all that keeps the place going. Besides the hotel there are two small stores, and a number of tent houses. A wharf was started and the outer part completed but the approach was not finished. As the flats extend far out into the Canal it became a question whether the outer portion of this wharf might not be across the boundary line in Canadian waters.[17]

The party followed much the same route as White-Fraser's to the Texas and Chickamin Glaciers. B.P.'s 15, 17, 18, and the supposed 16 were connected by triangulation, and all but 18, which was considered unsafe to climb, were occupied. In addition, the vista was cut from Mount Welker (B.P. 8) to the Salmon River, and Fremont Morse, the United States representative, did work along Portland Canal.

In March 1920, the boundary commissioners decided that more field work should be done between Portland Canal and the Blue River, the northern tributary of the Unuk River. Mining in the Stewart area was growing on a stable base, following the collapse of the wildcat speculation of the 1910 boom. In 1918, the Premier Mine, far and away the most important in the district, began shipping high-grade ore from their bonanza deposit. The mine lay in the Salmon River Valley, less than a mile inside Canada.

J.D. Craig and his party arrived at Stewart in late May 1920. It was a late season and there was snow everywhere. A climb was made to locate B.P. 4, at an elevation of 2,770 feet and on the ridge just above Stewart, but it was still buried under an estimated 25 feet of snow!

On 24 June, camp was moved to Ninemile, opposite the mouth of Texas Creek, on the road to the Premier Mine. The snow was still too deep to work on the ridges, and the men prepared a trail up the valley of Texas Creek, onto Texas Glacier, and over the divide to Salmon Glacier. On 6 July, a group climbed to Mount Bayard, B.P. 15, where a new-style, manganese-bronze post just over seven inches high was set to replace the bolt set by White-Fraser in 1905. Similar posts (B.P. 13 and 14) were set on the slope southwest of the peak by a party working from a simple temporary or fly camp located in the valley below the toe of Texas Glacier.

In mid-July, a cache was established at the ice falls on Texas Glacier for use in establishing another fly camp in the vicinity of Chickamin Glacier. On 24 July, the triangulation party left the cache for the new camp, but they lost their way in the fog on the divide and were forced to return to the cache. Several days later they crossed again, this time dropping pieces of playing cards on the snow for a guide in foggy weather, and established their camp in a patch of timber on the north side of Chickamin Glacier.

Everything seemed to be going smoothly when the brass arrived at the end of July, and, later, Craig described their visit in his report: "the camp was honored by a visit of inspection by the Commissioners, Messrs Barnard and McArthur, who were fortunate enough to encounter nothing but fine weather during their stay, which was only too short. A run by gasolene 'speeder' was made fourteen miles up the Bear River valley on the rails of the old Mackenzie and Mann road built in 1910, and proved very interesting. The next day's program included an inspection of the monument set at Eagle Point in 1905, a visit to the Premier mine, the 'show' mine of the district and dinner at the mess house there. . . . The following day the Commissioners inspected the vista in the vicinity of Cascade Creek and visited one of the monuments set in 1910, leaving for the north on the following day."[18]

It was a different story when Craig wrote to Commissioner McArthur on 12 August:

> there is very little to report as it began to rain shortly after your departure and it has been raining almost ever since. The boys got a good camp established over the Texas Glacier and stuck it out in the rain and fog at 3,800 feet until the end of the week and then returned to main camp. In the meantime the

river was rising steadily and though we were not actually flooded out, the river was cutting the bank at camp and on Sunday [August 8] we moved to higher ground opposite the roadhouse. Since then the bar on which we were camped has disappeared completely. The road is washed out between the mine and eleven mile for about a quarter of a mile, and there are two to five feet of water all over the road through the bush between Fish Creek and Five Mile. The Premier is of course completely cut off. They shut down today, I hear, having no gasolene and are making an attempt to get their horses to town as they have no horse feed and can get none up.

I came to town on Wednesday to wire the office re funds and cannot get back to camp, the second spell of heavy rain, which started that night is still going strong and the river is even higher than it was before. All of which is rather discouraging. I have however been able to get in a few days work on the line between 'showers' and the line is now opened out good and wide from the monument (B.P. 10) you were at down to Cascade Creek and looks well. There is no suitable place at the road crossing for a mark of any kind, but I think the vista is so well cut and so prominent that no further mark is necessary.[19]

It was 20 August before the triangulation party could return to the fly camp. By this time, a cable and trolley had replaced the washed out bridge across the Salmon River. Between 24 and 31 August climbs were made to B.P.'s 16, 17, and 18. Bolts and old signals were found at 16 and 17, but the former was found to be in the wrong place, the true point lying under deep snow and impossible to monument. An alternate point, B.P. 15A, about a mile from the true point was set. They could not reach the sharp summit on Mount John Jay (B.P. 18), and a reference monument was set on a minor peak, about 37.3 metres away and 5 feet lower in elevation.[20] Later in the season, the vista between Eagle Point (B.P. 1) and Point D (B.P. 7) was completed and three new monuments set.

Unuk River (B.P. 18 to B.P. 47)[21]

1905: Fremont Morse (United States) with fifteen men, including J.D. Craig, Canadian representative.

1908: O.M. Leland (United States) with twenty-one men, including F.H. Mackie, Canadian representative.

1909: O.M. Leland (United States) with twenty-seven men, including T.H.G. Clunn, Canadian representative.

1920: Jesse Hill (United States) with nine men, including J.A. Pounder, Canadian representative.

The Unuk River, about forty miles northwest of the head of Portland Canal, is the first important river cutting the Alaska Panhandle. On 17 May 1905, the Morse party and their outfit landed at the Unuk River Mining and Trading Company's dock, located near the mouth of the river and roughly twenty-five miles from the boundary. The mining company was building a road to their property on the Canadian side, and it was hoped they could supply transportation for the survey party. These expectations of an easy trip were dashed when it turned out the company had only enough teams and wagons to handle their own supplies. River travel was out of the question because of the swift current and many log jams, and the disappointed survey party were forced to back-pack until the company obtained additional teams about the end of June.

Late in July, the main camp was established about half a mile downstream from the boundary. Surveyors climbed Mount Stoeckl (B.P. 40) from a fly camp on its slopes and erected a signal in a blinding snowstorm on 15 August 1905. The weather cleared again on 23 August and Morse and Craig identified several boundary peaks including one thought to be B.P. 28. Later, this peak and Mounts Willibert (B.P. 23), Blaine (B.P. 24), and Lewis Cass (B.P. 47) were tied into the triangulation. In addition to photographic work, a considerable amount of plane table work was done in the vicinity of the boundary line. The vista was cut down the slope of Mount Stoeckl and on the heavily wooded slope across the river. Six monuments were set along this portion of the line.

When the survey results were computed during the following winter, it was discovered that the peak identified as B.P. 28 was actually Mount John Jay (B.P. 18), some twelve miles farther to the southeast. There was a mistake in the award maps, and, in fact, there was no peak at the point shown on the map, although there was one some five miles inland. With the monuments already in and the vista cut, the commissioners agreed that it should be retained and that B.P. 28 should be considered the highest part of the snow-covered ridge of Mount Middleton on the direct line between B.P.'s 40 and 18.

In the 1908 season, three sub-parties in overall charge of O.M. Leland operated on the Leduc River, Lake Creek, and Blue River, the last two of which are tributaries of the Unuk River. On Leduc, a tributary of the Chickamin, it took about forty miles of river travel to reach the boundary area. Ascending it proved incredibly difficult. Many of the bars were still covered with snow; brush and tree jams made frequent portages necessary, and rapids delayed progress since it sometimes took the entire party to manage a single boat, even when it was only partly loaded. Eight miles from the boundary, they gave up the boats and back-packed everything beyond. The trip had taken about six weeks instead of the estimated three. Mount John Jay (B.P. 18) to the south of the river could not be climbed, but Mounts Willibert (B.P. 23) and Blaine (B.P. 24) were occupied as camera stations. Cutting the vista across the Leduc proved difficult owing to steep slopes and poor footing in the rain-soaked brush. The boundary could only be marked temporarily since the monuments had not arrived in Ketchikan in time to be brought up river. More work was going to be required, so the party cached the non-perishable part of their outfit in the valley of Gracey Creek, a stream rising near B.P. 24 and flowing to the northeast, and back-packed into Lake Creek to join the sub-party working there.

For the Lake Creek sub-party, the first task was to move their outfit as far as possible by canoe. Perhaps the most troublesome part was the crossing of the swift Unuk River itself. Once on Lake Creek, the canoes could ascend about four miles to a narrow rocky gorge and, after a short portage, lined (that is, pulled on a rope by men walking on shore or wading) for another three miles. Beyond that, supplies were back-packed about eight miles to a camp at the forks of the creek. The main task for the party was to project the line from B.P. 18 (Mount John Jay) to B.P. 40 (Mount Stoeckl). Unfortunately, they found that a higher "Net Ridge" lay between the proposed B.P. 28 on Mount Middleton and B.P. 40, obscuring the former. Both the intermediate ridges were capped by snow slopes. Nothing worked: the two end points (B.P.'s 18 and 40) needed to project the line were seldom visible at the same time, and at other times when the sun came out a transit set up on Net Ridge or Mount Middleton would be thrown out of position by snow melting under it. Projection of the line would have to be postponed to another year, although some other work was completed. In late September, the combined Lake Creek and Leduc River sub-parties started down Lake Creek for the mouth of the Unuk.

The Blue River sub-party faced a different problem:

> Prior to this season the Blue River valley was almost unexplored. The lower part of the valley for a distance of about six miles above the Unuk was known to be filled with volcanic lava of comparatively recent origin, and it was the difficulty of traveling over this lava that prevented men's prospecting in the valley. It was considered impossible for men to carry supplies enough to maintain themselves for an extended trip over the lava. The surface is exceedingly rough, as may be gathered from the photographs, and aside from the slowness of travel in consequence, there is great difficulty owing to the wearing out of boots from the cutting action of the lava fragments. It is almost incredible that one or two days travel over the lava will make it necessary to repair a new pair of heavy boots. They are literally scratched to pieces. Also, the roughness of the chunks of lava prevents their slipping into stable positions and they roll under a man's feet and cause many falls, so that men's hands are often seriously cut.[22]

The party back-packed up the valley of the Blue, and, where possible, they used folding canvas boats on small lakes formed by the lava dams. The boats, fourteen feet long and weighing about eighty pounds, could be carried in two packs. They established and occupied a number of topographic stations. In the first half of August, the line between B.P.'s 40 and 47 was established from a temporary

Plate 16. A group from the *Danube* poses around the monument at B.P. 1, near the head of Portland Canal, which had just been cemented in place, August 1904.

Plate 17. Vernon Ritchie with a transit set up over the cone-type monument on Mount Cote, B.P. 62, Brabazon party, 1905.

Plate 18. J.D. Craig with his party behind him on one of Wrangell's boardwalks at the beginning of the 1908 season.

Plate 19. A lunch stop during river work, Craig party 1908.

Plate 20. Cutting the vista on the Craig River, a tributary of the Iskut River, Craig party 1908. The man on the right is holding up a leaf of the detested devil's club, all too common in the area.

Plate 21. A fly camp near timberline, Craig party 1908.

Plate 22.   Fremont Morse party's camp at Hugh Miller Inlet, Glacier Bay area, 1907.

Plate 23.   Camp on lava bed, Lava Fork of Blue River, probably Leland party, 1909.

Plate 24. D.H. Nelles using a topographic camera, Ratz party, Taku and Tulsequah Rivers area, 1906.

ate 25.   Hunting for the error in the readings, Ratz party, 1906.

Plate 26. Lining a canoe in swift water, Ratz party, 1906.

Plate 27. Working a boat through the ice of Glacier Bay, Morse party, 1907.

Plate 28. Back-packing on a glacier. The mens' pant legs are frayed and the toes of their boots worn through. H.S. Mussell photo, date and party uncertain.

Plate 29. Ice worms, *Mesenchytraeus solifugus*, similar to those seen by the W.M. Dennis party in 1912. The longer worms are about one inch in length.

Plate 30. Crossing an ice fall, probably the N.J. Ogilvie party, 1909.

Plate 31. "Overland rafts" with barrels for wheels used across the sandy portages on the inland water route from Yakutat Dry Bay, Brabazon party, 1906.

Plate 32. Triangulation station Bob, "a signal which made the chief laugh." Station Alex is indicated in the background, Craig party 1908.

Plate 33. Instrument and stovepipe signal at triangulation station Dean, about 23 miles southwest of Mount Ogilvie, B.P. 95, Leland party 1907.

station on a snow dome about one mile west of B.P. 40 where it was possible to see both peaks. From here, the line was extended to the ridge between the Lava Fork and the West Fork of Blue River. The three monuments to be set on the line were taken to their respective sites, but setting them was postponed until the following season so that the locations could be verified. In late September, supplies that could be used the following year were cached, and the sub-party started back for the mouth of the Unuk.

The 1908 season had been a disappointment. Very little work had been completed, and as a final blow, cold weather, new snow, and high water turned the trip to the mouth of the Unuk into a nightmare that lasted until late October.

In the 1909 season, Leland was back with a larger party. There would be the same sub-parties, but this year the Leduc River one would travel the Lake Creek route to their area. The teams and wagons of the mining company were used for transportation although considerable work was needed to clear the road of wind-falls and repair the bridges. Once again, they encountered the same difficulties in projecting the line from Mount Stoeckl (B.P. 40) to Mount Middleton (B.P. 28). It was a late season, and initially the signal at B.P. 40 was hidden by a deep bank of snow just to the east of it. Later, there were the usual problems with bad weather, but finally, on 9 August, B.P.'s 18 and 40 were both visible. The chief of the Lake Creek sub-party stationed on "Net Ridge," which blocked visibility from Mount Middleton, aligned his theodolite on the true line between B.P.'s 18 and 40. Next, he signalled the head of the Leduc River sub-party stationed on the snow-covered slope of Mount Middleton to a point on the true line. The line thus established was projected back towards B.P. 18 until it reached a rock outcrop that could be monumented, a point assumed satisfactory for B.P. 28. When the entire party reassembled at the mouth of the Unuk River in late October 1909, their work had been completed with the exception of a few days of vista cutting on the West Fork of the Blue River and the placing of the monument at B.P. 45.

Early in 1920, the commissioners decided that further work should be under-taken in the Unuk area to open out the vista, place new monuments, and correct B.P. 28, which had not been placed on the highest point of the snow-covered ridge of Mount Middleton as specified by the commissioners. In the spring, the United States commissioner made a contract with two experienced packers to deliver fifty-five hundred pounds of provisions to the boundary line using a thirty-foot Yukon poling boat built to their specifications in Ketchikan. The trip went smoothly; with one man and an Eskimo dog on the tow line and two men in the boat with poles, they succeeded in relaying the provisions to a cache near the boundary in seventeen days. The main party reached the mining company's now-abandoned storehouse on 17 May 1920. They had hoped to use the road, but it was out of the question since bridges were washed out, fills around rocky bluffs had caved in, and the snow in the woods was still too deep for trail-making. Consequently, the entire party made their way up river using the poling boat, stopping at four camps and making a double trip between each camp. The worst part was the canyon where Blue River enters the Unuk. In the last five hundred feet of the canyon, there is a vicious crosscurrent with eddies on each side. After a struggle, they managed to get the boat to a small island upstream. There, a rope was tied to a tree, and the supplies were ferried up by alternately allowing the boat to drift downstream and then hauling it up again hand over hand. On 1 June, the last boatload was taken from the fourth camp to the cache near the boundary.

At the boundary, they found that the vista had not been completed on the southeast side of the river, and the men spent much of June cutting it. There were more problems on the river. At the end of June, the two packers and their assistant quit, and a fourth man was ill with appendicitis. Jesse Hill, the party chief, left camp with the group early in the morning, and they were at the mouth of the Unuk the same afternoon. While Hill was in Ketchikan, the poling boat was repaired and fitted with a bracket for an Evinrude outboard motor. There were delays, and Hill and four new men did not reach the mouth of the Unuk River until 12 July. By then, it was in flood, and it took them three days to reach the foot of the First Canyon at the mouth of the Blue. Starting out next morning, they were unable to make any headway against the current, and once again they had to resort to the five-hundred-foot tow line. This time, two men went ahead and, from a convenient spot, let the line downstream attached to a float for the men in the boat to pick up. Then, with the rope tied to a tree, the men in the boat hauled her up, using the motor to keep away from the shore. The method worked, but just barely, and it took them two full days to ascend the mile-long canyon.

Late in August camps outfits were packed over the ridge north of Mount Middleton, and camps set up on Gracey Creek and the Leduc River. B.P. 28 was re-established at the crest of the ridge as specified by the commissioners, and from the station, the corrected line was run towards B.P. 24, and the new vista cleared in Gracey Creek. Cone monuments set in 1909 were removed by cutting their lugs, and the loose cones were built into cairns referencing the stubby bronze posts on the new line nearby. From the Leduc camp the vista was recut between B.P.'s 18 and 23, and five new monuments were set. By 1 September the entire party had reassembled at the Unuk River camp, and a few days later they moved down to the mouth of the Blue River. From there, light outfits were taken to the boundary area on the Lava and West Forks of the Blue using a folding canvas boat on Blue Lake. Two of the new manganese-bronze posts were set, and a cone-type monument, B.P. 45, left in the snow in 1909, was finally set in place. The vista on the West Fork was completed. There was one last brush with the river when the party moved out in late September; the boat was swept under an overhanging tree and swamped. They worked quickly and saved most of the equipment and all of the records and photographic plates. The water-soaked plates were developed in Ketchikan to prevent further deterioration.

Bradfield River — Iskut and Craig Rivers (B.P. 47 to B.P. 53)[23]

1907: J.D. Craig (Canada) with thirteen men, including D.W. Eaton, United States representative.
1908: J.D. Craig (Canada) with seventeen men, including D.W. Eaton, United States representative.
1909: F.H. Mackie (Canada) with nine men.

This section of the boundary, about eighteen miles long, could be reached either from the coast or by a roundabout route up a tributary of the Iskut River. J.D. Craig's party tried the coastal route first, and early in June 1907 the outfit was hurriedly unloaded from scows at a point just above the tide-flats on the North Bradfield River. Confusion reigned. "The balance of this day and most of the next were spent getting camp into shape and sorting out the supplies, which had got so badly mixed up in their various transfers from boat to dock, to boat, to scow and so on, finally to camp, that it was almost impossible to find anything."[24] From this camp, a base line and triangulation stations were prepared and supplies were relayed to a base camp about seven miles further upstream. At one point the river and a side channel were blocked by a log jam, and it had to be cut out using axes and saws, a dangerous operation in the swift water.

The first of the boating accidents that were to plague the party occurred on the second trip upriver and

> though nothing was lost but a case or two of canned goods, it might easily have proved very serious. A rowlock broke in one of the canoes at a critical point while rounding a point and the canoe was washed broadside on to a high "Sweeper" or tree overhanging the water. She promptly filled and went under, those in her having barely time to jump on the log. After turning completely over she came right side up on the lower side of a sweeper in an eddy, where she was promptly secured and after considerable difficulty worked over to the beach, while with the other canoes we picked up such stuff as was floating in an eddy about seventy-five yards downstream. . . .
>
> The speed of the river may be judged from the difference in time taken going up and coming down between "Cache Camp" and the main camp. It took three men from 7:30 A.M. until about 4:00 or 4:30 P.M. to take a load of about 700 pounds from the cache to camp, while the return trip was made regularly in between 35 and 40 minutes, the distance being about seven miles.[25]

From the camp on the North Bradfield, sub-parties fanned out to attempt to reach B.P.'s 47, 48, and 53, the three points controlling the section of the line. The route to 47 lay along a mountain torrent with a series of box canyons, which was fordable only at the glacier at the head. The sub-party occupied camera stations on prominent mountain shoulders but were unable to climb 47. The main party worked towards 48, but it could not be climbed either. The party working towards 53 were more successful; the valley they followed proved a convenient highway, and they succeeded in occupying camera stations in the unmapped area between the sources of the Bradfield, Katete, and Iskut Rivers although they did not reach the boundary line. Work was abandoned after rain set in on 17 September 1907, and Craig wrote of their retreat:

> That evening all the sub-parties reunited in the main camp, the first time they had all been together for two months. By the 20th the balance of the various fly camp outfits had been brought down to the main camp and they awaited a cessation of the heavy rain to start downstream. On the 21st the river rose rapidly to the highest stage of the season. An immense jam had existed, apparently for years, in the river about a mile above camp. During the afternoon this "went out" and for sometime the river was full of debris. Unfortunately, a great deal of this united in forming a new jam about a hundred yards below camp. As the water continued to rise and cut out the banks, many green trees floated downstream and lodged in the log jam making a veritable dam of it and about 10 P.M. just after a large drift of trees had gone down, the water backed up and rose so quickly that they were forced to throw their belongings hastily into the canoes and drag them through the bush about a quarter of a mile, to a spot just above water level where they built a fire and waited for daylight. It seemed as if the whole river was going through camp so great was the rush of the water. In the early hours of the 22nd the jam broke and the water receded rapidly. But what a sad wreck the camp was; tents all down and filled with sand, the cache of provisions washed away and scattered through the bush behind the camp for half a mile. It occupied them fully for a day gathering up the outfit, and another day "drying out." The most serious losses were a canoe from which they had been cut off by the rapid rise of water, and a considerable supply of provisions.[26]

There was another mishap on 24 September when a canoe was caught on a hidden snag. The five occupants managed to reach shore, but everything in the canoe was lost including several instruments and a box containing eight dozen exposed photographic plates. Efforts to recover the plates failed, and a small party waited in the area for a further ten days in the hope that the box might be found. The main party established camp at the mouth of the river: "The base was measured on October 10th. It was located on the grass tide flats at the mouth of the river and crossed one slough about 125 feet wide by triangulation. Good sized hubs were driven every hundred feet and lined in the usual way with a transit. The ends were marked by extra long hubs set very deep. The measure was done with an only remaining 100′ tape. As the spring balance was also missing they improvised one cut out of a couple of pieces of wild crabapple, some government 'red tape' and two heavy elastic bands, and by stretching these to the same limit at each 100 foot measurement we secured a uniform tension, which we found later by comparison with a standard spring balance at Wrangell, to be 19 lbs."[27] Finally, on 17 October 1907, after days of bad weather and no prospect of improvement in sight, the party returned to Wrangell, en route to the south.

In the 1908 season, Craig's party was more successful in reaching the area by way of the Stikine, Iskut, and Craig Rivers. Assisted by six Indians in a large canoe, the party moved their outfit to the border in seven steps, each taking about a week. It was heavy going, especially at a point about six miles from the border, where a portage about a mile long had to be cut around an impassable canyon. During the season Mount Pounder (B.P. 48) was occupied but not monumented, and the vista was cut across the Craig River. A sub-party returned to the North Bradfield River and re-occupied a number of the camera stations to replace the lost photographic plates. Their work completed, they rejoined the main party in September.

In the 1909 season, F.H. Mackie led the party on the Iskut and Craig Rivers, replacing Craig, who had been transferred to the survey of the 141st Meridian, where he remained until the project was completed. This year they used a launch to the mouth of the Iskut River, and they engaged Indians to aid in the freighting from this point. Tracking upstream began on 26 May 1909, and early in June one of the canoes was dumped while being manoeuvred around a pile of driftwood, and many of the heavier articles in it were lost, including several instruments. Mackie reported:

> Mr. Bates and I took apart and cleaned two of the three-inch transits and one camera which had got wet. We also adjusted our two three-inch transits and the five-inch Watt transit.
>
> The articles that we missed most, which were lost in the upset, were our camp dishes. We lost all our plates, cups and cutlery and had to use our pocket knives for knife, fork and spoon. . . .
>
> On June 7th we started up stream again and by noon reached an old camp ground of Mr. Craig's where we were lucky enough to find several table knives, forks and spoons as well as a few granite bowls. These came as a very welcome addition to our camp equipment, especially the bowls, as we had been using empty tins for drinking cups.[28]

Five members of the party reached the boundary about the middle of June and there was another unexpected prize; "We succeeded in getting across the river as the water was low and found some more dishes and cutlery in Mr. Craig's old camp. We found enough to nearly complete our outfit."[29]

A trolley was strung across the Craig River consisting of a half-inch rope tightened by a windlass. To cross, a man sat in a swing seat attached to a pulley and pulled himself across hand over hand along either the main rope or a lighter second rope strung beside it. The work of the previous season was resumed, but there was no improvement in the weather: "From June 24th the day we made our first climb until October 1st, there were only eighteen fine days. One or two of which broke fine and clear but clouded up before I could finish the station that I was occupying." On 1 October the party returned to the Iskut only to have it rain continuously until the seventh. The following morning, Mackie started out for Wrangell: "Arrived in Wrangell early in the afternoon as we had a down stream wind behind us all the way. Upon arrival I found that the Indians had taken my steamer trunk containing all my clothes, up the Iskut River by mistake instead of my small stationery trunk. It was lost with the mail at the mouth of the Little Iskut [Craig] River."[30]

The work of Mackie's party completed the Iskut River section of the boundary line. Although the triangulation had not been carried through to the Stikine, geographic control for the area was provided by the position of B.P. 53, obtained in the Stikine River work of 1904, and B.P. 48 from the Bradfield River work of 1907.

Katete River Area (B.P. 54 to B.P. 63)[31]

1904: G.R. White-Fraser (Canada) with fourteen men.
1905: A.J. Brabazon (Canada) with thirteen men, including J.M. Donn, United States representative.
1912: W.M. Dennis (Canada) with eight men, part-season only.

In late May 1905, a party led by A.J. Brabazon returned to the Katete River area to carry on the work begun by G.R. White-Fraser's party in the 1904 season. Brabazon, older than most of the party chiefs, was one of three former chiefs from the 1893–95 commission who were still doing active field work.[32] Bothered by stomach problems, he warned his crew members that he could be cranky at times. If anything, that was an understatement for as a French Canadian who had worked for White-Fraser the summer before put it: "I don't know what it is. Las' year I was gooth man, dis year I am one son of beech."[33]

The party set up their base camp at the abandoned North-West Mounted Police post on the Stikine River, a short distance above the boundary. A.G. Gillespie, an articled student with the party, described his first climb of the season:

> About the day after getting into camp, Mr. Brabazon asked me to come with him in one of the light Peterboro canoes. He was an expert canoeman himself and he was testing me. I evidently satisfied him as that evening he told me he wanted a signal on the top of Cote Mountain and that Scottie would go with me.
>
> We left camp next morning, shortly after 6. We had to cross the river and run down four or five miles to where a large slough entered the river. Here we

were to find a trail, marked by the party of last season. As Scottie didn't know anything about a canoe, he sat on the bottom and kept still.

We found the trail and started our climb. Cote is about 4,300 feet, and as we were not much above sea level, we would have about the whole of that altitude to climb; the summit would be about four or five miles back from the river; and there would be a fairly high ridge to ascend and descend before we got onto the main mountain.

We found the snow well down below the timberline. Before we left the timber, we cut three small trees, about ten feet long, but as they were cut high up, they were very thick at the butts and very heavy. The snow got deeper as we approached the summit, and before we got there, it became a desperate struggle as we sank almost to our waists, and could only manage a few steps between each rest. Fortunately, the mountain presented no climbing difficulties, other than the deep snow.

We reached the summit at five in the afternoon. We found the top of the bronze monument, planted the previous year, and lashing our trees strongly together in the form of a tripod, we planted it over the monument, draping some bunting around it, and our work was done. It only remained to get back to camp.

The view was superb. We could see miles away to the north up the valley of the Stikine, bounded on each side by great snow-covered mountains, and in every direction a sea of mountain peaks. I could just make out our camp, miles away, at the bend of the river. But something else I noticed. As I gazed down on the country, spread out before us like a map, I saw that the big slough paralleled the river from the point where we had left the canoe, to a point just above our camp. This meant that, if there were no obstacles, we could follow up the slough and so avoid the swift current of the river.

We did not wait long on the summit. It was easier now without carrying the heavy trees and going down hill. But when we came to climb the ridge, poor old Scottie gave up. Scottie was a good deal older than I was, and possibly not so strong. It looked a bit serious for a time — he declared he couldn't go another step and simply lay in the snow. I kept assuring him that it was only a very short distance . . . and then it would be all down hill, and soon out of the snow. Poor old Scottie! He was verra, verra Scottish. My memory vividly recalls that scene. Scottie and I struggling together up that last slope. "Go on, mon — go on and leave me." The old fool.

At last we got down to the canoe, and by this time it was getting late and we were hungry. Scottie lay down in the canoe and I took a chance that we could follow the slough. I had only a very slight current to buck until we got well up, then I noticed the current increasing, and began to fear that we were following up a stream and that there was no opening to the main river.

Finally, when the current was getting almost too strong to paddle against, we came to a gap, through which a strong stream joined the main river. We came out about half a mile above our camp and in a few minutes were across. It was about eleven when we finally got into camp.

It had been a terribly hard trip to start the season on. If we had been out for some time, we would not have felt it so much. We discovered afterwards that the party of the year before always took two days for the trip — but they did not have Brabazon as chief.[34]

A day or two after the Mount Cote climb, Brabazon, Gillespie, and two others set out to line a canoe up the Katete River. It was difficult going and they made camp for the night at the foot of an impassable box canyon on the west fork of the Katete, a few miles from the boundary. Next day they climbed the ridge between the forks and located the boundary line by shooting in the signal on Mount Cote (B.P. 62) and the summit of Mount Whipple (B.P. 54). In the meantime, the remainder of the crew back-packed the outfit to a campsite close to the boundary line. From it, the crew set to work cutting the vista across the heavily timbered slopes.

The vista was finished and the line monumented by mid-August. When the weather cleared soon after, Brabazon asked Gillespie to attempt to climb Mount Whipple, now free of snow. Gillespie and two companions lined a canoe a short distance up the east fork of the Katete River, setting out on foot from there. After a unpleasant struggle through devils club and alder, they camped for the night in a clump of juniper close to timberline, here at about two thousand feet above sea level.

Starting out before three the next morning, they reached a point about one hundred feet below the summit before Gillespie decided it was too dangerous and turned back. Next morning, after another night without a tent in the juniper clump, they skirted the mountain and climbed it from the other side, reaching the summit about ten in the morning.

What they took to be the summit in June turned out to be a cleft filled with snow, the true summit lying about thirty feet to the south. Try as he might, Gillespie was unable to set his small mountain transit up on the line from Mount Cote as marked by the signal on it and several other signals along the line. The best he could do was to balance the instrument precariously about a foot off the line. Fortunately, it was a beautiful day without wind and Gillespie was able to take the required bearings and complete the horizontal photography. Gillespie continues:

We got back to camp without adventure, but, as we had not brought much food, and had taken an extra day, we had nothing to eat in camp. Tommy Moore shot a whistler — a sort of glorified gopher, also called a ground hog — which we cooked in our coffee pot. The others managed to make a meal but it made me very sick in the stomach. We were very tired and spent the night under the juniper trees and next day made camp. Mr. Brabazon was very annoyed that the cairn which we left at our station on the summit was not on line, and I think he doubted the fact that it was impossible to set the transit up on line.[35]

The work on the Katete finished, the party returned to their base camp at the police post. Gillespie, told to take only a change of clothes when they started out in early June, finally got his kit bag back only to find that the pack rats had gnawed a hole in it and made a nest in the middle!

Early in September, the party started up the Iskut River tracking their canoes and boats all the way. It was miserable going; they staggered in the rapids and on the boulders and cut brush and lined along the banks in the deeper places. They were wet most of the time, their gumboots always full of water. It became a lost cause when the bad weather continued for almost six weeks. About all they accomplished was to measure a base line and carry the triangulation a few miles up the Iskut.

Brabazon, growing impatient, ordered Gillespie and Vernon Ritchie, another assistant, to climb a sharp peak, probably Iskut Mountain, in hopes of seeing the signal on Mount Whipple and tieing it in to the Iskut triangulation. Nearing the summit after climbing up a dangerous rock slide, they found the ridge above them was a knife edge, covered with new snow and extremely dangerous. They turned back and, years later, Gillespie wrote of Brabazon's reaction:

When Vernon and I got back to camp, Mr. Brabazon was very annoyed that we had not got to the top of the mountain. The weather changed, we had some cold rain, and snow high up on the mountains. It was time for the party to be going out of the country, but Brabazon sent Vernon and me to try and climb the mountain again. We took a different route, but found the going even more difficult and dangerous. It was blowing very hard, but we decided to read some angles and take photographs. With difficulty I managed to get the transit set up and used our canvas lunch bags full of stones tied to the tripod, to keep it from being blown away. Snow swirled round us, and it was bitterly cold. My fingers were stiff and awkward round the tangent screws on the transit, and Vernon's writing, as he recorded the readings was practically illegible. . . .

Brabazon was very cranky again when we got back and reported. For some reason he seemed to think the mountain could be climbed, and next day, just to show us, he took a man with him and said he would make the climb. However, they did not get very far and were soon back in camp.[36]

That finished it. The party packed up and left arriving in Wrangell about three days later after doing a little work on the way down.

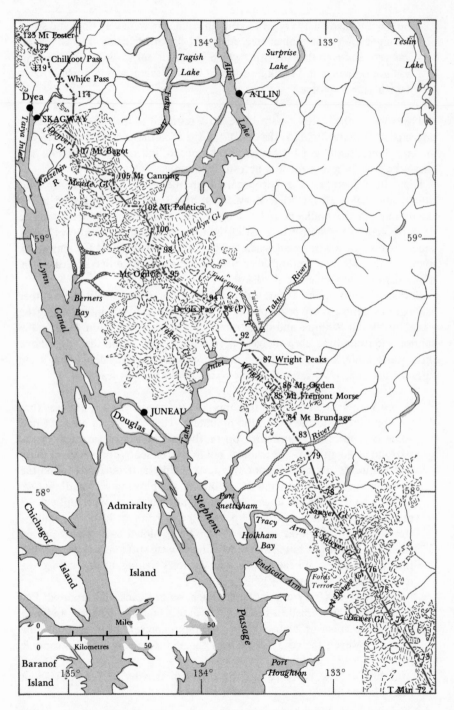

Map 5: Panhandle Boundary: Boundary Points 72 (T Mtn) to 123 (Mt Foster)

Subsequently the commissioners decided that the line between Mount Cote and Mount Whipple should be corrected, and in August 1912, a small Canadian party led by W.M. Dennis returned to the area. The station on Mount Cote was reoccupied and the boundary line run to the true summit of Mount Whipple, now free of snow. "The three copper bolts and four bronze monuments, described in Mr. Brabazon's report were blown out and their position changed to bring them on the new line. Some timber was cut near the [west] branch of the Katete to open the new line properly."[37] Surprisingly, despite the problems over the exact location of B.P. 54, it was not monumented in 1912, or, for that matter, in 1948 when the Katete vista was recut and improved.

Stikine River to T Mountain (B.P. 64 to B.P. 72)[38]

> 1904: Fremont Morse (United States) with fourteen men.
> 1907: W.F. Ratz (Canada) with thirteen men, including Radcliffe Hordern, United States representative.

In the 1904 season the Fremont Morse party working on the north side of the Stikine had monumented the boundary as far as Mount Talbot (B.P. 68), the last peak readily accessible from the river. In 1907, W.F. Ratz continued the work northwest into the snowfields and glaciers. Early in June, Ratz and most of his party landed at "Barley Cache," just south of Flood Glacier and about forty miles upstream from the boundary on the Stikine River. They had travelled from Wrangell aboard the Hudson's Bay Company steamer, *Mount Royal,* on her second trip of the season to Telegraph Creek. A base line was measured in the valley bottom, and the triangulation was extended westward towards the boundary line. Despite numerous crevasses, Flood Glacier proved easy travelling, and although none of the boundary peaks were climbed, stations were occupied almost to the boundary, often on tiny fragments of rock rising through the huge snowfield. Later, the base camp was moved about fifteen miles downriver. Fortunately, the good weather prevailed much of July and September, and at one point in the latter month observations were made from mountain summits on nine successive days — a near miracle in the Panhandle! The work continued until 10 October, by which time Ratz's work had been tied into Morse's work of 1904 and the Canadian work south of the river.

Endicott Arm and Tracy Arm (B.P. 73 to B.P. 78)[39]

> 1908: W.F. Ratz (Canada) with thirteen men, including Eberhardt Mueller, United States representative.
> 1909: N.J. Ogilvie (Canada) with sixteen men.

In the 1908 season Ratz and his party began work in the high country east of

Endicott Arm, about eighty miles south of Juneau. The boundary line in this area lay between Points P and T, simply left blank in the Tribunal Award and later covered in the Exchange of Notes of 25 March 1905. But there was a further problem; the section all lay between Peaks 7, 8, and T, where new boundary points were to be selected once more information was available.

The party's initial reconnaissance indicated that North Dawes Glacier, a dead glacier, could be travelled with relative ease, and the party began packing up it using sleds. By mid-June the camp had been moved to the snowfield at the head of the glacier, about seven miles west of the boundary. Towards the end of June supplies were transported up Dawes Glacier to a new camp. This proved more difficult. The glacier was very active, and large masses of ice were continually breaking from the face into the waters of Endicott Arm. On one occasion, the swell washed away a canoe with all its contents from a ledge fully thirty-five feet above high-water mark. For the first four miles, the steep slope of the glacier was broken into huge seracs separated by wide crevasses, and there was no route along the steep rock walls. Back-packers, carrying thirty-five pound loads, took eight hours to cover the four miles from the face of the glacier to the first camp.

Mueller, the United States representative, described the party's operation:

> On these trips up the various glaciers, from seven to ten men, including surveyors, would live in the side camp. Three or four men would be employed in packing provisions from the main camp, where one cook was always left behind, to these side camps.
>
> The packing of supplies on the glaciers was done on the backs of men. From the side camps on both the Dawes Glaciers, "fly trips" were made to reach peaks further inland. Since the packers already had all they could do to reach these two side camps, it was necessary for the observing parties living at these camps to carry the instruments and supplies themselves when penetrating further inland. So they would leave the side camps with their blankets, the instruments, and enough provisions for two days. This would be done on a day which seemed to promise good weather for the morrow. The night was then spent in the open. The peak was occupied the next day, and the return to the side camp made the day following.
>
> An observing party would consist of from 3 to 6 men, depending upon the number of packs to be carried up the mountain. The observer often carried one of the packs himself. The outfit at a new station would consist of a signal, camera and three-inch theodolite.[40]

Later in the season, the work was extended to Sawyer Glacier, north of Tracy Arm, and a triangulation net over thirty miles long was developed, a base line was measured, and the survey was connected to those of the Coast and Geodetic Survey. Work in the mountains had to be given up about the end of September after forty-two consecutive days of rain and snow. Despite the weather, the party had completed enough mapping for the commissioners to select the additional boundary peaks between 7 and 8 and 8 and T.

In 1909, a Canadian party of sixteen led by Noel Ogilvie returned to the area. W.F. Ratz was gone; he had died early in February of the year at the age of twenty-five after spending four incredibly difficult seasons on the boundary work. The routes they followed this season were much as those of the year before, although a heavy snowfall over the winter made travelling more difficult. One of the two fatal accidents of the boundary work occurred at triangulation station Bird, elevation 6,590 feet, which lies about four miles northeast of Fords Terror. A portion of the snowcap slid off the summit carrying with it Joseph Sheppard, one of the observers. He fell two thousand feet to the South Sawyer Glacier where his body could be seen at the base of the precipice, but it was impossible for the others to reach the surface of the glacier from the station. Two weeks later, a party succeeded in ascending the glacier from Tracy Arm only to find that more snow had broken off and apparently carried the body into a deep crevasse.

By the end of the season, the work was completed between T Mountain (B.P. 72) and B.P. 79, the latter just south of the Whiting River.

Whiting River (B.P. 79 to B.P. 84)[41]

1906: J.D. Craig (Canada) with ten men, including G.C. Baldwin, United States representative.
1907: W.F. Ratz (Canada) a sub-party of six men in charge of P.W. Greene, part-season only.

In the 1906 season, Craig and his party tackled the Whiting River. The river, emptying into an arm of Port Snettisham, already had a nasty reputation among local prospectors. The triangulation net was carried to the boundary using stations on both sides of the river. Boundary Peaks 79 and 83 were climbed but not monumented while Mount Brundage (B.P. 84) could not be climbed. Farther to the northwest B.P. 85 (Peak No. 4 of the Exchange of Notes of 25 March 1905) could not be identified. Near the end of the season, a base line was measured in the river flats, and the boundary was temporarily marked by a five-foot wide transit line and wooden posts on either side of the river.

In the 1907 season the task of cutting the vista across the Whiting was assigned to a small Canadian sub-party in the charge of P.W. Greene. Their troubles with the Whiting began when Greene and two others were bringing supplies upriver in late August:

While attempting to cross the river at a particularly swift point, where however, we had crossed twice before, our canoe capsized, and at the same moment hit a snag, badly smashing the stern. We drifted down the river for 300 yards before we made shore, not however without losing everything except a dunnage bag and the canoe.

Although securely fastened in bundles to the back thwart of the canoe, all our valuables, including the mail, survey expense vouchers, my summer's photographs, my return C.P.R. ticket to Ottawa, and many other articles were wrenched from it and lost; in fact everything in the canoe, including the supplies brought from Juneau, our blankets and dunnage and a rifle were all lost.

Having lost our paddles, we were unable to go after anything in the canoe, and although we ran along the shore we recovered nothing.

In the dunnage bag saved, fortunately, there was a small hatchet with which we made rough paddles and immediately proceeded up the river in the damaged canoe.

We spent a cold night in the open air and then proceeded at daylight.

During the morning a portage was encountered, a mile in length, formed by a change in the river bed since we had come down the river.

In our weak condition, having had nothing to eat since the previous noon, we were unable to portage the canoe, and so we were compelled to leave it, placing it on the highest ground available, intending to get it on our next trip down the river.

We climbed along the mountain side for the next ten miles, minus our boots, for we had kicked off our rubber boots in the river, and arrived in camp in the afternoon, after a day and a half without food.

I found that during our absence, the men had done more work than I had expected but were extremely low in provisions.

After consideration we decided it would be absolutely out of the question to return for fresh supplies, and we thought we could possibly finish the work with what provisions we had.

It was necessary to economize to the utmost and many of the mainstays of camp menu were missing. I take this opportunity of saying that the entire party worked splendidly and it was only due to their willingness that the work continued at all.

Although it poured rain for the next entire week with hardly an hour's cessation, we worked early and late in order to complete the work, if possible, under the existing circumstances.

On Saturday, August 31st [1907], the river started to flood. We had not quite finished the cutting on the side of Boundary Peak No. 6, there being about two days more work remaining.

The line was cut up through the first section of timber, to a height of 400 to 500 feet, where an open spot was reached, but beyond this, there were only two small patches of timber and scrub remaining.

However, our grub supply having practically disappeared, there being little else but dried fruit left, and having so far made every effort to complete the work, we decided it would be best to abandon it in this slightly unfinished state.

During the night of the 31st, the river rose considerably and for the second time during the season, flooded out the cook tent, so at daylight we loaded our outfit in one big canoe and started down the river in the pouring rain.

The trip proved very dangerous and rough, owing to the very high flood and we considered ourselves extremely fortunate in making the trip without an accident.

In places, we travelled fully 15 miles an hour and as we passed Mr. Craig's main camp of 1906, we noticed that it was under water to a depth of two feet. On reaching the point where we had previously left our small canoe, it was nowhere to be seen, the river covering the spot where we had left it. However, we could not have brought it out had we found it, as it would not have lived in the river in its present state.[42]

Taku and Tulsequah Rivers (B.P. 85 to B.P. 94)[43]

1905: W.F. Ratz (Canada) with seven men, part-season only.

1906: W.F. Ratz (Canada) with thirteen men, including Radcliffe Hordern, United States representative.

1907: W.F. Ratz (Canada), sub-party of six men in charge of P.W. Greene, part-season only.

1910: H.S. Mussell (Canada) with nine men.

1912: H.S. Mussell (Canada) with six men, part-season only.

On 16 August 1905, Ratz and his party set up camp on a small island in the Taku River, close to the boundary. Northwest of the river, B.P. 92 was identified and a signal was built on it. Across the river, B.P. 87 was identified, but it could not be climbed although three attempts were made. (The mountains were Peaks 1 and 2 of the Exchange of Notes of 25 March 1905, respectively.)

In late May 1906, a larger party, again headed by Ratz, started upriver using two canoes and a small launch. The canoes were able to reach the campsite near the boundary, but the launch had to turn back, defeated by shallow water and the strong current. After a second attempt failed, an Indian with a fishing skiff was engaged to bring up the remainder of the outfit. Signals were put up again on the stations of 1905, this time using a new type improvised for alpine areas. Made of six sections of telescopic stovepipe, the largest three and a half inches in diameter, they were held in place by a stone cairn around the base and two sets of guy wires with three wires each. Eight-ounce duck was used for the flag since the muslin normally used was too light to withstand the winds. Early in June, a new camp was established at the limit of vegetation on the south flank of Wright Glacier, just west of the boundary. B.P. 87 was finally climbed from this camp, but B.P.'s 85 and 86, flanking the glacier on each side, could not be identified with the data shown on the Tribunal maps. The decision on these had to be left for the commissioners to make after the mapping had been compiled the following winter. On its return to the Taku, the party separated with one group working up the Tulsequah River to extend the topography to the glacier at the head of it and the other group continuing work along the line itself. Boundary Peak 93 (Point P of the 1903 Award) was easily identified; Ratz writing of it: "Boundary Peak "P" is a magnificent peak towering fully a thousand feet higher than any other peak in the vicinity, its altitude being 8,584 feet. It is formed by three separate peaks of which the middle one is the highest, and from the arrangement of these peaks as viewed from the westward, the name "Devils Paw" seems very appropriate."[44] B.P. 94 was less certain, there were two peaks of nearly equal size, and the final decision had to be left for the commissioners.

The party left for Juneau in mid-October 1906. Their season had been a wet one with thirty-three fine days, thirty-one days with the clouds obscuring the summits but no rain, forty-one cloudy days with showers and forty-two days of heavy rain! Despite this, their work had established the boundary between B.P.'s 85 and 94.

In the 1907 season, Ratz returned briefly about the end of May to set four monuments in the Taku River valley. A sub-party of six men remained behind to widen the transit lines to the full twenty-foot vista across the valley of the Taku and its tributary the Sittakanay River.

In the 1910 season, Mussell's party extended the mapping into the area northwest of Devils Paw, which was impossible to reach from the coast. The party were able to work their canoes to a point about two miles below the Tulsequah Glacier. From a base camp near its foot, equipment and supplies were packed over the relatively smooth surface of the glacier to an upper camp near the head. From here, it was a slow and difficult task to reach the nunataks, tiny islands of rock rising above the snow and ice, that were used as triangulation stations. The most distant, "7800," was at that elevation on the summit of Llewellyn Glacier, about fourteen miles from the base camp and less than eight miles from Mount Ogilvie (B.P. 95). Their work on the glacier completed, the party completed the triangulation down the Tulsequah River to join that done in 1906.

Early in September 1912, Mussell returned with a small party and spent about six weeks occupying some of the stations and completing the cutting of the vista in the Taku River valley.

East of Lynn Canal (B.P. 95 to B.P. 108)[45]

1907: O.M. Leland (United States) with sixteen men.

A network of triangulation stations was built up along Lynn Canal using the Coast and Geodetic stations from 1890 plus a number of new ones, all within five miles of tidewater. From these, all the Boundary Points between 95 and 108 were identified and shot in. However, since the distances from these triangulation stations to the boundary points involved were long, sometimes over thirty miles, it seemed important to occupy at least one station either on, or close to, the actual boundary line. In mid-June 1907, the first camp was set up near the mouth of Katzehin River, and work continued on a trail to Meade Glacier. The glacier could be travelled on, but it proved difficult to reach a suitable station since the mountains rose abruptly from the snowfields. Finally, after several unsuccessful attempts on other peaks, a route was found up Mount Canning (B.P. 105), and the heavy packs were carried to a fly camp near the summit. After a wait of several days during a snowstorm, there were two good days for observations. The mountain, composed of shattered granite, had two peaklets both at an elevation of about 6,927 feet, and the copper bolt marking the station was cemented in the western one, formed by a huge block about ten cubic yards in size. In addition, a camera station was occupied about seven miles to the southwest. The mountain work was completed in early August, and later that month the main party moved south to complete the work along Lynn Canal.

Skagway River, White and Chilkoot Passes (B.P. 109 to B.P. 123)[46]

1904: O.M. Leland (United States) with four men.
1905: O.M. Leland (United States) with twenty men, including C.A. Bigger, Canadian representative.
1906: O.M. Leland (United States) with seventeen men, including G.R. White-Fraser, Canadian representative.

Leland had worked in the White Pass in 1904, but the boundary remained unmarked, pending a final decision by the commissioners. In late June 1905, Leland and his party set up camp near Denver station, about five miles from Skagway on the White Pass and Yukon Railway. They had to be prepared to move camp at a moment's notice. It was unusually dry and the hazard was forest fires, all too often started by sparks from passing locomotives. South of Skagway River, B.P.'s 109, 110 and 111 were identified, but none was climbed despite a number of attempts. Later, they moved camp to the Skagway River, east of Glacier station. A party climbed B.P. 114 and placed a monument on its four-foot wide summit. In addition, two monuments were set and the vista was cut across the Skagway River. The scraggly patch of timber, about two-thirds of a mile across and consisting of balsam and hemlock that seldom reached two feet in diameter, was the only stand of trees along the line from the Taku to the Chilkat River, a distance of about 135 miles!

Rather than a single turning point in the wide flats at the summit of the White

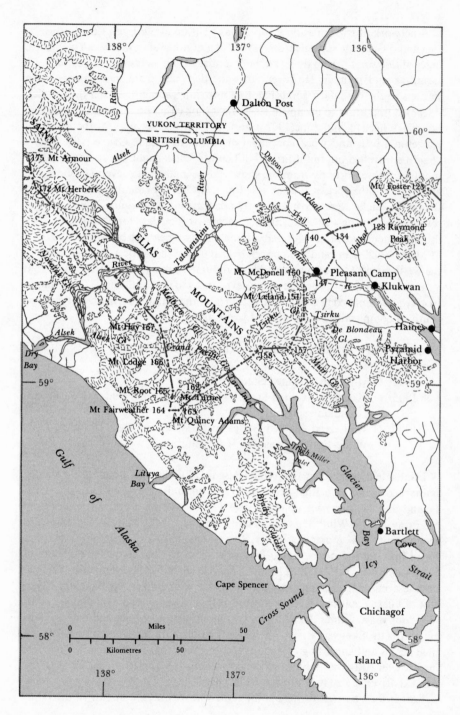

Map 6: Panhandle Boundary: Boundary Points 123 (Mt Foster) to 175 (Mt Armour

Pass, the commissioners agreed on a narrow line, 2262.9 metres long and trending slightly north of west, that was more easily referenced to B.P.'s 114 and 119. Provisional boundary marker No. 2, considered the summit of the White Pass, lay along the line and was marked by an obelisk-type monument (B.P. 117). It lay close to the White Pass tracks and was flanked by two large flag poles. Provisional markers Nos. 1 and 3 were made into permanent marks by cutting the iron pins off about a foot above the ground and incorporating them in large cairns. Its work in the White Pass completed, the party left for Seattle in mid-September 1905.

At the beginning of the 1906 season, Leland's party worked in the vicinity of Chilkoot Pass, and later they did preliminary work in the Meade Glacier area on the east side of Lynn Canal. By mid-June, the entire party was involved in back-packing their supplies over the Gold Rush route to the Chilkoot Pass. A team of horses had been obtained from the sole resident of Dyea, and the outfit was hauled by wagon for a few miles. Beyond, the bridges from '98 were so dilapi-dated that the teamster refused to risk them. Travelling much as the 98ers, the surveyors shuttled their outfit past the still-standing buildings at Canyon City and Sheep Camp to "The Scales" at the foot of the steep ascent to the pass. In the Chilkoot Pass, the two provisional markers of 1900 were retained, and the bronze cones B.P. 120 and 121 were set on the slopes on either side of the pass.

B.P.'s 119, 122, and 123 were occupied, although the weather was so poor it was a rush to complete the work, some stations being occupied five or six times before the required observations were obtained. Owing to the scarcity of timber, signals consisting of eight to ten sections of six-inch stove-pipe held in place with guy wires were used. Modified and strengthened, this type of signal became the standard for mountain work. Upon completion of the triangulation, a messenger was sent to a party in the Chilkat River area to give them the exact geographical location of B.P. 123 and the azimuth from that point to B.P. 128.

Chilkat Glacier to Mount McDonell (B.P. 123 to B.P. 150)[47]

1904: C.A. Bigger (Canada) with twenty-two men.
1904: J.A. Flemer (United States) with fourteen men.
1905: J.A. Flemer (United States) with seven men.
1906: D.W. Eaton (United States) with nine men.
1910: N.J. Ogilvie (Canada) with eight men.

By the end of the 1904 season, Bigger's and Flemer's parties had marked the boundary line from Mount McDonell, past Pleasant Camp and northeast to Mount Ashmun, a direct distance of about sixteen miles. In 1905, Flemer, by now more accustomed to the vagaries of the Chilkat River, returned to extend the line to Raymond Peak (B.P. 128) and the triangulation to the bend of the Chilkat River, about four miles to the southeast.

The 1906 season was a frustrating one for Eaton and his party. It was Eaton's third season in the area; the first two he had spent as Flemer's assistant. This time, their task was to bridge the gap between Mount Foster (B.P. 123) and Raymond Peak (B.P. 128) across the glaciers at the head of the Chilkat River. The weather was against them, and they only saw the mountain tops on four days in July. Then, on reaching stations near the Chilkat Glacier, they found, as expected, that there were no points on the line from which B.P. 123 and 128 were both visible and that it would therefore be necessary to know the exact geographic position of B.P. 123, as determined by Leland's party, before the line could be projected. Leland's messenger arrived with the information on 14 September, and during the next two days, the line was established and marked across the Chilkat River. Later a portion of the vista was cut, and two bronze cones, B.P.'s 126 and 127 were set on opposite sides of the river.

In the 1910 season, Ogilvie and his party set bronze bolts (B.P.'s 124 and 125) in rock ridges on either side of Chilkat Glacier. The triangulation up the Chilkat River was strengthened and extended, by the addition of new triangulation stations but there was no hope of placing permanent markers in the snow-fields and snow-covered ridges in the ten-mile gap between B.P.'s 123 and 124.

Tsirku River (B.P. 151 to B.P. 157)[48]

1904: C.A. Bigger (Canada) reconnaissance only.
1905: W.F. Ratz (Canada) with seven men, part-season only.
1910: O.M. Leland (United States) with eight men.

The Tsirku River, a tributary of the Chilkat, was used by the surveyors in 1904, 1905, and 1910. The river lies in a narrow valley with Tsirku glacier at the head, smaller glaciers extending down to the river on the south side, and a hopeless tangle of stunted hemlock and alder in the thousand-foot gap between river and snow line on the north side. At certain seasons, the men could ascend the river to within five miles of the boundary line. After completing their work on the west side of the Klehini, one of Bigger's parties had succeeded in reaching the boundary on the Tsirku on 17 September 1904, but it was too late in the season to do more than occupy camera stations on the accessible hilltops.

In late May 1905, Ratz's party landed at Haines and then travelled to Klukwan, opposite the mouth of the Tsirku, in large Indian dugouts under sail. With two Indians and one member of the party in each canoe, they ascended the Tsirku to the first snow bridge, a distance of about twenty miles, at which point the Indians refused to go farther. Beyond, the party hauled their outfit on some Yukon sleds found in an old cache. When they set up their base camp on 3 June 1905, there was five feet of snow on the ground, and it did not leave the valley for another three weeks. The party were able to carry the triangulation from the Chilkat River to the boundary area, and they were able to determine B.P.'s 152 to

156. Two bronze cones (B.P. 152 and 153) were set on the north side of the Tsirku Valley. Their work finished by the end of July, they left for the Taku River area.

In June 1910, an American party led by O.M. Leland tackled the Tsirku River. This time their outfit was hauled in three Peterborough canoes and five cottonwood dugouts. The canoes, carrying between 1,000 and 1,200 pounds were hauled by two men on a tow line while a third steered the canoe and, on occasion, waded in the stream to prevent an upset in the many rapids. Each dugout, carrying 650 pounds, was pulled by one Indian while a second poled. They established their camp near the boundary in late June and made preparations to take advantage of any clear weather. It finally came on 25 July, and in the six clear days that followed, the survey party occupied B.P.'s 154 to 157 as well as three new triangulation stations. One more day would have done it, but the weather closed on 31 July, and with their tents being torn to pieces by wind, rain, sleet, and snow, the observers were forced to return to the main camp. There was another break in the weather after 9 August, and ten days later, their work completed, the party started downriver. A flood forced the party ashore before nightfall:

> The next morning, a very early start was made. The flood had passed and it was hoped to reach Nugget Creek without difficulty. A small load of supplies was left behind to lighten the boats, and two Indians who had been expected before but had not arrived were sent after it when we met them in the forenoon. There were several narrow escapes, but just below the face of DeBlondeau Glacier, all three boats were caught out in the river by a terrible flood of floating ice accompanying a rise of several feet in the river. The larger ice fragments reached about four feet in diameter. It was miraculous that we escaped with the boats. We had to stand in the shallow water of the gravel bars, retreating to the highest spots, but cut off from the banks of the valley by deeper streams crowded and jammed full of ice. Our legs were bruised by the ice which we strove to keep from smashing the boats. Finally after about two hours, the quantity of ice became smaller and we succeeded in reaching the east bank of the river where we camped, exhausted, thankful for our lives.[49]

In the work they found that B.P.'s 152 and 153, set by Ratz in 1905, lay from fifteen to twenty feet west of the true line between B.P.'s 151 and 154, possibly because Ratz had sighted on a shoulder of B.P. 154 that hid the true summit. Leland did not move the monuments, and later the commissioners, showing less concern than in the Katete area, decided to accept the line as monumented as the true boundary.

Muir Glacier to Mount Hay (B.P. 157 to B.P. 167)[50]

1907: Fremont Morse (United States) with seventeen men, including D.H.

Nelles, Canadian representative.
1912: W.M. Dennis (Canada) with eight men, part-season only.

In the 1907 season, a long stretch of the boundary, almost from the Tsirku area to the Alsek River, was sighted in from a triangulation net carried up Glacier Bay by Morse's party. Many of the shots were long, sometimes in excess of fifty miles, but for the most part the boundary peaks were prominent and readily identified. The plan to carry the triangulation up the glaciers towards some of the boundary peaks had to be abandoned owing to a lack of time.

In the 1912 season, W.M. Dennis and his party returned to the area to carry the triangulation inland following Grand Pacific and Melburn Glaciers. On 25 May the party started up Glacier Bay travelling in a twenty-two-foot launch and two canoes, but they were forced to pull in and camp at Hugh Miller Inlet. In his report, Dennis summarized the problems they faced:

For 25 miles below the glacier the inlet was blocked entirely by ice. This made movements very dangerous, as the canoes and launch were always crowded by small ice through which they were slowly pushed or over which the canoes were often carried. It was always necessary to keep as far as possible from the larger bergs, as their actions are very erratic. As the top melts away, the position of their centre of gravity changes, so that without warning they begin to roll over to take a new position of equilibrium. This action always causes great commotion and noise. Thousands of tons of water are carried up to pour off into the sea. As it rolls up to a new position, tremendous bending moments and shearing stresses are produced, generally accompanied by fracture along some plane as the ice is almost always built in layers. If this plane at the moment of fracture is usually inclined to the horizontal, the top portion, say 7,500 tons, slides down the slope into the sea. The drop of the centre of gravity of this party [*sic*] may be 30 feet, with the production of 450,000,000 ft. lbs. of work. As one can easily see, this energy will likely disturb the equilibrium of other bergs in the vicinity, spreading similar action over a considerable area. As the bay is always full of ice, constant vigilance is necessary to avoid disaster to small boats.

On this trip many of the dangerous and difficult conditions typical of the southwestern part of the Canada-Alaska boundary were met with. It was found early that there was only one route past the face of [Grand Pacific] Glacier by which the upper part could be reached. This route led for about one-third of a mile along the steep face of bench some 500 feet high. Years previously the surface of the glacier had been some 700 feet higher than it is now and had left a body of ice about 200 feet thick on top of this bench. This ice, protected on top from the sun by a thickness of about 30 feet of the original lateral moraine, wasted only on its outer face, and as soon as the sun began to melt this face, the rock would begin to roll down the face of the bench throughout its full length. For a week and a half, 9 men crossed the face of this bench, about one-third of the way up the slope, each day, with a 65 lb. pack, and returned in the evening. There were many narrow escapes as those men had to avoid a continuous rain of rocks while on a very uncertain footing.

On three different occasions the life of our one incompetent was saved by the quick action of his nearest companion — once from a turbulent stream which, about 100 yards below the rock from which the man stumbled, loses itself for 2 miles under the glacier's 600 feet of ice — again from a fall of 150 feet when he tripped on a fragment of rock while crossing a sloping ledge and again from drowning, when in an ice pack, the bow of the canoe having slid upon some submerged arm of ice, his thoughtless act turned the canoe over. This man was very tall and slight and, on one occasion, one of the other men, being impatient that he should have to look after another man as well as take care of himself remarked: "It will be easy to take you out when it does happen, we can double you up three times to make a decent pack."

On July 4th, when crossing the glacier just above the Nunatak about 9 miles inland from the boundary we noted in the morning a few specimens of ice worms. On our return in the evening we found their distribution covered the glacier completely across, except over part of the Nunatak where the ice was only about 20 feet thick. Here there were none. Elsewhere, where the ice was hundreds of feet deep, the worms were so thick as to give a slight tinge to the color of the glacier. There would be easily a worm to every square inch of area. They could also be seen many feet down in the water holes in the ice. These worms were about the size and length of an ordinary pin. Some specimens were preserved and, on our return to Ottawa, some were sent to McGill University. On the following day, July 5th, the worms on the glacier had entirely disappeared.[51]

The worms were identified as *Mesenchytraeus solifugus,* an annelid worm.

Despite the difficulties, the party had carried Morse's triangulation forward nearly twenty-two miles to a station on Melburn Glacier, about twelve miles across the boundary line. On 28 July 1912, they broke camp and sailed for Juneau, en route to other projects in the southern part of the Panhandle. Their work supplied the material needed to complete a phototopographic survey of the area east of the boundary between Mount Root (B.P. 165) and Mount Hay (B.P. 167), an inaccessible area, hidden from observers working along the coast.

Alsek River (B.P. 167 to B.P. 172)[52]

1906: A.J. Brabazon (Canada) with eleven men.
Fremont Morse (United States), Party No. 4 in charge of L. Netland.

1908: Fremont Morse (United States) with nineteen men, including G.R. White-Fraser, Canadian representative.

From Mount Hay (B.P. 167) to Mount Herbert (B.P. 172) the Panhandle boundary is a straight line just over fifty-one miles long. Most of it is through high country or glaciers with the exception of the Alsek River, which has cut its way through the Saint Elias Mountains to empty into the Gulf of Alaska at Dry Bay. In 1906, two parties, a Canadian and an American sub-party, attempted to mark the boundary on the Alsek. It was a disappointing summer for both.

The Canadian party led by Brabazon reached Yakutat on 9 May 1906, ahead of the Americans who were delayed when most of their outfit was burned in the fires following the San Francisco earthquake of 18 April 1906. There must have been more to Brabazon than his bad temper for three of the crew from the 1905 season were back; his son, A.G. Gillespie, and Vernon Ritchie. The son may have had little choice, but Gillespie had turned down an opportunity to work on the Vermont border in order to return to Alaska. He later wrote of the start of the season:

> We arrived at Yakutat Bay at about three in the morning [of 9 May], a dismal time to arrive, but it was made worse by a heavy snow storm. We had to unload all our outfit into boats, as there did not seem to be a wharf. In the process we lost a hundred pound sack of sugar over the side, which went to the bottom like a stone.
>
> We landed on the beach. The settlement consisted of an Indian village and a huge salmon cannery and a general store. The missionary gave us permission to use the schoolhouse for living quarters, which was fortunate, as otherwise we would have had to put up tents in the snow.
>
> From Yakutat Bay we had a journey of about sixty miles down the coast to the mouth of the Alsek River. As it was impossible to use the canoes — there being practically no break in the sandy shore line, which extended the whole way and where the surf was forever rolling up and breaking on the beach — we had to accomplish this journey over land, making use, where possible, of any lagoon or creek.
>
> There was a railway belonging to the cannery, which when in operation, ran for about eight miles down the coast, but as at the time of our arrival the cannery and railway had not yet come out of hibernation, Mr. Brabazon decided we would make a start. We had approximately eight tons of supplies and about fourteen in the party.
>
> From time immemorial the Indians have travelled from Yakutat to the mouth of the Alsek at Dry Bay, and have dug channels and widened small creeks, so that a loaded canoe can travel many miles on the journey, but there were many portages, and some long ones over miles of sand.

[After losing a few days trying to move to the railhead by canoe] Brabazon decided it would save a great deal of hard work to wait for the railway to operate. We made a camp on the open sand flats, and waited, but it was not long before the railway was running. It had only the engine and one flat car, a narrow gage. On each side were ditches full of water, and it was amusing to see the salmon in the ditches trying to beat the train. When the boiler needed water, the train would stop, and the Indian fireman would take a few buckets of water from the ditch and pour them into the engine.

As soon as the supplies were dumped at the end of the railway, we started again for Dry Bay. It was a very interesting but hard journey. We had bought some empty barrels and putting axles through two of them from top to bottom, made a sort of overland raft, which we found very useful on the long flat, sandy portages. With seven men to a raft, we could haul about 700 pounds of freight.

The coast was very wild between Yakutat and Dry Bay, being inhabited by only a few Indian families. We picked up a small Indian boy for guide, as the route is quite tricky. At one place, we travelled up a river for some distance, and then with a short portage of a few yards, we got on another river and went down it. The last river we travelled, which took us out at Dry Bay, was beautiful, being of uniform depth of about two feet, with clear water, and smooth white, sandy bottom, without any stones or gravel.

We made camp near the mouth of the river, and were surprised to find American surveyors in camp, about three miles away on the sand flats. This party had been brought down to Dry Bay by a small steamer, and had made the entrance at high, slack water. They were fortunate in getting in, as at times there are days and days when it is impossible to enter.[53]

The two parties worked together in preparing a base line and then began their triangulation. Early in July, Gillespie and two men were sent to look at the canyon of the Alsek formed between a rock wall and a glacier at a point about twenty miles upstream:

As we came up near the glacier, we came into what might almost be called a small lake, formed by an almost right angle bend in the river. This was a new kind of surrounding to us all. A huge great glacier extended along the south side of this small lake and when I entered I noticed a peculiar thing, which was that apparently very recently the lake had been ten or twelve feet higher than at present. This was shown by what was undoubtedly new drift left high up on the sides. There was something rather uncanny about it, so when we made camp that night, we carried our canoe well back from the river and pitched our tent up on a ridge.

That night, when we were sound asleep, we were suddenly awakened by the most awful noise. As I rushed out of the tent, I felt my hair stand on end. The noise was terrifying. I thought at first the great mountain across the river was falling down. Then the waves came roaring across the lake — huge great waves — rushing over the gravel towards us. We then realized what had happened. The glacier had "calved," and thousands of tons of ice had fallen into the lake. It was a lesson to us, but fortunately, though we had to cross the lake several times, we were only caught in the canoe once when the ice broke. We turned the bow of the canoe into the waves and rode them out.

Above this lake, there was a bad canyon to negotiate. On the right bank, was a sheer rock cliff, hundreds of feet high, and on the left, the ice wall of a hundred feet or more. To make the passing of this canyon even more hazardous, there was an active rock slide down which, at irregular intervals all day long, rocks of all sizes came hurtling and plunging into the river. It was a truly nasty place to pass. The whole party was now camped just below the canyon and how to get through was the puzzle.

While we were waiting, an American geologist, attached to the American party, with two men in a light canoe, came along to go up the river. We told them that it was almost impossible to get through the canyon and the active rock slide. However, they camped the night near us, and next morning started up the river, with rather a superior manner. They had not been gone very long before they were back. They had lost everything, but were lucky to be alive. The rocks had come down, smashing their canoe to match wood and one of the men was rather badly cut on the shoulder. We took them down the river to the American camp — their season's work was over.

After waiting nearly three weeks [until early August], the weather got cold and, as usually happens on these snow and ice-fed rivers, they rise and fall considerably with the temperature. The river dropped and by good fortune, a long gravel bar showed up in the middle of the river, between the ice and the rock slide.

Four of us took a canoe up the river, as near the rock slide as we dared, and then by hard paddling, were able to make the gravel bar. . . . We tracked the canoe up the bar till we stood in water almost to our middles. Then the bow man holding the canoe, the others climb in and get their paddles ready, the bow man scrambles in and by desperate paddling, we were able to gain the bank above the rock slide. As this had proved successful, we struck camp and all day until late in the evening we were moving our camp above the rock slide. If the ice had ever crashed while we were in the canyon, we would all have gone. We knew the danger, and were thankful to make a rough camp that night at 10 P.M., among the boulders, well above the dangerline.

The travelling was now extremely rough, the river very swift and the shore strewn with huge boulders, making tracking very difficult. We had an accident, which might have been disastrous. Three of us were tracking the canoe, which contained all our field work up to date. The canoe got out of hand in an eddy, and took a sheer. We could not hold it, and two of us were dragged into the river and forced to let go. It went off like a runaway horse, plunging over the big waves, and heading for the ice. Fortunately, one of the crews below saw it coming, and hastily chucking out part of their load went after it and managed to bring it to shore.

For three days we moved up the river, only making three or four miles a day. Finally, we made camp on a good site just below another canyon, much the same as the last, with a glacier on the south side and rocky cliffs on the north.[54]

The American party followed the Canadians through the canyon and set to work connecting the triangulation above and below it. Meanwhile, the Canadians ascended the second canyon and did reconnaissance work to mouth of the Tatshenshini River, some eight miles beyond the border and thirty miles from the top of the first canyon. The weather improved somewhat, but both parties were delayed by heavy fogs that hung in the river bottoms. Most frustrating of all, Mount Herbert (B.P. 172) was not visible from any of their stations, and they were unable to identify Mount Hay (B.P. 167) owing to an error in the award maps supplied to them.

Their problems continued. The American party returned to Dry Bay on 24 September 1906 to embark for Yakutat aboard the *Stockholm*, a gasoline launch chartered from Seattle for the season. Heavy seas prevented them from crossing the bar until late next day; then, after a dark and stormy night, they found themselves lost at sea with a broken-down engine and a sick captain. When the engine was finally started and land sighted, they were off Sitkagi Bluffs at the tip of Malaspina Glacier, thirty-five miles the other side of Yakutat. They finally reached Yakutat after forty-four hours at sea with much of the credit for their safe arrival due to the party's cook, who had manned the wheel for twenty-three hours straight.

The Canadian party left the Alsek in late September and retraced their slower and less exciting route through the streams and lagoons to Yakutat. Their loads were lighter and they made better time, but on their last night under canvas, a gale with driving, cold rain blew all but one of their tents to ribbons.

In the 1908 season Morse and his party returned to the Alsek. By late June they were through the lower canyon, the bane of the 1906 season. This time it was easy; the season was late, and the river was low enough that they could row their four twenty-five-foot Peterborough canoes through it. Later when the river rose and rowing became impossible, the slides were quiet, and there were no difficulties in lining the canoes along the shore. Even better, the location of Mount Herbert (B.P. 172) and Mount Hay (B.P. 167) had been determined in 1906 and 1907, respectively, and the length and azimuth of the line joining them had been computed. In the field, the triangulation was completed through to the boundary with the geographic position of each station being calculated as the work pro-

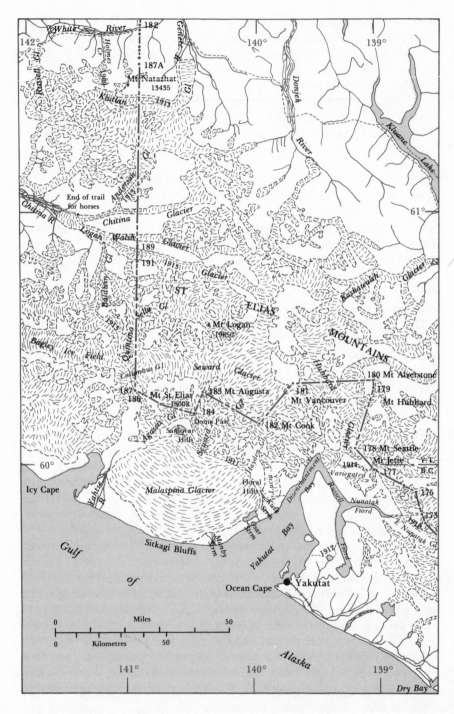

Map 7: Panhandle Boundary: Boundary Points 172 (Mt Herbert) to 187
141st Meridian: White River to flank of Mt St Elias (Monuments 182-191)

gressed. Using all this information, the exact intersection of the boundary on a new base line was determined. From this point, the boundary line was projected along the known azimuth, four monuments were set and the vista was cut. It was all done without direct observations on B.P.'s 167 and 172, neither of them visible from the triangulation stations close to the border.

Their work completed, the party suspended operations on 10 September 1908 and made a swift return to Dry Bay. A gale prevented their crossing the bar until the fifteenth, but, once they were across, a nine-hour run through heavy seas brought them to Yakutat, first stop on their return voyage to Seattle.

Mount Herbert to the 141st Meridian (B.P. 172 to B.P. 187)[55]

> 1906: Fremont Morse (United States) with thirty-four men.
> 1911: H.S. Mussell (Canada) with five men.
> 1911: W.M. Dennis (Canada) with five men.
> 1912: H.S. Mussell (Canada) with six men, part-season only.

In 1906, the year of all the problems on the Alsek River, three other United States parties under the overall charge of Fremont Morse operated in the area from Yakutat Bay to the Alsek. The San Francisco earthquake had disrupted their preparations since much of their outfit was burned and provisions already delivered to the dock were confiscated for disaster relief. Nothing further could be done in San Francisco, and a new outfit was hastily assembled in Seattle, the entire party of thirty-five sailing from that city on 26 May aboard the steamship, *Bertha.*

Supported by the launch *Stockholm,* chartered for the season, the parties developed a triangulation net from the toe of the Malaspina Glacier southeast to the mouth of the Alsek River. The Malaspina Base of the United States Coast and Geodetic Survey, laid out in 1892, was recovered, including one station with the signal still standing. A number of new stations were occupied along the low-lying coastal strip and in the flanking Brabazon Range to about five thousand feet in elevation. The much higher elevations of the "S" peaks of the 1903 award, some of them to almost sixteen thousand feet, proved a great advantage, and despite shots of up to forty miles, about eighty-six miles of the boundary between B.P.'s 172 and 182 was established.

In the 1911 season, W.M. Dennis and his party attempted to make their way to the huge snowfield lying north and east of Mount Seattle (B.P. 178). Working their way past the ice in Disenchantment Bay and the snout of Hubbard Glacier, they made camp two miles south of Variegated Glacier and began relaying their supplies up it on 1 July. To do this, the party divided into two groups of three. The rear group packed supplies from the cache behind to the temporary camp and the following day carried them to a forward cache. Meanwhile, the forward group packed beyond on days unsuitable for survey work, but on fine days they were always in camp at the foot of the mountain they were to climb. Five attempts were made to climb Mount Jetté (B.P. 177) but it was finally abandoned as too dangerous. Years later, Dennis wrote of their frustration:

> Although the surface of the Variegated climbs gradually from Russell Fiord, it drops as a cascading glacier from about 5,000 feet to the snow field in the rear which has an elevation of about 3,000 feet. This cascade is caused by a ridge of [Mount Jetté] which, running north, turns east to form the wall of a short canyon, of which Irish station forms the other wall. This ice fall prevented us from getting off the glacier, had the steep glaciated walls held any attraction for us. With our base camp 25 miles behind, with a month's food supplies on hand, back-packed therefrom, and with the gateway to an open snow plain and a record season's work only one-half mile ahead, we were forced to turn back. We arrived in camp July 19th.[56]

Following their retreat from the Variegated Glacier, Dennis and his party moved to a camp on Nunatak Fiord to occupy camera stations south of Mount Jetté. Despite their frustrations, they had obtained much of the information needed to complete mapping in the area.

On 24 June 1911, a second Canadian party led by H.S. Mussell succeeded in landing through the surf of the west side of Disenchantment Bay at a point about twenty-five miles north of Yakutat. From their landing near the foot of Galiano Glacier, the men, assisted by ten Indians, cut a trail across the tangled brush on the moraines of Atrevida and Lucia Glaciers. An aerial tramway was rigged across a glacial stream issuing from the latter, but the Indians refused to risk it and left. Relaying only essential equipment and supplies, the party found a route through the Floral Hills and across Hayden Glacier to Malaspina Glacier. Here, sleds could be used in the early morning until the snow became too soft to travel, generally about 9 A.M. About thirty miles up the Malaspina, they tried to reach Dome Pass through what appeared to be a gap in the Samovar Hills. Turned back by steep cliffs, they began to work their way around the hills to Seward Glacier, finding the latter so crevassed that they had to resort to back-packing and relaying. Finally, they found a campsite against the rock where the ice was comparatively smooth and there was some shelter from the bitterly cold winds. Here, silk tents were slung between alpenstocks and braced by the heavy packs. Cooking and heating was done with alcohol stoves. Four stations were occupied before B.P. 184 could be identified. Only 4,830 feet in elevation, it was dwarfed by Mount Augusta (B.P. 183) at 14,070 feet and, at first, it was taken for a small shoulder of that peak. Later, B.P. 184 itself was occupied as a camera and triangulation station, its position determined by shots on the towering Boundary Peaks nearby. The station was the missing link; all the others from Mount Cook (B.P. 182) to Mount St. Elias (B.P. 186) had been identified in Fremont Morse's work along the coast in 1906, and the new triangulation and camera stations would suffice to complete the topography. Their work done, the party abandoned most of the camping equipment and retreated to Disenchantment Bay, spending four nights in the open en route. When they reached their cache at Floral Hills "it was a great treat to get back to a few delicacies of civilization like milk, sugar and canned fruit. One man ate two large tins of canned peaches."[57] After several days waiting for a launch, the party was back in Yakutat on 16. August.

In the 1912 season, Mussell and his party returned to Yakutat in early June with plans to occupy stations at the head of Nunatak Glacier. They found Disenchantment Bay completely blocked by ice which, according to the local Indians, would probably remain for several weeks. There was nothing for it but to make an eleven-mile portage across the Yakutat Peninsula from Humpback Creek to Russell Fiord.

> From here we started a trail across the peninsula . . . and packed a 20 foot canoe and outfit across. Some very thick bush was encountered and windfalls so progress was not very fast. It was also a paradise for all kinds of insects that never left us alone night or day. After 16 days of trail cutting and packing we found ourselves at Russell Fiord again. The last of the journey was down a steep gulley for about 700 feet and very rough going. This was responsible for 25 holes being punched in our canoe. The canoe was made of cypress and while being very light it would dry out much faster than cedar but it was too brittle a wood for a rough passage. With cedar there is a certain amount of elasticity and when it gets an ordinary bump it will give while with cypress it means a hole every time. Our tacks had been lost on the trip so it was repaired with hobnails which served the purpose fine.
>
> Camp was made at the foot of Nunatak Glacier — where firewood was scarce, and from here we started to pack up the ice. This glacier had been one of the many routes into the Yukon during the gold rush days and it was littered from one end to the other with tin cans, discarded clothes, and sleds. The crest of the glacier just on the Canadian side . . . was reached on July 28th and a fine heather patch was located for a camp ground. There was no brush so alcohol was used for cooking purposes. Five stations were occupied with camera and transit in the next two weeks but owing to smoke over the Alsek valley and a haze which we took to be caused by volcanic activity to the westward it was very difficult to secure good photographs.[58]

The party's work supplied the last of the information needed to complete the topographic mapping from B.P. 175 southeast to the Alsek River area. On 22 August 1912 they were back in Yakutat, waiting for a steamer to Juneau. From there, the party was to complete a small assignment in the Taku area before returning to Vancouver.

THE COMMISSIONERS' CERTIFICATE OF 26 NOVEMBER 1951

At the close of the 1920 season, the fieldwork had been completed to the satisfaction of the commissioners and preparation of the final report and maps was underway. Thirteen maps at a scale of 1:250,000, or about four miles to the inch, with a contour interval of 250 feet were prepared to cover the work. By early 1928, eleven of the thirteen maps had been completed and signed by the commissioners, while the other two were held back for political rather than technical reasons.[59]

Differences had arisen over the interpretation of the Line A-B of the 1903 award, a matter outside the scope of the commissioners' duties. The United States began to have second thoughts about this section of the award not long after it was handed down.[60] Was it the intent to leave them without a full three-mile limit south of Dall Island, Prince of Wales Island, and some smaller islands in Dixon Entrance? Canada claimed that it was and the question remains unresolved to this day. The Commissioners certificate of 1951, together with accompanying report and maps, deftly sidesteps the issue by describing the boundary from Point B (Tongass Passage) north to Mount St. Elias, ignoring Line A-B.

Plate 34. Observing at a line projection station near Monument 92, 1910. The second man is operating the heliograph.

Plate 35. Heliograph station, probably near Monument 22, 1911 season.

Plate 36. Observing at Yukon River, East Base, 1907. The carefully measured base line, 1,498.7423 metres long, straddled the 141st Meridian at Boundary.

Plate 37.   Packing up on a camp move, D.H. Nelles, precise levelling party, 1910.

Plate 38.   Inspection party crossing the white ice of Russell Glacier near Skolai Pass, 1913.

late 39. The vista south of Ladue River, 1910 season. The line is still visible on the hillside in the middle distance.

Plate 40. Finishing touches, trowelling the cement around a new boundary monument, monumenting party, 1910.

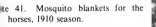

e 41. Mosquito blankets for the horses, 1910 season.

Plate 42. Freighting on the so-called wagon-road from Whitehorse to Kluane late in the spring of 1909.

Plate 43. Season's end, September 1910. Survey parties boarding the *Susie* at the mouth of the Tatonduk River.

Plate 44. Breakup on the Porcupine River at Rampart House, May 1912. The American launch, *Midnight Sun*, had wintered here.

Plate 45. Chiefs of parties; Thomas Riggs, Jr. (United States) left and J.D. Craig (Canada) right, with Mike Pope of the American contingent. Rampart House, probably 1912.

Plate 46. Riggs and Craig at the Arctic Coast, 18 July 1912. The small pennant are for Princeton and Queen's universities. *Insert:* After posing for the commemorative photograph, the two men took a dip in the ocean.

Plate 47. Collecting dry willows for firewood, Hospital Camp on the Malcolm River, 25 miles south of the Arctic Coast, 1912

ate 48. Freighting from McCarthy to the Chitina
Glacier, 1913 season. The sled is placed on another
temporary sled to keep the load above water.

Plate 49. "Care needed in moving" instrument station
near Monument 189, 1913 season.

te 50. Packing supplies across Anderson Glacier, 1913.

Plate 51. "The great towering mass of Moun
Elias," photographed from a camera sta
about 26 miles to the north, Baldwin p.
1913.

Plate 52. Back-packing to the saddle
west of Mount St. Elias, Baldwin
party, 1913.

Plate 53. Camp in the saddle at an elevation of 13,500 feet, Baldwin party, 191

7

The 141st Meridian: A Single Straight Line
(1906–13)

The 141st Meridian was not included in the 1904 agreement to mark the boundary in the Alaska Panhandle. Two years later, on 21 April 1906, it was covered in a convention between Great Britain and United States.[1] Under it, the position of the 141st Meridian would be determined at a single point, using the telegraphic method, and this line would be projected north to the Arctic Ocean and south to the flank of Mount St. Elias, overlooking the Pacific Ocean. Once again, King and Tittmann were designated commissioners for the project.

Using telegraphic methods, far greater accuracy would be possible than with the astronomic methods used by Ogilvie and McGrath. The commissioners selected Boundary, on the south bank of the Yukon River about three miles west of Ogilvie's observatory, as the site for the longitude determination. From it, there were telegraph connections to Vancouver, B.C., via Dawson, and to Seattle, via Eagle and a cable from Valdez. Some work had already been done; in 1905 the longitude of both Vancouver and Eagle (Fort Egbert) had been tied to a station in Seattle. Now, the difference in longitude would be determined between three stations, Boundary, Eagle, and Vancouver. Calculation of the results would take time, and if surveys were to go ahead in the 1907 season it would be necessary to start the work in 1906 without waiting for formal ratification of the convention. On 19 August 1906, just three days after formal ratification, F. A. McDiarmid, of the Dominion Observatory in Ottawa, began observations at the Boundary site.[2] His astronomical transit was installed on a cement pier, located about 20 feet south of the river and 352 feet to the east of Ogilvie's line of 1895-96.

Time signals would be transmitted to and from Vancouver over two thousand miles of telegraph line, much of it a single strand of iron wire strung between insulators nailed to tree trunks after a swath of branches had been lopped off. For hundreds of miles, the line ran through isolated country lying behind the Alaska Panhandle and was patrolled by lonely men based at repair stations about thirty miles apart. Breaks in the line were common with snow, wind, water, and fire some of the causes. In addition, with so many operators along the line there was a human element as well, and one earlier attempt to clear the line and transmit a time signal from Washington failed when a lonely lineman broke in and hammered out on his key: "Has anybody seen Hootalinqua Mary?"[3]

Both the weather and the telegraph lines co-operated in 1906, and by 3 September seven differential longitude determinations had been obtained both between Boundary and Vancouver and between Boundary and Eagle. Later, when the results were computed over the winter, it was found that Ogilvie's line of 1887–88 lay 218 feet west of the meridian, his 1895–96 line some 370 feet to the west and McGrath's 1889–91 line some 477 feet to the east.[4] All were remarkably accurate considering the conditions the earlier work had been done under.

1907 SEASON — YUKON RIVER SOUTH TO SCOTTIE CREEK (MONUMENTS 112 to 157)[5]

In this first season, few Canadian surveyors were available and the bulk of the work was done by American parties. To help offset the costs, the Canadian government supplied subsistence for the entire force.

An initial party, charged with laying out the north-south azimuth of the line, arrived in Dawson on 13 April 1907 after travelling by ship from Seattle to Skagway, rail to Whitehorse, and thence by stage to Dawson. Next day, using hired teams, the party set out on the ice of the Yukon River for Boundary. It was hard going; they had to contend with rough ice, deep snowdrifts, and, in places, ice that was covered with a foot of slush. At Forty Mile there was another delay when the Royal Northwest Mounted Police, enforcing a glanders quarantine, ordered the Dawson teams sent back, which meant a wait of several days for a local team.

After reaching Boundary on 20 April, the party set to work to lay out the azimuth of the line. There were still problems with snow; caught without snowshoes, the men had to struggle through more than a mile of soft spring snow to set up and maintain a sighting target, made up of a box which had a light inside visible through a narrow slit. The azimuth was established through a sequence of sightings on the target and various stars made by observers from both countries. Once the north-south line was marked out on the ground, actual line projection could begin. When the work ended seven years later, the line had been projected north to the Arctic Ocean and south to the flank of the St. Elias Mountains where snow and ice made work along the line itself out of the question.

The main party, consisting of twenty-six men with Thomas Riggs, Jr., in charge, left Seattle on 25 May 1907 aboard the steamer *Dolphin*, and they were joined next day in Vancouver by ten Canadians. A. J. Brabazon, transferred from the Panhandle work, was the Canadian chief of party. One of the first problems was over wages, Riggs writing: "To avoid any ill feeling among the men [we] had decided . . . . that the wages of men employed in the joint party should as far-as possible be uniform. The pursuance of which idea the lowest monthly wage paid was $75.00 . . . . The wages of the country being $5.00 per day and board, this was about as low a scale as could be paid and still hold the men."[6]

The main party reached Boundary on 12 June 1907. Once the work along the line began, the men would be assigned to one of a number of smaller parties. These could include: Projection, Reconnaissance, Triangulation, Topography, Vista and Stadia, and Monumenting, all under the control of two chiefs of party, representing the United States and Canada. Forty-eight pack-horses, purchased in eastern Washington, would be used for transportation. The field work differed from that in the Panhandle where most of the parties worked in isolation. Here, all would be following the 141st meridian, each assigned one or more of the many tasks involved. Canadian and American parties would be working close together, and at times, a good-natured rivalry ensued. In practice, the parties were somewhat flexible, and when the need arose, duties could be changed or men shifted from one to the other.

The projection party would mark the boundary line at points on ridges, roughly ten to twenty miles apart, leaving other parties to complete the survey along the boundary line, cut the vista, and place the monuments.[7] The line was projected by optical methods using a 6¼-inch repeating theodolite with a micrometer eyepiece. Heliographs, used for communication by flashing a modified Morse code and for signals marking stations on the line, linked a rear station on the line, the instrument station, and the new point where the line was to be established. The theodolite was set up over the final station on the line and sighted back to the rear station. The instrument's telescope was next rotated and the fore-heliograph man signalled to a point on the approximate line. This was usually accomplished in two or three moves following instructions signalled to him by heliograph. Once in position, he would mark two stations about five feet apart on opposite sides of the approximate line and set his heliograph over one of them. Observers representing both countries would take "sets" of multiple readings on the signal from the fore-heliograph until there was agreement within five seconds of angle on the deviation of the station from the projected line. The fore-heliograph was then positioned over the second point and the procedure repeated. The fore-heliograph man would then signal the exact distance between the two points to the instrument party who, using this as a base and knowing the micrometer deflection for the two points, calculated the position of the true line with respect to the points. This information was signalled to the fore-heliograph man, who then measured the offset from one of the points, marked the position of the true line, and erected a signal over it. Using this method, the boundary line was projected for a total of 555.5 miles between 1907 and 1912, inclusive. This involved a total of forty-five sightings, averaging 12.35 miles in length with the longest 45.0 miles and the shortest 0.3 miles. In all but three of the sightings, the lines determined by the American and Canadian observers lay within a foot of the line as it was finally marked. The glaring exception was on a projection of 24.1 miles across the flats of the Old Crow River where the discrepancy was almost 4.7 feet on either side.

The reconnaissance party was responsible for the selection of triangulation stations and the erection of signals.[8] The work was done using a plane-table, basically a drawing board mounted on a tripod, and an opensight alidade, a brass ruler with sighting holes at each end. Starting from a station on a measured base line, lines or rays were drawn to points that might be suitable for triangulation stations. These points were occupied in turn, the plane-table oriented by backsighting along rays drawn from the earlier stations. Signals were then put up on the points chosen as triangulation stations. Generally, these consisted of a pole, twelve to sixteen feet long, with targets of white and black signal cotton facing the principal lines of sight. Where possible, a tripod of poles was used to support the signal, but where these were unobtainable a stone cairn was substituted. When done by a capable man with a good sense of topography, the plane-table method proved a quick and efficient method of covering an area with a triangulation net.

The triangulation party began their work from a carefully measured base line.[9] From stations at the ends of this line, the nearby triangulation stations were observed using a 6½-inch theodolite, similar to the type used for line projection. With the length of the base line known, horizontal and vertical distances between the triangulation stations could be calculated. Next, some of the observed stations would be occupied and the triangulation net carried along the boundary line as a series of interlocking triangles. During the survey of the 141st meridian, a total of seven base lines were measured, and careful controls were used to ensure the accuracy of the observations. Later, in the office, the field results were adjusted mathematically to reduce the probable errors to a minimum.

The topography parties were responsible for mapping a belt along the boundary four and a half to five miles wide at a field scale of 1:45,000 and a contour interval of one hundred feet.[10] Most of the work between the Arctic Ocean and Mount Natazhat was done using plane-table mapping, while in the mountains to the south photo-topographic methods were used. In the latter, the camera proved indispensable because of uncertain weather conditions and the time required to sketch the rugged country using the other method. Geographic control for the work was provided by the triangulation.

The vista and stadia parties were responsible for the establishment of the line between the main projection stations, measurement of horizontal and vertical distances along the line using optical methods, and, in timbered areas, the cutting of the vista with its twenty-foot clear skyline, that is, with nothing except low underbrush left standing within ten feet of the line on either side.[11]

The monumenting party erected permanent monuments at sites selected by the chief of the stadia party.[12] Where possible, an attempt was made to have monuments at an average of about three miles apart and intervisible, so that at least one other monument could be seen from a monument site. Monuments were the same kind as those used in the Panhandle. During the work, a total of 11 large obelisk-type monuments, sixty-three inches high, were set, one at the Arctic Coast and the others at important river crossings, and a total of 191 smaller conical monuments, thirty inches high. But the monuments had to be set in cement, and only rarely could all the required materials be found near the site. If none were there, the total weight needed to set in cone-type monument rose to an impressive eighteen hundred pounds made up of: the monument, fifty-five pounds; mixing tools, forty-five pounds; water three hundred pounds; sand, four hundred pounds; stone, eight hundred pounds, and cement, two hundred pounds. It was no wonder that the party's horses soon became the "goat train." The horses quickly learned to recognize the pickets and signals left by the instrument parties, and after a hard climb, they would mill around the first signal they came to, waiting to be unpacked and growing indignant if they were forced to move on to another site.

Pack-trains were the main means of transportation for about 550 miles of the boundary line from the Arctic Ocean to the flanks of the St. Elias Mountains. Much of this country was not well suited to their use, but at the time, there was no better alternative. Throughout its entire length, the boundary line cuts across the grain of the country, alternating between ridge and valley bottom. The boundary trail, in places more like a roller coaster, ran within a few miles of the line, groping for the best route around the many obstacles. In places, high upland surfaces above tree line were easy travelling, but intervening valley bottoms with their permanently frozen ground and thick moss cover were difficult. Even worse, once the horses' hooves had punched through the insulating moss, the ground below thawed to a stinking mass of black muck. Time and time again, new routes had to be found around sections of the trail that had become impassable. Stream and river crossings were another hazard that could change almost from hour to hour. Natural feed for the horses was poor along much of the route, and the pack-trains themselves could afford to carry little more than the oats needed to catch the foraging horses in the mornings. Fortunately, in a number of sections, men using poling boats were able to bring feed and supplies up to the line.

As the number of parties in the field increased, so did the number of horses, reaching a maximum of 166 in the 1911 season. Each pack-train, generally consisting of fewer than 20 horses, was the responsibility of the packer and his assistants. On camp moves, they and, at times, the cook rode saddle horses while the rest of the men on the party walked, often the easiest way to travel the rough trail. Each pack-horse carried a load of about 250 pounds, much of it in alforjas, or canvas bags with leather ends, hung on either side of a simple wooden "sawbuck" pack-saddle. Other items such as blankets, tents, and sacked goods were either piled carefully on top of the main load or slung from the pack-saddle. The entire load was then covered with a pack-cover, a large canvas or linen tarpaulin, and everything was held in place by a cinch with a long rope, tied around the load in a diamond hitch. The hitch, an ingenious one, is named for the diamond of rope formed over the top of the load as the rope is tightened against the load and the free end tied. If the load is properly balanced on each side of the horse and if the diamond is thrown properly, the pack may stay in place for the entire move. However, even the best-behaved and most orderly pack-train can be turned into a stampede in seconds after a single horse brushes a wasp nest, catches the scent of a bear, or is "spooked" by part of the load working out from under a pack cover or some totally inexplicable cause. Then, an hour or more could be lost while the horses were caught and tied, the spilled loads picked up here and there through the brush, and the entire outfit repacked. Much depended on the packer; a good one could make time on the trail and still keep his horses in good condition. Other packers, less skilled, seemed unable to do so. One of the more serious problems was sored horses. The sores, sometimes inches across, developed where the pack-saddle pressed against the horse's back, and loads had to be cut until they healed. Even then, the spot remained weak, and it was all too easy to develop a new sore.

Using pack-horses set definite limits to the size and weight of objects that could be carried. Items such as long tripods for the survey instruments were the bane of the packer's existence. To carry them he would have to find a place somewhere in the load where the horse would still have enough freedom to move without rubbing against them. Some substitutions were necessary; the surface of the dining and kitchen work tables consisted simply of pieces of canvas with laths tacked to them about half an inch apart so that they could be rolled for packing. At each camp, a rough frame for the dining table would be made from local spruce, with rails that the table top could be unrolled on, and log benches were used as seats. For cooking, they had light stoves, made from sheet steel and not much over a foot in height. These came with telescopic stove pipes that could be packed in the tiny oven on a camp move. Folding metal stoves had been tried, but they were discarded after it was found that it was almost impossible to set them up again after they became warped from use or had been damaged as the stove-horse battered them against trees en route. Men on the parties showed considerable ingenuity in making their camps comfortable using little more than local trees, axes, and a few nails.

There were limits to their diet as well. Items such as canned fruits and vegetables, with their high water content, were out of the question because of weight. Few fresh goods would stand up to weeks on the trail. As a result, in a hundred days in the field, a party member could expect to eat about four hundred pounds of food. The principal items were eighty-eight pounds of flour, sixty-four and a half pounds of sugar, fifty-four pounds of bacon, seventeen pounds of ham, fifty-four pounds of beans, nineteen pounds of butter, fifteen pounds of cereal, and ten pounds of evaporated milk, the latter almost the only item with a high water content.[13] It was a monotonous diet, and it is little wonder that game animals such as sheep, moose, caribou, mountain goat, and, on occasion, bear were a welcome addition to the food supply.

Mosquitoes and many varieties of biting flies plagued the parties until well into the month of August each year. The men, at least, could escape at night using special sleeping tents with a sewn-in floor and a tunnel entrance closed by a draw string. There was no escape for the horses, and at times when the flies were bad they could not stand still long enough to feed or rest. Mosquito blankets, various concoctions of "fly-dope," and smudges were all tried in attempts to give the animals some protection. The smudges proved the most effective, and the horses would stand for hours in the thick white smoke, venturing out now and then to grab a mouthful of feed.

By late June 1907, the initial confusion was over, and the newly organized parties had moved south along the boundary line leaving Riggs, the United States chief of party, and three others behind to occupy nearby triangulation stations. They faced one of the usual start-of-season problems: "By an oversight no cooking utensils were left so for five days we were obliged to cook in a gold pan, tin cans and a shovel."[14]

It was an initial "shaking down" season, but when it ended the line had been projected south for about 130 miles, the triangulation for 61 miles, line-cutting had been done, and monument sites had been selected for 52 miles, and the topographic survey was complete for 46 miles. The projected line had gone through the Sixtymile gold field but "in only one place has the change of boundary affected any mining interests, this being on Poker Creek [near Monument 126A] where a miner who had bought a Crown claim and who for years has been paying royalty, renewal and license fees now finds himself moved bodily claim and all into American territory."[15]

The horses all came through the season only to be lost in a furious blizzard on the way to Tanana Crossing where it had been planned to winter them. It was the first instance of a recurring problem; it was prohibitively expensive to take

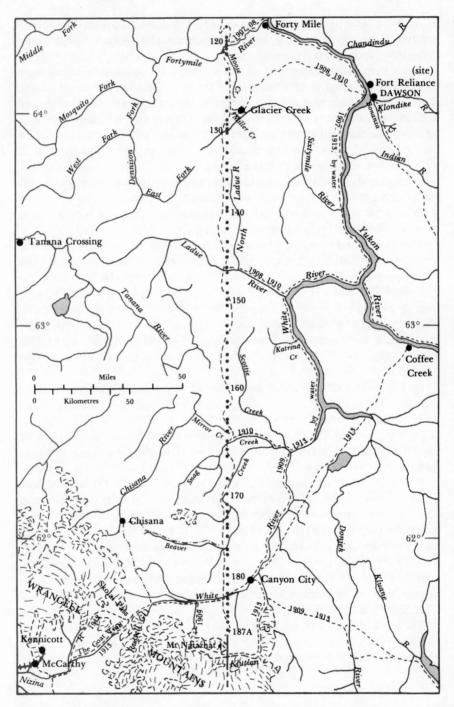

Map 8: 141st Meridian: Fortymile River to Klutlan Glacier (Monuments 118-18

the horses Outside at the end of each season, and attempts to winter them in the north met with indifferent success.[16] Some years the horses would "come through" in good condition, while in others most would be lost. Much depended on snow conditions during the winter. Snowfall was generally light, but if a hard crust prevented them from pawing for feed, many would starve. Other years, the horses would venture out to feed in patches were the snow had burned off on steep, grassy, south-facing slopes, but here the hazard was a broken leg from a fall on an icy patch.

1908 SEASON — YUKON RIVER SOUTH TO WHITE RIVER (MONUMENTS 112 TO 184)[17]

This season, the Canadians had the larger appropriation and put more men in the field than the Americans. In an attempt to extend the working season, the topographic party was sent in over the winter trail, and they were at work by the middle of May, gaining about a month. Since they were without horses until the arrival of the main party, all their supplies had to be back-packed or dragged on hand-sleds some twenty-five miles from their depot on the Sixtymile River. To make matters worse, the snow was so deep that they needed snowshoes to reach many of their stations.

In June, Canadian supplies were hauled over the wagon road from Dawson to the Sixtymile area and from there special supply pack-trains shuttled them to the south. Early in June, a river steamer landed crews at the mouth of the White River which they ascended in small boats. At Katrina Creek, approximately forty-five miles upstream, the main party was met by the pack-trains while a fore-heliograph section of the projection party continued another one hundred miles upriver on to Canyon City. With the parties strung out over about 150 miles of the line, there were predictable problems. Riggs, the United States chief, reached a camp near the White River on 29 June:

At this camp the mosquitoes were frightful, the poor horses being driven nearly frantic. We built a number of smudges around which they would hover, merely leaving the smoke for a few minutes at a time for the purpose of feeding.

Upon my arrival in camp, I found that Mr. Reaburn's cook . . . being unable to stand the mosquitoes had left that morning, so there was nothing to do but return immediately to Dawson to engage another cook.

I started back the next morning . . . my diary shows the following entries:
July 2nd — Arrived Dawson
July 3rd — Engaged T. and arranged to leave in morning.
July 4th — T. too drunk to go. Engaged M.
July 6th — Arrived Gilmore's camp 11 P.M.[18]

The twelfth of August was another day of troubles for Riggs:

Three and a half hours heart breaking climb to "Flat" [west of Monument 152]. Got set up and found part of the eyepiece to be missing and nowhere to be found. Rigged one up with string and paper out of a vernier glass and occupied the station . . . . Got back to camp about seven. Found some good grass across a little creek. After supper started to take the horses across. "Roany" fell into the creek and would not get out. We worked until 11 with pries, rope and Spanish windlass, but the best we could do was to get him to his feet in the middle of the stream. Got too dark to do anything more so we left him, hoping that he would get out by himself.
August 13 — Cloudy
. . . Went out to see what had become of "Roany" while Mack was washing the dishes. Found him still standing in the stream. I tried to turn him up the bank but he fell over, so I patted him good bye and shot him.[19]

Then, later in the season, there was difficulty in finding food caches put out by others:

The next day (August 25th) I reoccupied "Scottie" [near Monument 158] hoping that better weather conditions would make the signal visible.

While engaged in the cheerful occupation of reviling the Reconnaissance party for not putting up better signals, Mr. Reaburn suddenly appeared over the rim of rocks looking very gaunt, ragged and dirty. From him I elicited the information that food and plenty of it was earnestly and quickly desired. They had been out of supplies for two days and were hungry.

As our supplies were down to almost nothing, in fact only beans remaining, and as the position of the cache on Snag Creek was very doubtful, if it was there at all, the only thing remaining for us to do, was to back track to Ladue Creek, where Mr. Oliver had supplies to last him to the end of the season.[20]

Unknown to Reaburn, the cache on Snag Creek, boated up in the spring, had been left farther downstream than agreed upon, but to search for any distance along the creek bank as it wanders in a saucer of muskeg would have been extremely difficult. No doubt the boat crews, after following countless meanders, must have been certain they were much closer to the border than they actually were. For them, short of a astronomic determination, it would be next to impossible to tell when they were close to the projected boundary line. The last point set lay some twenty-five miles to the north! The retreat to the Ladue meant an early end to the field season, and once there, the crew members built rafts and floated downstream to Dawson.

1909 SEASON — LADUE RIVER SOUTH TO MOUNT NATAZHAT (MONUMENTS 150 to 187 A) AND YUKON RIVER NORTH TO CATHEDRAL CREEK (MONUMENTS 111 TO 99)[21]

This year A. J. Brabazon did not return as Canadian chief of party, his place taken by F. Lambart and subsequently by J. D. Craig, the latter transferred from work in the Panhandle. Craig and his American counterpart, Thomas Riggs, Jr., would continue as chiefs of party until completion of the project in 1913.

During the season there was a determined attempt to finish up as much as possible south from Boundary on the Yukon River. The work had outrun the river systems, and this year supplies were freighted over the winter roads and trails leading west from Whitehorse. A total of fifty-one men and eighty-three horses made the three hundred-mile trip. In addition to party members, there were transport teams and also three drivers to handle supplies for use on the trip in, camp outfits, and the mens' gear. They used wagons as far as Kluane Lake, which they crossed by sleigh over the ice, and beyond everything was packed on the horses. Most of the men walked the entire distance.

The journey took almost three weeks, the first nine or ten days being on the so-called wagon road where manhandling the wagons out of mud-holes was the order of the day except on higher portions of the trail where the problem was deep snow. The smaller Canadian party made the trip a few days ahead of the United States parties and had to break trail much of the way. The trip was completed just in time, with the last party crossing the sole remaining ice bridge on the White River on 21 May 1909, half an hour before it collapsed into the swollen waters of the river.

At Canyon City, Riggs supervised the splitting of the United States group of thirty-four men and fifty horses into six parties: "Every party now had its own separate organization, including its allotment of provisions and horses, the head packer however still keeping a watchful eye on the grain which was more precious and nearly as expensive as gold, especially as the natural forage had not yet started. It was very amusing to hear some of the reasons advanced by the various packers why their horses should receive more oats than the others."[22]

A base line straddling the 141st Meridian was laid out on the south bank of the White River, and the triangulation was carried south into the high mountains west of Mount Natazhat. Later, it was carried north to join the work done in 1908 and westward along the White River to Skolai Pass, the latter a distance of approximately thirty miles. The gap of almost one hundred miles in the topography was filled by parties working from both ends, who met on 24 August in

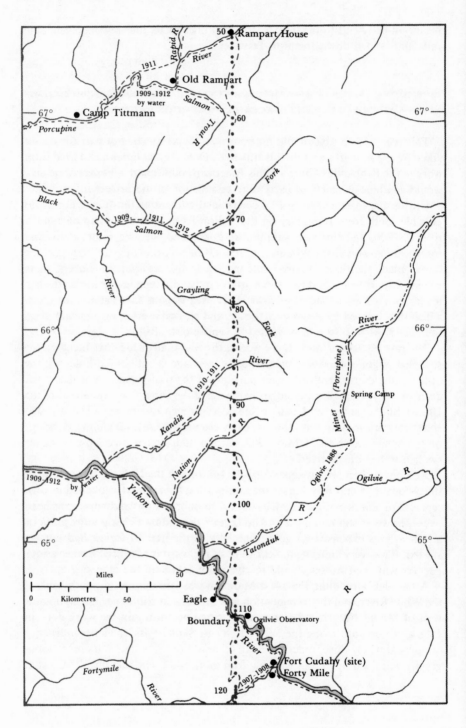

Map 9: 141st Meridian: Porcupine River to Fortymile River
          (Monuments 50–123)

the muskeg at Mirror Creek, about six miles south of the point where the present-day Alaska Highway crosses the boundary.

South of White River, the line ran directly into the high peaks of the St. Elias Mountains, and if the line was to be projected at all, it was going to be a mountaineering task. One of the first objectives was Mount Natazhat, over thirteen thousand feet in elevation and some three miles west of the line. A route to the Klutlan Glacier, lying south of the peak, was found up Holmes Creek, about twelve miles west of the line. A small camp was set up across the divide, but three men returning to it on 11 August found "the tent down and everything wet or frozen. We shovelled away the snow for a small space with snowshoes, put up the tent as best we could and crawled into our scanty bedding. During the night it snowed twenty-five inches, and continued snowing the greater part of the next day. Even with the coal-oil lamp burning full blast and three men in the little seven by seven tent, the thermometer registered only 32°."[23] The attempt on Natazhat had to be abandoned.

At the end of the season, the American parties returned overland to Whitehorse with the exception of one small group, which followed the river route to Dawson like the Canadians. It had been a successful season; line projection, triangulation, and topographic mapping had been completed from Boundary on the Yukon River south to Natazhat Ridge, a distance of 215 miles. The remaining 57 miles of vista cutting and 101 miles of monumenting would be completed in the 1910 season.

1910 SEASON — YUKON RIVER NORTH TO PORCUPINE RIVER (MONUMENTS 111 to 47) AND YUKON RIVER SOUTH TO NATAZHAT RIDGE COMPLETED (MONUMENTS 112 TO 187 A)[24]

Work north of the Yukon River commenced in the 1909 season, and the line had been projected some forty miles. In addition, a small reconnaissance party had rented a launch and attempted to ascend the Black and Porcupine Rivers. The former proved too shallow to depend on, but the Porcupine was considered navigable by good-size steamers during the high waters of early June. In 1910, the parties planned to start work from the mouth of the Tatonduk River, about twenty-five miles downstream from Boundary. To get the longest possible season the entire crew travelled the winter road to Carmacks, just over one hundred miles north of Whitehorse. Here they could board the steamer *Casca* which had wintered at Hootalinqua to avoid the late breakup of the ice on Lake Laberge. Riggs wrote of the overland trip:

> The first contingent of the party left Whitehorse on foot on May 10th [1910] and was followed the next day by the balance of the men. On the 14th Mr. J. D. Craig and I left Whitehorse by stage, making two posts a day, arriving at Carmacks at the same time as the last of the main party.

Five miles out of Carmacks our stage was stopped on a steep grade by evidence of an accident: the cribbing on the road had broken and one of the freight wagons carrying personal belongings and instruments had been rolled about a hundred feet down the steep incline, bringing up against a tree. Blood was scattered on the rocks and we feared a fatal accident to some of the men. Soon men were seen coming back and I learned that G., one of the cooks, had been hurt. I found him on board the *Casca*. There being no physician nearer than Dawson it devolved on me to patch him up to the best of my ability. I found that his forehead and nose had been severely cut, probably from the kick of a horse and that one rib was cracked. He was able to proceed with the party to Dawson where I turned him over to Dr. Thompson, who said that he would shortly be fit for duty.

Leaving the party on the *Casca* to wait the breaking of the ice in the Rink Rapids and at Hellsgate, we crossed the river with Mr. H. Wheeler, the Superintendent of the mail service and drove to the Pelly River.

At the Pelly we procured a canoe and by striking an occasional lead through the icejam we got into Selkirk at 10 o'clock, leaving there at eleven. Below . . . we got mixed up in an ice jam and were obliged to land until it became light enough to avoid the floating cakes of ice.

The run of the next hundred miles to Stewart River through the ice was quite exciting, but after leaving the Stewart the river was passably clear. We arrived in Dawson at 3:30 on May 20th, having been almost continually travelling by canoe for two days. We were the first ones to arrive by water during the year and bringing the first mail to come down the river.

The *Casca* with the party and the livestock came in at noon on the 23rd. Two of my men were down with measles. At first the health officer was inclined to order us to quarantine for two weeks, but as the symptoms by which the trouble could be accurately diagnosed had practically all disappeared, he finally allowed us to establish our own quarantine in the woods. We left Dawson at midnight.

Some little delay was encountered at Eagle owing to the *Casca* being a British bottom and in consequence forbidden to land men and supplies at more than one American port. By putting up a bond however this matter was left to future adjustment and we were allowed to proceed. We arrived at Sheep Creek [Tatonduk River] at 5:30.

Everything:— outfit, forage, provisions, horses were unloaded on the beach in confusion. The only attempt made that night to bring order out of the chaos was to put up a few cook tents and issue the bedding.[25]

Next day, a permanent camp was established, and the group of fifty men, together with seventy-five horses and fifty to sixty tons of camp outfit and supplies, were divided into eight parties. After a few days spent sorting equipment and shoeing horses, they started inland. With the parties on the move, there was a friendly race between the projection party's fore-heliograph section and the reconnaissance party, first one and then the other forging ahead.

A steamer carrying a small triangulation party reached Rampart House on 22 June, marking the beginning of a new area of transportation on this river. In addition to supplies for the party, it carried about fifty tons of staples and feed for use in the 1911 season. The three men on the party were forced to spend three weeks of their short season packing everything up from the beach to a storehouse after the local Indians, certain they had a corner on the market, demanded prohibitive rates. Despite the delay, the party completed sufficient observations to join their triangulation with that carried from the south.

Beginning early in the season, the parties to the south were handicapped by an epidemic of hoof-rot among their horses. A running sore would develop from a slight scratch just above the hoof and gradually spread around it, ending in the hoof dropping off. Before the packers discovered how to treat it using carbolic acid crystals, nearly a third of the horses were lost and many of the remainder weakened.[26]

On 30 August 1910, the projection party, reduced to six horses, reached the south bank of the Porcupine River. Delayed by storms and the poor condition of their horses, they had already been on short rations for two days. "That same evening we crossed to Rampart House where a most hospitable and festive reception was given us by Mr. Gilmore and Mr. Cadzow, the trader. The horses were also given a feast of hay and oats and were soon on the road to recovery. They were the first quadrupeds of this kind ever seen in that part of the country and were a never ending source of wonderment to the native, who wondered and asked: 'Where you catchum?' "[27] Fortunately, the party were able to obtain a scow from the trader and, loading the six horses, made the 225-mile trip down to Fort Yukon in a little over four days.

At the end of the season, the other parties retreated south to the mouth of the Tatonduk River. Riggs wrote:

> The trip out was a nightmare. The horses were failing fast as the sustenance had departed from the frozen grasses. Hardly a day passed that some horse did not play out and have to be shot. Toward the end of the trip the weather became very cold. Huge fires had to be built in the morning to thaw out the frozen pack rigging, packers froze their fingers while tugging on the frozen ropes. A third of the horses were in the "hospital train," the men were all carrying packs, every extra ounce had been abandoned and, had it not been for the oats caches along the way, not a horse would have survived. As it was Reaburn and I would bring up the rear and shoot the horses as they fell out of the train. The tenderfeet were disheartened and afraid.[28]

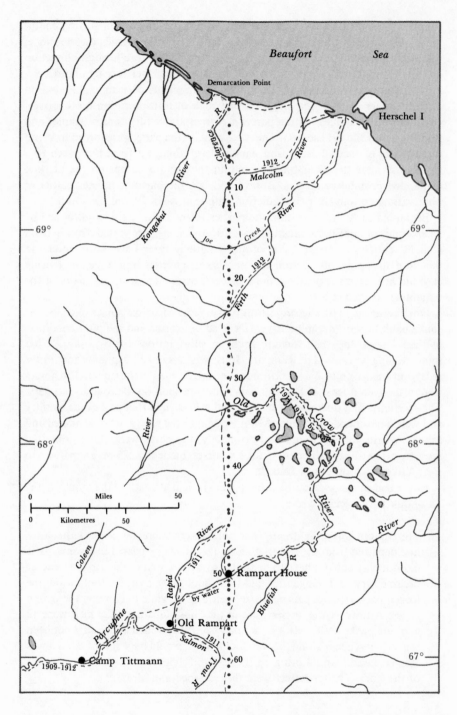

Map 10: 141st Meridian: Arctic Coast to Porcupine River (Monuments 1-63)

On 23 September 1910, the parties at the mouth of the Tatonduk were picked up by the *Susie*, which already had the men from Fort Yukon aboard. Despite difficulties, the work between the Yukon and Porcupine Rivers had been completed with the exception of the monumenting and vista cutting. In addition, D. H. Nelles had completed a line of precise levelling between Whitehorse and Monument 126, on the ridge between the Fortymile and Sixtymile Rivers. His work had taken three years, and when it was complete, it was found that the assumed elevation used since 1907 was only 38.4 feet below the true elevation as determined from sea-level observations at Skagway.

1911 SEASON — PORCUPINE RIVER NORTH TO MALCOLM RIVER (MONUMENTS 47 to 8) PLUS SOME WORK BETWEEN THE YUKON AND PORCUPINE RIVERS.[29]

This season, main operations were based at Rampart House on the Porcupine River. In addition to the boundary surveys proper, small parties took advantage of the transportation system to commence geologic mapping of the boundary strip. D. D. Cairnes of the Geological Survey of Canada was assigned the section from the Yukon River north to the Porcupine River and A. G. Maddren of the U.S. Geological Survey from the latter river north to the Arctic coast.

Over the winter, both governments had launches built at Whitehorse. The craft were sternwheelers, about forty feet long and with an eight-foot beam, the Canadian *Aurora* powered with a twenty-five horsepower gasoline engine and the United States *Midnight Sun* by a slightly heavier motor. Although able to carry little more than their own supplies and fuel, they were each capable of pushing a thirty-five-foot scow with a load of eight tons or more. In addition, two smaller launches were chartered for the season.

As in the 1910 season, the chiefs planned to send the men and horses overland from Whitehorse to Carmacks. The main supplies would be shipped via St. Michael, but until these arrived, the parties would depend on supplies freighted over the ice of Lake Laberge for shipment as soon as the river opened. Unfortunately, the ice on the lake failed, leaving freight stranded at the upper end and another lot halfway down. Riggs and Craig, the chiefs of party, made their way over the rotten ice to the foot of Lake Laberge and sorted out as much as possible of the survey outfit from the seven-hundred-odd tons piled up there. They shipped it aboard the *Lafrance* only to have her ground and later burn in the swift "Thirtymile" section of the Yukon River below the lake. Luckily, the survey freight was saved and brought to Dawson by barge.

The main party reached Dawson on 26 May and left for Fort Yukon the following day aboard the *St. Michael*. Replacement supplies were picked up at Dawson and in small lots at some of the settlements on the Alaskan side. En route, the pack-train for the vista and monumenting party was landed at the mouth of the Tatonduk River, and most of the men of that party landed at the mouth of the Kandik River to make their way upstream to the line in poling boats. The main group transferred to the steamer *Reliance* at Fort Yukon, landing at Rampart House on the evening of 1 June. The steamer *Vidette* arrived from Dawson on the sixth bringing the remainder of the crew, stock, and an additional fifty tons of freight and feed.

In 1910 the advance parties of the survey had arrived at Rampart House unannounced, at least as far as the native population was concerned. During the winter of 1910–1911, however, the news seemed to have spread that the survey was coming in full force, and there was congregated at Rampart House a motley assemblage of natives and their dogs, and the parties received a cordial if unconventional welcome.[30]

When the horses were unloaded and turned loose, there was a general scramble of the Indians for their cabins. Most of them had never seen a horse before. For two days not a squaw or child was to be seen, then gradually becoming bolder, they would venture a short distance from the cabins. By the end of the week the older children were tying tin cans to the horses' tails. At the first toot of the steamer all the dogs had taken to the hills from where they made the sleeping hours of daylight hideous with their long drawn wolfish howls.[31]

The usual two or three days of more or less orderly confusion ensued in getting the one hundred and fifty horses shod, outfits sorted and allotted, and supplies distributed to the various parties, numbering about eighty men in all, and what a wonderful time it was for the Indians! . . . They were puzzled to know the wherefore of horseshoes. "The moose and the caribou didn't need them." Having no word in their language for horse, they simply called them the "big dogs," and several of them were very desirous of becoming owners of horses, for the fact that they could carry a load of two hundred and fifty pounds appealed to them, but their enthusiasm waned when they found they would not eat fish, which of course is the staple food of the country for man and beast. The "bronco busting" by the packers and the breaking of the horses to the pack-saddles caused intense admiration and amazement and the first Indian to trust himself on a horse's back was a local hero for some days.[32]

During the following week, the parties all got away for their work north and south of the river. The American launches, working on the Old Crow River, had succeeded in landing about twenty tons of supplies at a point only a few miles from the line. The Canadian launch, troubled by falling water on the Black River, had been unable to make a planned trip to the line and brought her freight to Rampart House to be sent south by pack-train. A smaller Canadian launch, arriving with mail in early June, was used by the chiefs of party in an attempt to get up the Old Crow River to the line, but by then the spring high water was over and "there was no practical results to the trip, except a first hand knowledge of the Old Crow Flats, with special emphasis on the fact that there the flies and mosquitoes were extremely plentiful."[33]

There was still no sign of the supplies shipped via St. Michael and Craig and Riggs, growing anxious, went to Fort Yukon in a small launch, meeting the *Tanana* there on 13 June. After washing her boilers, she set out for Rampart House carrying about 80 tons of freight and towing a barge with about 225 tons. But by now there was trouble with low water, and the barge had to be dropped the second day out. The *Tanana* herself was worked upstream to a point just below where Turner had been dropped in 1889. She unloaded and returned to the barge in an attempt to relay everything upstream as far as possible. Meanwhile, the launches began relaying the remaining distance to Rampart House. The *Tanana* made good progress relaying from the barge, even making one trip to Rampart House when the river rose for a brief period, but she hit a rock and sank on her next trip upstream. Fortunately, she was only in a few feet of water, and after refloating her, the captain retreated to Circle and telegraphed for a smaller boat to complete the work. Her replacement, the *Reliance,* was sent up and, taking advantage of another period of higher water, managed to get the rest of the freight to Rampart House. Here, the impasse with the Indians over help in handling the freight continued. As a result the entire three hundred tons had to be handled by the half-dozen members of the various parties who happened to be in Rampart, every man available turning in, even to the chiefs and cooks, assisted at times by the launch crews.

In late July, just when other problems seemed to be solved, the physician attached to the American party discovered an Indian girl suffering from what he diagnosed as smallpox. Riggs, arriving at Rampart House soon after, took charge in the absence of Craig and Dan Cadzow, the trader. He dispatched the American launch downstream with instructions to find Craig and with telegrams to be sent from Circle. Then he and the doctor ordered the infected camps burned, isolated the occupants, issued new clothing and rations to them, and bullied the entire tribe into taking baths. All the Indians who could travel were sent to the hills with strict instructions to return if any eruption appeared on their skin. A strict quarantine was imposed forbidding anyone to land at Rampart House or any of the residents to go downriver.

The Yukon government acted promptly, and the *Midnight Sun* arrived nine days later carrying Craig, a mounted policeman, and a male nurse plus vaccine and disinfectants. Four new cases of smallpox were found that day and despite the vaccinations, within a few weeks there were forty-three cases with new ones a daily occurrence. Instead of trying to isolate the sick as before, whole families were quarantined on an island in the Porcupine River, and their old campsites were burned over. Later, a hospital was built on the island. Fortunately only one child died, and the scourge disappeared over the following winter.[34]

The survey parties were at or north of the Old Crow River. Other than having orders to bypass Rampart House on their trip out, they carried out the field work as usual. Mosquitoes were the immediate problem; the chief of one of the triangulation parties wrote:

> A report of the season would be sadly incomplete without some mention of the ever present mosquito. It was a common saying in camp that when he alighted it was always with his feet last. At any rate we all wore gloves and veils, even the observations had to be made in them. These were seldom removed except in the sleeping tents. At meal times smudges of damp moss and gunny sacks were built on the windward side of the table and in this way those of us with exceptionally strong lungs could dine in comparative peace. The same system of smudging was applied to give the horses relief. Even the shaggy malamute dog took the precaution to bury his nose in the moss before going to sleep.[35]

At the end of the season, the parties reassembled at Camp Tittmann, about sixty-five miles downstream from Rampart House. From there, they travelled to Fort Yukon on the *Delta*, transferred to the larger *Sarah*, and arrived in Dawson on 24 September. From Dawson, all the horses were shipped to Coffee Creek on the Yukon River to be driven overland to a winter range on the upper White River.

The main party had talked their way past a quarantine ordered at the mouth of the Porcupine River by the government of Alaska. Riggs, following about a week later after overseeing two launches taking loads of lumber to Rampart House, had a more difficult time:

> Mr. Boulter [of the Bureau of Education] had recently established a quarantine, five miles up from the mouth of the Porcupine bristling with rifles and bearded guards. We meekly obeyed their threats and called at quarantine, but as there was no one there to inspect us, and knowing that the doctor was at Fort Yukon, and as it was getting late we proceeded to town. At Fort Yukon Mr. Boulter, pompously ordered us back to quarantine for inspection. Not knowing just what authority he had, and not wishing to get the survey into any disrepute through any action of mine, we took the doctor *on board* and went out of sight of town where the doctor examined us and gave us a clean bill of health. This was the only official recognition on the part of the U.S. of any service rendered in protecting the health of the whole Yukon valley.

Even though we now had a clean bill of health, we did not go into the town, as our own regulations called for a two weeks isolation which we proposed to take out on board of the launch.

We left Fort Yukon on the 23rd, arriving Dawson on October 1st. Dr. Thompson, the Medical Health Officer, expressed himself as perfectly satisfied with our precautions and we were told that it was no longer necessary to remain in isolation.[36]

Despite the many problems, the 1911 season had been reasonably successful. North of the Porcupine River, the projection party were within twenty-five miles of the Arctic Coast and might have reached it if there had not been a totally unexpected delay of two weeks while the party searched for their lost horses. The topography and triangulation parties were close behind. South of the river, there had been delays when it became necessary to shuttle everything down the line from Rampart House and about sixty miles of monumenting and vista cutting were still incomplete.

1912 SEASON — OLD CROW RIVER TO THE ARCTIC COAST (MONUMENTS 32 TO 1),
TRIANGULATION FROM THE WHITE RIVER TO CHITINA RIVER AREAS, INSPECTION AND
MINOR WORK BETWEEN THE ARCTIC COAST AND YUKON RIVERS (MONUMENTS 1 TO 111)[37]

This season, everyone connected with the survey was anxious to see it completed through to the Arctic coast. Early in April 1912, a small United States party that had wintered at Rampart House used dog teams to move supplies to the Surprise Creek area, about twenty-five miles north along the line. The American launch, overhauled at Rampart House, was sent to the mouth of the Old Crow River as soon as the Porcupine River opened. During the several day wait for the Old Crow to open, the Canadian launch arrived from Dawson. Working together, the two craft succeeded in getting a considerable amount of supplies to the vicinity of the line.

The men, together with new horses to replace a large number that had died over the winter on the White River, made the usual overland trip from Whitehorse to Carmacks, arriving at Dawson on 22 May 1912, after a stop to pick up the surviving horses at Coffee Creek. Five days later they reached Rampart House aboard the *Tanana*: "A scene of desolation met our eyes, where the previous year the beach had been crowded with Indians eager to see so many white men and to them, that unknown animal, the horse; now there was not an Indian to be seen. Their houses had been burnt down to eliminate any danger of infection from smallpox and the natives themselves had been sent into the hills to avoid congregating together until absolutely all danger was over."[38]

Over the next ten days, the various parties left to continue their work. "There was considerable excitement when the supply train left as this was composed almost entirely of green horses. The bucking which ensued would have done credit to a Wild West Show, and two loaded horses distinguished themselves by rolling head over heels from the top of the first steep hill all the way to the flat, a distance of about 500 feet, the only damage done was that the saddles were badly broken and the contents of their packs were spilled and wrecked."[39]

Craig and Riggs, the chiefs of party, started north on their inspection trip on 14 June. Soon after they encountered one of the unsolved mysteries of the north: "One of the packers while relaying had discovered an old camp with a few pots and kettles strung around and a short distance below that an old rifle. Near the camp was a little wind break built of brush and back of this lay the bleached skeleton of a man. The shape of the head and the excellent condition of the teeth led us to believe it to have been a native, but we were in doubt afterwards as we also found traces of writing material and note books which, however, were perfectly illegible."[40]

Working this far north, there was none of the hot summer weather common in the Yukon River drainage, and on 11 July Riggs wrote in his diary: "The spring frosts stopped day before yesterday and autumn frost started today."[41] About this time, they arrived at the combined camp of the topography and reconnaissance parties on the Malcolm River, about thirty miles from the coast itself, to find the reconnaissance chief seriously ill with possible congestion of the lungs. They took over his work and the last point on the line, right at the Arctic Coast, was set on 18 July 1912. Here, Craig and Riggs posed in front of flag poles with the flags of United States and Great Britain. In addition, perhaps on a bet, the two took a dip in the Arctic Ocean amid remnants of the floes that had jammed the coast less than a week before. Party members searched the nearby shoreline, hoping to find some sign of the early explorers. There was nothing, although Demarcation Point was crowded with deserted dwellings, or barabaras, and must have had a population of several hundred Eskimos at one time. Riggs wrote:

It was with rather a lost feeling that we arrived at the shore of the Arctic Ocean and saw the practical completion of the work on which we had been engaged for so many years. Our camp on the Arctic was in a sheltered cove where plenty of drift wood was found which comes from the Mackenzie River. Strange to relate the forage for the horses was extremely good. While short and not plentiful still the horses seemed to thrive on the tundra grass and be in better condition than at any time since we started.[42]

The final report adds the following description:

The Arctic coast is paralleled by a strip of tundra which, in the vicinity of the line, is from twelve to fifteen miles wide, and travelling over this was found to be very trying to both man and beast. It sheltered myriads of mosquitoes which arose in clouds whenever the wind dropped sufficiently to allow them out, and whether or not it was that the blood of white people and of southern horses was specially palatable to them, they certainly had most ravenous appetites. "Seeing" conditions at the coast were bad, and delayed projection and triangulation greatly. The air seemed to be in a state of continual disturbance, caused possibly by the contrast between the air-conditions over the tundra, heated almost continuously by the sun, and the adjoining expanse of ice and ice-cold water of the ocean. Haze was very persistent, and mirages were frequent, beautiful and at times awe-inspiring. On one occasion, when moving camp along the coast, one of the pack-trains made a detour of several miles to avoid an imaginary lake. Needless to say, the packer in charge was not allowed to forget this for some time. The sun at midnight when it approached the northern horizon assumed most fantastic shapes, but its rays, even at noon-day, seemed to be powerless to counteract the piercing effects of the prevailing east and northeast winds.[43]

Monument No. 1, one of the large bronze obelisks, was set in the tundra about two hundred feet south of the Arctic shore. The parties completed their work as quickly as possible and began the three-week trip to Rampart House, the last one leaving the coast on 6 August. En route, the inspection party checked the work and numbered the monuments in sequence.

About 50 miles east of the line, D'Arcy Arden and Harper Reed were still tending a light on Herschel Island where they had been sent early in the summer in an attempt to join the island to the triangulation. On 20 June the launch *Aurora* dropped them and their six dogs off on the north bank of the Old Crow River, about 25 miles from the boundary. From there they had walked across the divide to the Firth River, followed it to its mouth, and crossed the ice to Herschel Island on 1 July, the last day the ice held. They erected a twenty-six-foot pole and target on the high point of the island and remained at the station night and day showing their light at every possible opportunity when it might be seen. They saw nothing from the mainland, and finally on 6 August, they received a note from Mr. Gilmore of the American triangulation party that all the parties would be leaving the Arctic coast for Rampart House and there would be no further possibility of contact by heliograph. They had to wait until the thirteenth before it was possible to sail a whaleboat to the mainland, and then they travelled overland the entire way, arriving at Rampart House on the afternoon of 31 August after covering about 160 miles in thirteen and a half days of actual travel.

Their work in the northern section completed, the parties left Rampart House for the last time at the end of August 1912 aboard the steamer *Delta*. South of Porcupine River, a Canadian team had completed the monumenting and vista cutting in early July and then started south from Rampart House for the Yukon River, inspecting the work and numbering the monuments as they went. Reaching the Yukon River about 10 September, they rafted to Eagle where they

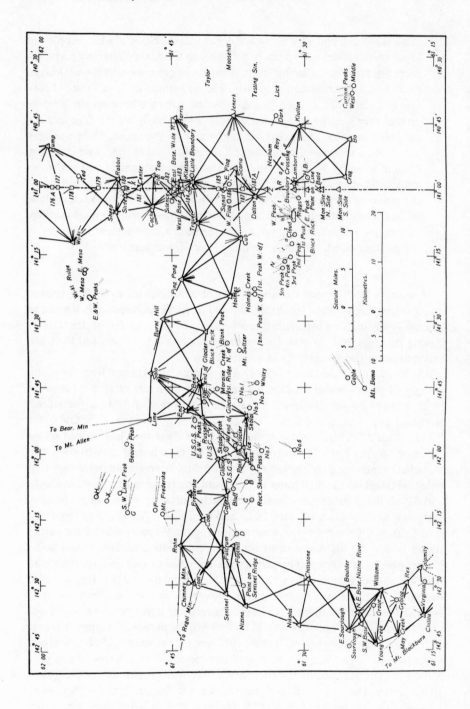

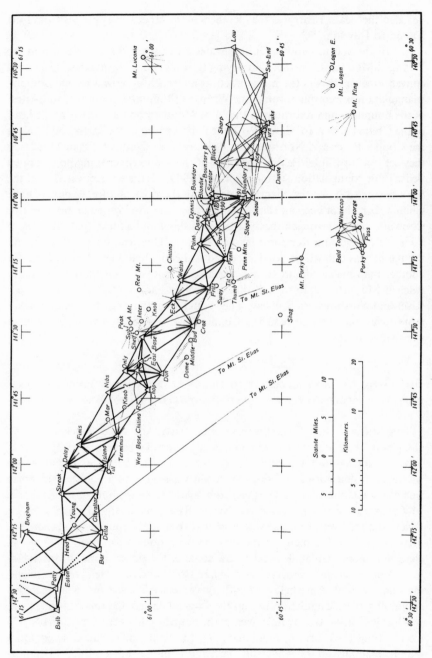

Triangulation Net used to carry the 141st Meridian Survey through the Wrangell Mountains

boarded the steamer carrying the members of the other survey parties from Fort Yukon to Dawson.

Far to the south, another United States party spent the 1912 season in the Wrangell Mountains. Rather than trying to work south of Natazhat ridge using conventional methods, the most practical approach appeared to be a looping triangulation net cutting through the Wrangell Mountains about fifty miles west of the boundary and returning to the 141st Meridian on the glaciers at the head of the Chitina River. In March 1912, the party arrived in McCarthy, Alaska, on the Copper River and Northwestern Railway from Cordova. From McCarthy they set out for Skolai Pass at the head of the White River using horse-drawn sleds. Four triangulation stations from the 1909 work were recovered, and the net was carried down the Nizina River to join the work of another party on the Chitina. It had not been an easy season. One group lived for some time on two sheep and some ptarmigan they managed to shoot and a lucky find of a sack of flour left cached in a tree some six years before. One man fell over a cliff, and though he was unhurt, he decided he had had enough and left the survey as did another man pulled unhurt from a crevasse. If that were not enough, the party reached McCarthy only to find that snowslides had knocked out the Copper River and Northwestern Railway. They could do nothing else but walk for sixty more miles and then descend the Copper River for eighty-five miles in small overloaded boats.

1913 SEASON — MOUNT NATAZHAT TO MOUNT ST. ELIAS (MONUMENTS 189 TO 191)
INSPECTION BETWEEN YUKON RIVER AND MOUNT NATAZHAT (MONUMENTS 111 TO 187A)[44]

This season, aside from the inspection party, the work concentrated on completing the line in the gap of about eighty-five miles between the ridge west of Mount Natazhat and Mount St. Elias. In March 1913, a number of parties left McCarthy using horses and sleds to freight their outfit to a point on the north side of the Chitina Glacier, some eighteen miles west of the boundary line. From McCarthy, their route crossed the Nizina River, cut overland to the Chitina River, and followed the braided flats of that river to the foot of the glacier. The final camp, base for many of the season's operations, was under 3,000 feet in elevation, more than 10,000 feet below some of the points along the boundary line. Deep snow and temperatures down to -40° Fahrenheit delayed the freighting, and it was late April before everything was ready. The season's work included continuing the triangulation net up the Logan Glacier (the final station, Low, was located almost twenty miles east of the boundary line at an elevation of 8,675 feet); setting three bronze monuments on the flanks of Logan Glacier; topographic mapping up the Anderson Glacier; and photo-topographic work covering the area between Logan Glacier and Mount St. Elias. In addition, a group attempted to climb Mount St. Elias. The peak, sighted and named by Vitus Bering in July 1741, had been climbed only once, by the Duc d'Abruzzi and his party in the summer of 1897.

The new attempt was made from the north by five Americans and two Canadians led by A.C. Baldwin. On 13 June 1913, they set out on Baldwin Glacier, a tributary of Logan Glacier, dragging their outfit on two seven-foot Yukon sleds. They were using special lightweight equipment and carried a month's provisions, with the main items being rice, sugar, bacon, pilot bread, dehydrated cranberries, and tea. About six miles up the glacier the party was blocked by soft snow, four to six feet deep. Three of the party, wearing snowshoes and roped together for safety, went ahead and tramped out the trail for the next six or seven miles, and the following morning they found that the sleds could be hauled over the now-frozen trail without using the awkward snowshoes. It took only two days to reach the divide. Baldwin wrote of the trip beyond:

Gaining the summit of a 10,000-foot peak about seven in the evening, we caught our first glimpse of our goal. We were overlooking a wide valley sweeping in graceful curves southwestward towards the Pacific. From side to side it was probably twenty miles in width. A main stream of ice flowed through it, and this we took to be Columbus Glacier. Many smaller streams flowed into the main one, and all were covered with a mantle of snow whose whiteness was emphasized by the numerous black peaks that seemed just able to hold their heads above the flood of snow.

Near the head of the valley was the great towering mass of Mount St. Elias, rising nearly eleven thousand feet above the valley floor. In the evening light it recalled a huge white ghost, though in shape it resembled a great sea lion, lying head erect, and facing the east . . . .

The days spent crossing the snowfields were much the same as far as the work was concerned. Sledding was begun shortly after midnight and was continued until the snow became too soft to travel on. The elevation ranged from seven to eight thousand feet and there were no crevasses in the glaciers. No animal life existed except a few flies and moths, and a black insect about one-sixteenth of an inch in length that at times animated the snow. On the exposed rocks there was sometimes found a species of moss with a purple blossom . . . .

The temperature conditions were peculiar. At midnight a wind was generally blowing, and it was cold enough to freeze water in pails and form a strong crust on the snow. At two or three o'clock the eastern sky would begin to glow, and as the sun crept higher and finally rose above the mountains it warmed the chill glacier air. By eight or nine o'clock the snow would be soft, and sledding difficult. The direct rays of the sun and the light reflected from the snow burned our faces and raised new blisters each day.

In the afternoon, the tents would sometimes be uncomfortably warm, but as soon as the sun disappeared, the temperature dropped rapidly, and in a short time ice would be formed.

By June 22 we had traveled across fifty miles of this kind of country beyond timberline, and had reached the base of Mount St. Elias. During all this time the sky had been clear, but on the 23rd a thick fog settled down over the peaks and the weather became unsettled.

Our camp was now at an elevation of 7,500 feet, and to the east the western shoulder of St. Elias rose 9,000 feet in sheer height, too steep for the snow to cling to. At intervals, from the dizzy heights an avalanche of snow would be seen creeping down the wrinkled sides. Seconds afterwards a dull roar would be heard, and, as the moving mass gained in proportions and speed, it swept everything before it, and reaching a precipice, would shoot out in a stream like foaming water and disappear in the depths below. Long afterwards, clouds of snow-dust hung in the air and the dull rumbling continued.

It was useless to attempt to climb this west face, and therefore, on the 23rd, a reconnaissance was made up a steep glacier that led to a saddle with an elevation of 12,000 feet. The entire day was spent crossing crevasses and cutting steps and locating a feasible pack-route. Late in the afternoon we reached the saddle, and through the fog could dimly see a slope that lead to the high shoulder, and appeared to be climbable.

The following day camp was moved by sleds to the 9,500-foot level and then back-packing was begun. Camp was raised 2,000 feet at a move, packs of about forty pounds each being taken twice a day over this stretch. On the 28th of June, at five o'clock in the morning, we succeeded in getting the camp outfit to an elevation of 13,500 feet.

Looking to the south from this camp we could see below us the great Malaspina Glacier, and beyond it the Pacific Ocean. The Yahtse River was plainly visible, and in the sunlight, with every streamlet flashing, it suggested an arm of the sea. Icy Bay was also a noticeable feature, and stretching away to the west was the Coast Range at about our own level. Turning to the north, we could trace our route over the snowfields as far as the Logan divide. Beyond there appeared on the horizon Mount Wrangell and Mount Blackburn and many other snow-covered peaks rivalling them in height, while one sharp peak in particular, seemingly more distant than the others, was very conspicuous. In every direction we could see a hundred miles or more, except to the northeast, the west shoulder of St. Elias cutting out the view there. It rose abruptly from camp 3,000 feet, while farther to the right, three miles distant and 4,500 feet above camp, stood our goal, the terminal cone of the mountain.

Rising at midnight on June 29th to get an early start for the final dash, we found that a dense fog had filled the valleys, and storm flurries were in evidence about the summits. Before an hour had passed snow began to fall, and it was midnight of the following day before the sky cleared, and even at that early hour the sun was lighting the summit of St. Elias. The instruments, food, and extra clothing were made up into packs, giving each man about twenty pounds, and about one o'clock A.M. the ascent began.

Although cameras were taken along, the difficulties of the first part of the climb proved so engrossing that picture making was forgotten entirely. We scaled a succession of cliffs, which one of the men declared were so steep that he was leaning backwards most of the time. Hands were used quite as much as feet, and to secure a firm grip on the rocks, mittens were often removed, and although we were not aware of it at the time, several finger tips were frost-bitten. When outcrops of rock were not being traversed, the route lay over ice-slopes where the cutting of steps was necessary.

After nine hours of difficult climbing we were within a few hundred feet of the top of the west shoulder, and the rest of the climb to the summit appeared to be over a gradual slope presenting no obstacles. Four of the party only were feeling slightly the effects of the altitude, and all were confident of making the remainder of the distance, when a storm, such as is known only at high altitudes, overtook us. At first we were loath to admit that it was anything but a slight flurry, and continued the ascent. It soon became evident, however, that it was to be of more than temporary duration and that even if the summit were reached instrument work would be impossible, and so, at an elevation of a little over sixteen thousand feet, we reluctantly turned back.

The descent was accomplished not without considerable danger, and great care was necessary to keep our footing, and in one place one of the men, who had been weakened by mountain sickness, slipped on an ice-slope and was well started on a swift glissade, when one of his companions below stopped him. Camp was finally reached at five in the afternoon.

Rations were now very low and, in order to make it possible to attempt another ascent, three of the men, who had been most affected by the rarity of the atmosphere, were sent to the base camp. Three others remained with me to await fair weather, but the storm continued unabated. We rolled ourselves in our robes for warmth, and only ventured out about once in every twelve hours to eat a little rice and bacon. At midnight on the 3rd of July the bacon was gone, and only a handful of the rice remained; eighteen inches of snow had fallen, and it was still coming down. The last hope of scaling Mount St. Elias had vanished, but we still hoped to be able to secure a round of photos at camp level. About three A.M. the clouds suddenly raised, and a camera station near camp was occupied. Then the packs were made up and we hastily descended to lower altitudes.

At one place where in going up we had jumped a crevasse possibly four feet wide, when coming down we found its width doubled. No bottom could be seen, and there was no alternative but to jump it again. The landing on the opposite side was a 3-foot ledge which sloped into a second crevasse. The man in the lead tied one end of the climbing rope around his waist, and taking a 50-foot run, jumped the yawning opening, and landed with great precision on the narrow ledge. The packs were passed over on the rope and the others crossed safely.

Reaching the lower camp that evening, an inventory of provisions showed that only four days' rations remained, so the next morning, the Fourth of July, we headed back towards timber and the main cache, occupying two camera stations that day. The following day a thick fog was hanging over the snow fields, but the shortness of rations made it necessary to keep moving, and during this day and the two following days we sledded through the fog, unable to see more than a few feet in any direction, but fortunately able to keep our course by following the tracks we had made coming in nearly a month before.

On the fourth day we reached the Logan Glacier, and made a fire of wood for the first time in thirty days, and though our camp was pitched in only a small patch of willow, we all agreed that this looked larger than any forest any of us had ever seen.

The following day, after crossing the glacier, we found the balance of the party, who were very anxious about us and prepared to start out on a relief expedition.[45]

By luck, Elbow, Baldwin's camera station on the spur of Mount St. Elias, proved to be only 128.2 metres west of the 141st Meridian. Subsequently, the commissioners decided that the boundary should be placed on the Meridian at the latitude of the station. Another piece of good fortune took the form of a series of photographs taken by the official photographer of the Abruzzi expedition in 1897. The focal length of his lens was determined graphically and the topographic information obtained was used to supplement Baldwin's limited coverage.

Farther north, a Canadian party headed by F. Lambart worked in the Mount Natazhat area. Travelling to the area by the winter trail from Whitehorse, they set up camp at the foot of Klutlan Glacier. The boundary was projected south across the Klutlan Glacier and, on 18 June 1913, when conditions looked favourable, they made an attempt to climb Mount Natazhat. Hopes that photography from its 13,435 foot summit would provide a tie with Mount St. Elias and the Southeast Alaska Datum ended as the clouds gathered. "All the anticipated pleasure of reaching the summit had vanished, and our only thought was to finish and get down as quickly as possible. This we certainly did in short order, remaining at the summit only ten minutes, during which time we made six exposures with a hand camera and set a pole with a large flag. During the return journey, which took five hours, we were enveloped much of the time in clouds, and it was intensely cold, with a heavy wind from the northeast."[46]

Despite this disappointment, the party succeeded in extending the triangulation south of Klutlan Glacier and completed enough photo-topography to join up with topography done by a United States party working up Anderson Glacier. At the end of the season the party took to small boats and floated down the White and Yukon Rivers to Dawson.

During the summer of 1913, Craig and Riggs carried out the final inspection of the line from Boundary south to the spur of Natazhat Range. Supplies had been cached in advance at the Ladue River and Canyon City in hopes that the outfit could move at a more leisurely pace, free of the necessity of relaying supplies. It was not to be. Initially, there were problems with a thick pall of smoke from forest fires hanging over the country which cut visibility between stations, and soon after the party was caught up in a minor stampede. Riggs wrote:

It was while we were in camp on the main Ladue, that we got our first word of the new Chisana gold strike. James and Nelson, two sourdough prospectors, had taken out 200 ounces of dust in a few hours, on Chathenda Creek, which is a tributary of the Chisana or Shushanna River. Dawson had gone wild over the news and every person who could beg, borrow or steal an outfit was headed for the new diggings. In Dawson they had resurrected an old sketch map of mine, from which they had made blue prints and were selling them for a dollar each. The report had been circulated, that by following the "Government trail" shown on the map, that the diggings could be reached in five days from Glacier. The shortest time from Glacier is not less than 16 days and the government trail even by courtesy cannot be called a trail. In consequence, the stampeders who had outfitted for a five days trip were considerably damaged by the time they struck our camp. Every stampeder seemed to think that a government outfit was being run for their especial benefit, and hardly a day passed without our having from one to twenty men in camp demanding all manner of assistance. We would try to conceal the camp by getting well off into the woods, but to no avail. As soon as the cook tent was pitched, we would be besieged by a bunch of hungry miners. As soon as the fry pan was on the stove, we would not have been surprised to see stampeders coming down a tree, where they had been lying in wait.

Many would lose their outfits, then we would have to put them on their course and let them have enough provisions to last them until they could reach a source of supply. There were men without enough clothing to cover them decently, without shoes or bedding, but all were hurrying toward the new Eldorado, anxious to be among the first to stake.[47]

The new diggings, less than thirty miles due west of the boundary, could be reached by trails along the White River or by another trail following Beaver

Creek that left the boundary line about fifteen miles farther north. Gold fever struck the men of the survey party too, but all were loyal enough to wait until the end of the season to set out.

As the inspection party moved south, the monuments were numbered; eight new ones were placed, and the surveying was strengthened where required. The large obelisk-type monument on the north bank of the White River, which had tilted as the ground thawed beneath it, was straightened and improved by a heavy crib foundation. The final monument, No. 187A, about ten miles south of the White River was set on 21 August. Their work completed, the party set out for McCarthy on the Copper River and Northwestern Railway. Their route followed the White River to its source at Russell Glacier in the core of the Wrangell Mountains, crossed Skolai Pass along the east side of the glacier, then Chitistone Pass, following "The Goat Trail" to the upper Chitistone River and down that river to the Nizina River and McCarthy.

> The trail over Skolai Pass is on the route traversed by prospectors on their way from McCarthy . . . to the Chisana country. On a much smaller scale, the stampede was the same old story of the great Klondike gold rush of '97 and '98. People absolutely unfit to be let loose in the mountains thronged the trail; ill-equipped and ignorant of camping, treating their horses in the worst way imaginable, filthy and thieving. Four men had been drowned in the Nizina and Chitistone Rivers, and one heard on all sides the most lurid tales of the awful trail.
>
> There is no doubt that the trail looks bad, and a slip in places would result fatally, but when we were once going over it, we found that it was no worse than a score of others along the boundary.
>
> Probably the most satisfied person on the trail was the head packer. For the entire trip from Skolai Pass to McCarthy, he had donned his best — wide Mexican sombrero with silver band, bear skin chaps with huge silver clasps, silver mounted saddle and bridle, and silver spurs on high heeled boots. Buffalo Bill had nothing on him at all. At the head of his pack-train of well kept, well equipped and well trained horses, he was the envy and admiration of all observers.[48]

The trail had proved easier than expected, but Riggs had a new respect for the opaque, silt-laden waters of the rivers flowing from the glaciers:

> When we crossed the White River . . . to repair the monument, the ford had been about two feet deep, that night on recrossing, the water was nearly to the backs of the horses and running like a mill race. On the far bank, Mr. Craig's horse stepped in quicksand, which caused Mr. Craig to do a vaude-ville stunt of landing on his head in the mud. The incident was a camp joke

for several days, but that was before we heard from stampeders what terrible and dangerous rivers the White and Nizina are: later when I was finding a crossing ahead of the pack-train through the quick sands of the Nizina and my horse floundered into soft sands and a deep hole, everybody was very much concerned, and instead of giving me the laugh, they built a huge fire to dry me out, and I was overwhelmed with offers of dry clothing and with other kind attentions. Strange to relate, the fire was built not a hundred yards from a grave bearing the inscription: "James Sullivan, drowned August 27th, Buried by friends." and this was August 29th.[49]

When they reached McCarthy, the party was paid off, and most of the men headed back for the Chisana, victims of gold fever, while those who remained travelled by rail to Cordova and thence to Seattle. It was over, and later Riggs, one of the very few to have been on the project all seven years, mused in his report: "the years spent in the survey of the 141st Meridian even with all their hardships and almost unsurmountable difficulties have resulted in being the happiest years of my life . . . . I can do no more than repeat part of my telegram from McCarthy on August 31st: 'Regret my work completed.'"[50]

THE COMMISSIONERS REPORT OF 15 DECEMBER 1918

The commissioners submitted their final report and duplicate prints of the accompanying maps to their respective governments on 15 December 1918. There were thirty-eight maps at a scale of 1:62,500, or about one mile to the inch, using a hundred-foot contour interval and showing a strip of topography about five miles in width. They began with No. 1 at the Arctic Coast continuing south to No. 38 at Mount St. Elias. The four sets of maps submitted were printed on special paper and each was signed by the commissioners. Numbers 1 to 32 had been signed by King and Tittmann, the original commissioners, and the re-mainder by their successors, J.J. McArthur for Canada and E.C. Barnard for the United States. The latter expressed his feelings in the final paragraph of his letter of transmittal:

It is most gratifying to record that the location of the International Boundary along the 141st Meridian, and the preparation of the maps and report have been accomplished in a spirit of hearty co-operation, and to state that the cordial relations that so long existed between the former Commissioners have been continued by their successors.[50]

It had been a remarkable achievement by an equally remarkable group of men.

Afterword

On land, the Alaska boundary was quickly accepted once it was marked on the ground. Despite some loose talk, it has never been seriously challenged, even at the height of the Klondike Rush. In the years since then some of the freedom of the north has been lost as each country tightened control of people and freight moving across its boundaries. In World War II some of this control was set aside as United States soldiers and equipment were rushed to northern British Columbia and the Yukon to work on the Alaska Highway. In a way it resembled the Klondike Rush, complete to entrepreneurs conniving to smuggle liquor to thirsty highway builders.

The water boundary along Line A-B in Dixon Entrance is a different matter. The United States is still unwilling to admit they have no rights south of it, and, occasionally, the United States Coastguard has seized Canadian vessels that have ventured within three miles of the islands to the north of the line.[1] Canada, in turn, has protested the incidents, but the main issue remains unresolved. At Cape Muzon two concrete monuments reference Point A; placed there in 1913 by a Canadian party with a United States representative.[2] Some official United States maps simply do not show the offending section of the boundary while others do but with the notation *(Approximate Boundary)*, whatever that may imply. Lord Alverstone, who endured so much trying for a complete settlement, would not be amused.

Since 1925, the Alaska Boundary has been maintained under a treaty between United States and Canada.[3] From time to time, new monuments have been set, others repaired or replaced, and sections of the vista re-opened to the full twenty-foot width. In recent years, helicopters, radio communication, power tools and newly developed surveying instruments have all made fieldwork easier, but even yet, many of the old skills are still required. One new approach that failed was an attempt to clear the vista using defoliants sprayed from a helicopter.

Second growth had obscured the boundary line and the pilot was unable to follow it within acceptable limits.

In 1943, the U.S. Coast and Geodetic Survey completed first-order triangulation from Skagway over the White Pass and along the Alaska Highway to the boundary area. At last, there was a direct tie between work on the 141st Meridian, done on the Yukon Datum with its single astronomic determination, and the work on the Panhandle, done on the Southeast Alaska Datum. When both were converted to the 1927 North American Datum, the present standard, the discrepancy on Mount St. Elias (B.P. 186) proved to be 22.6 metres (74.1 feet) in latitude and 62.7 metres (205.7 feet) in longitude![4] A probable cause is that the party working from the north in 1913 and the party working from the southeast in 1906, sighting from comparatively low elevations, did not observe the same point on the snow-covered dome of Mount St. Elias.

In 1977, there were new differences between United States and Canada as both countries sought to extend their boundaries seaward to a new two-hundred-mile limit. In August 1977 the two countries appointed special negotiators with a mandate to reach a comprehensive settlement on (1) maritime boundaries delimitation (2) complementary fishery and hydrocarbon resource arrangements as appropriate, and (3) such other related matters as the two governments may decide.[5] Subsequently, differences arose, and in November 1978, the negotiators were directed to give priority to Atlantic fisheries and boundary issues.[6] To date, no agreement has been reached on Alaskan boundaries or even on the form that future negotiations might take. There is no help from the past; neither the 1825 Treaty nor the 1903 Award offer any guidance as to where the new boundaries should run.

Appendix

Treaty Between Great Britain and Russia, Signed at St. Petersburgh, February 28/16, 1825.

[Translation.]

AU NOM DE LA TRÈS SAINTE ET INDIVISIBLE TRINITÉ.

Sa Majesté le Roi du Royaume Uni de la Grande Bretagne et de l'Irlande, et Sa Majesté l'Empereur de toutes les Russies, désirant resserrer les liens de bonne intelligence et d'amitié qui les unissent, au moyen d'un accord qui régleroit, d'après le principe des convenances réciproques, divers points relatifs au commerce, à la navigation, et aux pêcheries de leurs sujets sur l'Océan Pacifique, ainsi que les limites de leurs possessions respectives sur la côte nord-ouest de l'Amérique, ont nommé des Plénipotentiaires pour conclure une Convention à cet effet, savoir:—Sa Majesté le Roi du Royaume Uni de la Grande Bretagne et de l'Irlande, le Très Honorable Stratford Canning, Conseiller de Sa dite Majesté en Son Conseil Privé, etc.

IN THE NAME OF THE MOST HOLY AND UNDIVIDED TRINITY.

His Majesty the King of the United Kingdom of Great Britain and Ireland, and His Majesty the Emperor of all the Russias, being desirous of drawing still closer the ties of good understanding and friendship which unite them, by means of an agreement which may settle, upon the basis of reciprocal convenience, different points connected with the commerce, navigation, and fisheries of their subjects on the Pacific Ocean as well as the limits of their respective possessions on the northwest coast of America, have named Plenipotentiaries to conclude a Convention for this purpose, that is to say:—His Majesty the King of the United Kingdom of Great Britain and Ireland, the Right Honourable Stratford Canning, a member of His said

Et Sa Majesté l'Empereur de toutes les Russies, le Sieur Charles Robert Comte de Nesselrode, Son Conseiller Privé Actuel, Membre du Conseil de l'Empire, Secrétaire d'Etat dirigeant le Ministère des Affaires Etrangères, etc.; et le Sieur Pierre de Poletica, Son Conseiller d'Etat Actuel, etc. Lesquels Plénipotentiaires, après s'être communiqué leurs pleins-pouvoirs respectifs, trouvés en bonne et due forme, ont arrêté et signé les Articles suivant:

Art. I. Il est convenu que, dans aucune partie du grand Océan, appelé communément Océan Pacifique, les sujets respectifs des Hautes Puissances Contractantes ne seront ni troublés, ni gênés, soit dans la navigation, soit dans l'exploitation de la pêche, soit dans la faculté d'aborder aux côtes, sur des points qui ne seroient pas déjà occupés, afin d'y faire le commerce avec les indigènes, sauf toutefois les restrictions et conditions déterminés par les Articles qui suivent.

II. Dans la vue d'empêcher que les droits de navigation et de pêche exercés sur le grand océan par les sujets des Hautes Parties Contractantes ne deviennent le prétexte d'un commerce illicite, il est convenu que les sujets de Sa Majesté Britannique n'aborderont à aucun point où il se trouve un établissement Russe, sans la permission du Gouverneur ou Commandant; et que, réciproquement, les sujets Russes ne pourront aborder, sans permission, à aucun établissement Britannique, sur la côte nord-ouest.

Majesty's Most Honourable Privy Council, etc., and His Majesty the Emperor of all the Russias, the Sieur Charles Robert Count de Nesselrode, His Imperial Majesty's Privy Councillor, a member of the Council of the Empire, Secretary of State for the Department of Foreign Affairs, etc., and the Sieur Pierre de Poletica, His Imperial Majesty's Councillor of State, etc. Who, after having communicated to each other their respective full powers, found in good and due form, have agreed upon and signed the following Articles:

Art. I. It is agreed that the respective subjects of the High Contracting Parties shall not be troubled or molested, in any part of the Ocean, commonly called the Pacific Ocean, either in navigating the same, in fishing therein, or in landing at such parts of the coast as shall not have been already occupied, in order to trade with the natives, under the restrictions and conditions specified in the following Articles.

II. In order to prevent the right of navigating and fishing, exercised upon the ocean by the subjects of the High Contracting Parties, from becoming the pretext for an illicit commerce, it is agreed that the subjects of His Britannic Majesty shall not land at any place where there may be a Russian establishment, without the permission of the Governor or Commandant; and, on the other hand, that Russian subjects shall nót land, without permission, at any British establishment, on the north-west coast.

III. La ligne de démarcation entre les possessions des Hautes Parties Contractantes sur la côte du continent et les îles de l'Amérique nord-ouest, sera tracée ainsi qu'il suit:

A partir du point le plus méridional de l'île dite Prince of Wales, lequel point se trouve sous la parallèle du 54e degré 40 minutes de latitude nord, et entre le 131e et le 133e degré de longitude ouest (méridien de Greenwich), la dite ligne remontera au nord le long de la passe dite Portland Channel, jusqu'au point de la terre ferme où elle atteint le 56e degré de latitude nord: de ce dernier point la ligne de démarcation suivra la crête des montagnes situées parallèlement à la côte, jusqu'au point d'intersection du 141e degré de longitude ouest (même méridien); et finalement, du dit point d'intersection, la même ligne méridienne du 141e degré formera, dans son prolongement jusqu'à la Mer Glaciale, le limite entre les possessions Russes et Britanniques sur le continent de l'Amérique nord-ouest.

IV. Il est entendu, par rapport à la ligne de démarcation déterminée dans l'Article précédent:

1. Que l'île dite Prince of Wales appartiendra toute entière à la Russie.

2. Que partout où la crête des montagnes qui s'étendent dans une direction parallèle à la côte depuis le 56e degré de latitude nord au point d'intersection du 141e degré de longitude ouest, se trouveroit à la distance de plus de 10 lieues marines de l'océan, la limite entre les possessions Britan-

III. The line of demarcation between the possessions of the High Contracting Parties, upon the coast of the continent, and the islands of America to the north-west, shall be drawn in the manner following:

Commencing from the southernmost point of the island called Prince of Wales Island, which point lies in the parallel of 54 degrees 40 minutes, north latitude, and between the 131st and 133rd degree of west longitude (meridian of Greenwich), the said line shall ascend to the north along the channel called Portland Channel, as far as the point of the continent where it strikes the 56th degree of north latitude; from this last mentioned point, the line of demarcation shall follow the summit of the mountains situated parallel to the coast as far as the point of intersection of the 141st degree of west longitude (of the same meridian); and, finally, from the said point of intersection, the said meridian line of the 141st degree, in its prolongation as far as the Frozen Ocean, shall form the limit between the Russian and British possessions on the continent of America to the north-west.

IV. With reference to the line of demarcation laid down in the preceding Article it is understood:

1st. That the island called Prince of Wales Island shall belong wholly to Russia.

2nd. That whenever the summit of the mountains which extend in a direction parallel to the coast, from the 56th degree of north latitude to the point of intersection of the 141st degree of west longitude, shall prove to be at the distance of more than 10

niques et la lisière de côte mentionnée ci-dessus comme devant appartenir à la Russie, sera formée par une ligne parallèle aux sinuosités de la côte, et qui ne pourra jamais en être éloignée que de 10 lieues marines.

V. Il est convenu en outre, que nul établissement ne sera formé par l'une des deux Parties dans les limites que les deux Articles précédents assignent aux possessions de l'autre. En conséquence, les sujets Britanniques ne formeront aucun établissement, soit sur la côte, soit sur la lisière de terre ferme comprise dans les limites des possessions Russes, telles qu'elles sont désignées dans les 2 Articles précédents; et, de même, nul établissement ne sera formé par des sujets Russes au delà des dites limites.

VI. Il est entendu que les sujets de Sa Majesté Britannique, de quelque côté qu'ils arrivent, soit de l'océan, soit de l'intérieur du continent, jouiront à perpétuité du droit de naviguer librement, et sans entrave quelconque, sur tous les fleuves et rivières qui, dans leurs cours vers la mer Pacifique, traverseront la ligne de démarcation sur la lisière de la côte indiquée dans l'Article III de la présente Convention.

VII. Il est aussi entendu que, pendant l'espace de 10 ans, à dater de la signature de cette Convention, les vaisseaux des deux Puissances, ou ceux appartenant à leurs sujets respectifs, pourront réciproquement fréquenter, sans entrave quelconque, toutes les mers intérieures, les golfes, havres, et criques sur la côte mentionnée dans l'Article III, afin d'y faire

marine leagues from the ocean, the limit between the British possessions and the line of coast which is to belong to Russia, as above mentioned, shall be formed by a line parallel to the windings of the coast, and which shall never exceed the distance of 10 marine leagues therefrom.

V. It is moreover agreed, that no establishment shall be formed by either of the two parties within the limits assigned by the two preceding Articles to the possessions of the other; consequently, British subjects shall not form any establishment either upon the coast, or upon the border of the continent comprised within the limits of the Russian possessions, as designated in the two preceding Articles; and, in like manner, no establishment shall be formed by Russian subjects beyond the said limits.

VI. It is understood that the subjects of His Britannic Majesty, from whatever quarter they may arrive, whether from the ocean, or from the interior of the continent, shall forever enjoy the right of navigating freely, and without any hindrance whatever, all the rivers and streams which, in their course towards the Pacific Ocean, may cross the line of demarcation upon the line of coast described in Article III of the present Convention.

VII. It is also understood, that, for the space of ten years from the signature of the present Convention, the vessels of the two Powers, or those belonging to their respective subjects, shall mutually be at liberty to frequent, without any hindrance whatever, all the inland seas, the gulfs, havens, and creeks on the coast mentioned in

la pêche et le commerce avec les indigènes.

VIII. Le Port de Sitka, ou Novo Archangelsk, sera ouvert au commerce et aux vaisseaux des sujets Britanniques durant l'espace de 10 ans, à dater de l'échange des ratifications de cette Convention. Au cas qu'une prolongation de ce terme de 10 ans soit accordée à quelque autre Puissance, la même prolongation sera également accordée à la Grande Bretagne.

IX. La susdite liberté de commerce ne s'appliquera point au trafic des liqueurs spiritueuses, des armes à feu, des armes blanches, de la poudre à canon, ou d'autres munitions de guerre; Les Hautes Parties Contractantes s'engageant réciproquement à ne laisser ni vendre, ni livrer, de quelque manière que ce puisse être, aux indigènes du pays les articles ci-dessus mentionnés.

X. Tout vaisseau Britannique ou Russe naviguant sur l'Océan Pacifique, qui sera forcé par des tempêtes, ou par quelque accident, de se réfugier dans les ports des parties respectives, aura la liberté de s'y radouber, de s'y pourvoir de tous les objets qui lui seront nécessaires, et de se remettre en mer, sans payer d'autres droits que ceux de port et de fanaux, lesquels seront, pour lui, les mêmes que pour les bâtiments nationaux. Si, cependant, le patron d'un tel navire se trouvoit dans la nécessité de se défaire d'une partie de ses marchandises pour subvenir à ses dépenses, il sera tenu de se conformer aux ordonnances et aux tarifs de l'endroit où il aura abordé.

XI. Dans tous les cas de plaintes relatives à l'infraction des Articles de

Article III for the purposes of fishing and of trading with the natives.

VIII. The port of Sitka, or Novo Archangelsk, shall be open to the commerce and vessels of British subjects for the space of ten years from the date of the exchange of the ratifications of the present Convention. In the event of an extension of this term of ten years being granted to any other Power, the like extension shall be granted also to Great Britain.

IX. The above-mentioned liberty of commerce shall not apply to the trade in spirituous liquors, in fire-arms, or other arms, gunpowder, or other warlike stores; the High Contracting Parties reciprocally engaging not to permit the above-mentioned articles to be sold or delivered, in any manner whatever, to the natives of the country.

X. Every British or Russian vessel navigating the Pacific Ocean, which may be compelled by storms or by accident, to take shelter in the ports of the respective Parties, shall be at liberty to refit therein, to provide itself with all necessary stores, and to put to sea again, without paying any other than port and light-house dues, which shall be the same as those paid by national vessels. In case, however, the master of such vessel should be under the necessity of disposing of a part of his merchandise in order to defray his expenses, he shall conform himself to the regulations and tariffs of the place where he may have landed.

XI. In every case of complaint on account of an infraction of the Articles

la présente Convention, les autorités civiles et militaires des deux Hautes Parties Contractantes, sans se permettre au préalable ni voie de fait, ni mesure de force, seront tenues de faire un rapport exact de l'affaire et de ses circonstances à leurs Cours respectives, lesquelles s'engagent à la régler à l'amiable, et d'après les principes d'une parfaite justice.

XII. La présente Convention sera ratifiée, et les ratifications en seront échangées à Londres dans l'espace de 6 semaines, ou plutôt si faire se peut.

En foi de quoi les Plénipotentiaires respectifs l'ont signé, et y ont apposé le cachet de leurs armes.

Fait à St. Pétersbourg, le 28/16 février, de l'an de Grâce 1825.

(L.S.)   STRATFORD CANNING.

(L.S.)   LE COMPTE DE NESSELRODE.

(L.S.)   PIERRE DE POLETICA.

of the present Convention, the civil and military authorities of the High Contracting Parties, without previously acting or taking any forcible measure, shall make an exact and circumstantial report of the matter to their respective Courts, who engage to settle the same, in a friendly manner, and according to the principles of justice.

XII. The present Convention shall be ratified, and the ratifications shall be exchanged at London within the space of six weeks, or sooner if possible.

In witness whereof, the respective Plenipotentiaries have signed the same, and have affixed thereto the seal of their arms.

Done at St. Petersburgh, the 28/16th day of February, in the year of Our Lord, 1825.

[L.S.]   STRATFORD CANNING.

[L.S.]   COMTE DE NESSELRODE.

[L.S.]   PIERRE DE POLETICA.

Source: International Boundary Commission, *Joint Report upon the Survey and Demarcation of the Boundary between Canada and the United States from Tongass Passage to Mount St. Elias,* pp. 194–96.

Notes

CHAPTER ONE: BRITAIN AND RUSSIA ESTABLISH THEIR BOUNDARY

1. Appendix.
2. Great Britain, Colonial Office, *Memorandum on the Boundary between Canada and Alaska showing the Contention of the Canadian Government in Respect Thereto, 1899* (London: Colonial Office, 1899), appendix No. I, pp. 60–65.
3. Sir C. Bagot to G. Canning, 17/29 October 1823, ibid., appendix No. XVII, pp. 111–12.
4. Sir C. Bagot to G. Canning, 12 August 1824, ibid., pp. 129–31.
5. G. Canning to S. Canning, 8 December 1824, ibid., pp. 138–42.
6. Margaret A. Ormsby, *British Columbia: a History* (Toronto: Macmillan of Canada, 1958), p. 59.
7. Captain John Franklin, *Narrative of a Second Expedition to the Shores of the Polar Sea in the Years 1825, 1826, 1827* (London: John Murray, 1828), p. 139.
8. Allen A. Wright, *Prelude to Bonanza* (Sidney, B.C.: Gray's Publishing, 1976), pp. 24–25.
9. Somewhat different descriptions of the incident are given in: Alaska Boundary Tribunal, *The Case of the United States . . . plus Appendix* (London: 1903), pp. 267–315; Gloria Griffen Cline, *Peter Skene Ogden and the Hudson's Bay Company*

(Norman: University of Oklahoma Press, 1974), pp. 112–19; and R. M. Patterson, *Trail to the Interior* (Toronto: Macmillan of Canada, 1966), pp. 74–78.
10. Quoted in Great Britain, Colonial Office, *Memorandum on the Boundary between Canada and Alaska . . . 1899*, p. 5.
11. Ibid., appendix No. XX, pp. 147–49.
12. C. C. Chipman, commissioner of the Hudson's Bay Company, to W. F. King, 1 & 13 February 1893, International Boundary Commission (Canada) Papers, File 1301 (4).
13. Wright, *Prelude to Bonanza*, pp. 49–55.
14. George M. Dawson, *Report on an Exploration in the Yukon District, N.W.T. and Adjacent Northern Portion of British Columbia, 1887*, Geological Survey of Canada Report No. 629 (Ottawa: Queen's Printer, 1898), p. 60.
15. F. A. Kerr, *Lower Stikine and Western Iskut River Areas, British Columbia*, Geological Survey of Canada, Memoir 246 (Ottawa: King's Printer, 1948), p. 80.
16. Patterson, *Trail to the Interior*, pp. 83–84.
17. Dawson, *Report on an Exploration . . . 1887*, p. 60.

CHAPTER TWO: CANADA AND UNITED STATES MARK THE 141st MERIDIAN

1. Clifford Wilson, "The Surrender of Fort Yukon," *The Beaver*, Outfit 300 (Autumn 1969): pp. 47–51.

2. Clifford Wilson, *Campbell of the Yukon* (Toronto: Macmillan of Canada, 1970), pp. 111–17.

3. Ibid., p. 134.
4. United States, Congress, Senate, *Report of a Reconnaissance of the Yukon River, Alaska Territory* by Capt. Charles W. Raymond, 42nd Congress, 1st Session, Executive Document No. 12, 1871, p. 7.
5. Ibid., p. 9.
6. Wilson, "The Surrender of Fort Yukon," p. 48.
7. United States, Congress, Senate, *Report of a Reconnaissance of the Yukon River, Alaska Territory* by Capt. Charles W. Raymond, p. 6.
8. Ibid., pp. 13–14.
9. Leroy N. McQuesten, *Recollections of Leroy N. McQuesten of Life in the Yukon 1871–1885* (Dawson: Yukon Order of Pioneers, 1952), p. 9.
10. Descriptions of Fort Yukon are given in: Frederick Whymper, *Travel and Adventure in the Territory of Alaska* (London: John Murray, 1868), pp. 217–27; and William H. Dall, *Alaska and Its Resources* (Boston: Lee and Shepherd, 1870), pp. 102–4. Bompas, a native of London, England, had arrived at Fort Simpson on Christmas Eve, 1865. Consecrated a bishop about 1874, he served in the north until his death in 1906.
11. United States, Congress, Senate, *Report of a Reconnaisance of the Yukon River, Alaska Territory,* by Capt. Charles W. Raymond, pp. 44–45.
12. Ibid., p. 16.
13. Wilson, "The Surrender of Fort Yukon," p. 51.
14. United States, Congress, Senate, *Report of a Reconnaissance of the Yukon River, Alaska Territory* by Capt. Charles W. Raymond, p. 16.
15. Ibid., p. 17. A third man, Private Michael Foley had been assigned to Raymond's party at Sitka on the trip north, p. 13.
16. Ibid., p. 17.
17. Ibid., p. 18.
18. Ibid., p. 19.
19. Ibid., pp. 20–21.
20. United States, Department of State, *Alaska Boundary Tribunal, The Counter Case of the United States, Appendix* (Washington: Government Printing Office, 1903), pp. 89–90.
21. Schwatka, *A Summer in Alaska,* p. 10.
22. Ibid., pp. 10–11.
23. Ibid., pp. 83–84.
24. Ibid., p. 98.
25. Ibid., p. 105.
26. Ibid., p. 106.
27. Ibid., p. 309.
28. Ibid., p. 278.
29. Ibid., p. 245.
30. United States, Congress, Senate, *Report of a Military Reconnaissance in Alaska, Made in 1883 by Lieutenant Frederick Schwatka, U.S. Army,* 48th Congress, 2nd Session, Executive Document No. 2, 1885.
31. Schwatka, *A Summer in Alaska.* One feature, Selwyn River, was named after a Canadian, A.R.C. Selwyn, at the time director of the Geological Survey of Canada.
32. Wilson, *Campbell of the Yukon,* p. 70.
33. George M. Dawson, *Report on an Exploration in the Yukon District, N.W.T. and Adjacent Northern Portion of British Columbia, 1887,* Geological Survey of Canada Report No. 629 (Ottawa: Queen's Printer, 1898), p. 142.
34. R. C. Coutts, *Yukon: Places and Names* (Sidney, B.C.: Gray's Publishing, 1980), p. 158. Subsequently, an artificial lake formed behind a hydro-electric power-plant and dam at Whitehorse and an insignificant creek about seventy miles to the northwest have been named after Schwatka.
35. Great Britain, Colonial Office, *Memorandum on the Boundary between Canada and Alaska showing the Contention of the Canadian Government in Respect Thereto, 1899* (London: Colonial Office, 1899), appendix No. VII, p. 72.
36. International Boundary Commission, *Joint Report upon the Survey and Demarcation of the International Boundary between the United States and Canada along the 141st Meridian from the Arctic Ocean to Mount St. Elias* (Ottawa and Washington: King's Printer and Government Printing Office, 1918), p. 227. In 1887 some doubt seems to have arisen whether the post was in Canadian territory, and the buildings were burned and a new post built opposite the mouth of the Salmontrout River. Soon after, the buildings were taken down and moved to the present site, just east of the 141st Meridian.
37. Clifford Wilson, *Campbell of the Yukon,* pp. 121ff.

38. Leroy N. McQuesten, *Recollections of Life in the Yukon, 1871–1885,* (Dawson: Yukon Order of Pioneers, 1952), p. 5.
39. George M. Dawson, *Report on an Exploration in the Yukon District, N.W.T. and Adjacent Northern Portion of British Columbia, 1887,* pp. 179ff.
40. Ibid., p. 181.
41. William Ogilvie, *Early Days on the Yukon* (London and New York: John Lane, 1913), p. 37.
42. Ibid.
43. William Ogilvie, *Exploratory Survey of Part of the Lewes, Tat-on-duc, Porcupine, Bell, Trout, Peel, and Mackenzie Rivers* (Ottawa: Queen's Printer, 1890), p. 3.
44. Ibid., p. 5. John J. Healy in a deposition made 20 May 1903 stated that some years before 1887 Hudson's Bay Company representatives had killed a number of Indians at Pyramid Harbour, in United States, *Alaska Boundary Tribunal, The Counter Case of the United States, Appendix,* pp. 233–36.
45. Ogilvie, *Exploratory Survey . . . ,* pp. 5–6.
46. Ogilvie, *Early Days on the Yukon,* pp. 53–54.
47. Dawson, *Report on an Exploration in the Yukon District . . . ,* pp. 5–6.
48. Ogilvie, *Exploratory Survey . . . ,* p. 10.
49. Ibid., pp. 11–13.
50. Ibid., p. 11.
51. I.B.C., *Joint Report . . . 141st Meridian from the Arctic Ocean to Mount St. Elias,* p. 224, and John D. Spittle, "Royal Engineer Observatory New Westminster — Determination of the Longitude," *The Link,* The Corporation of Land Surveyors of the Province of British Columbia, Vol. 4 (June 1980): 30–35. The latter includes a sample calculation for a moon culmination.
52. Ogilvie, *Exploratory Survey . . . ,* pp. 13–15.
53. Ibid., p. 16.
54. Ibid., p. 52. The area was mapped by the Geological Survey of Canada in 1961 and 1962.
55. Ibid., p. 54.
56. Ibid.
57. Ibid., pp. 55–56.
58. Ibid., p. 59.
59. Ibid., p. 62.
60. R. G. McConnell, *Report on an Exploration in the Yukon and Mackenzie Basins,*

N.W.T., Geological Survey of Canada Annual Report 1888–1889, New Series, vol. IV, report D (Ottawa: Queen's Printer, 1891), pp. 113–14D. Surprisingly, Ogilvie does not mention the meeting in his report.
61. Ogilvie, *Exploratory Survey . . . ,* p. 8.
62. McConnell, *Report on an Exploration . . . .* Maps incorporating the work of Dawson, Ogilvie, and McConnell accompany this report. Dawson's report includes maps from Fort Selkirk south to the Stikine River, and Ogilvie's is without maps. This may have annoyed Ogilvie.
63. Ogilvie, *Early Days on the Yukon,* p. 60.
64. Israel C. Russell, "A Journey up the Yukon River," *Bulletin of the American Geographical Society* 27 (1895) p. 144.
65. Ibid., p. 146.
66. Ibid., p. 147.
67. Ibid., p. 150.
68. National Archives of the United States, Coast and Geodetic Survey, RG23, Series 22, Volume 586: Turner to Mendenhall, 1 January 1890.
69. Ibid.
70. J. Henry Turner, "The Alaskan Boundary Survey, III. The Boundary North of Fort Yukon," *National Geographic Magazine* 4 (1892) p. 191.
71. National Archives of the United States, Coast and Geodetic Survey, RG23, Series 22, Volume 606: Turner to Mendenhall, 20 November 1891.
72. United States, Coast and Geodetic Survey, *Annual Report of the Superintendent for the Year Ending June 1891* (Washington: Government Printing Office, 1892), pp. 86–90.
73. National Archives of the United States, Coast and Geodetic Survey, RG23, Series 22, Volume 606: Turner to Mendenhall, 8 December 1891.
74. Ibid., RG23, Series 34, Volume 608, Monthly Reports and Journals 1891.
75. Ibid., 11 October 1889.
76. Ibid., RG23, Series 22, Volume 620: McGrath to Mendenhall, 27 February 1892.
77. International Boundary Commission, *Joint Report upon the Survey and Demarcation of the International Boundary . . . along the 141st Meridian from the Arctic Ocean to Mount St. Elias,* p. 232.
78. National Archives of the United States,

Coast and Geodetic Survey, RG23, Series 34, Volume 608, Monthly Reports and Journals, 1891.

79. International Boundary Commission, *Joint Report upon the Survey and Demarcation of the International Boundary between the United States and Canada . . . along the 141st Meridian from the Arctic Ocean to Mount St. Elias*, p. 232.

80. National Archives of the United States, Coast and Geodetic Survey, RG23, Series 34, Volume 608, Monthly Reports and Journals 1891.

81. Ibid.

82. Ibid., RG23, Series 22, Volume 585: McGrath to Mendenhall, 15 June 1890.

83. Ibid., McGrath to Mendenhall, 23 August 1890.

84. Ibid., Series 22, Volume 605: McGrath to Mendenhall, 20 June 1891.

85. Ibid., McGrath to Mendenhall, 4 October 1891.

86. International Boundary Commission, *Joint Report upon the Survey and Demarcation of the International Boundary between the United States and Canada . . . along the 141st Meridian from the Arctic Ocean to Mount St. Elias*, p. 233.

87. Ogilvie, *Early Days on the Yukon*, pp. 152–53 and Canada, Sessional Paper 13–1897, No. 9, *Extracts from Reports of Wm. Ogilvie, D.L.S.*, pp. 40–54.

88. Ogilvie, *Early Days on the Yukon*, pp. 144–50.

89. Ibid., p. 153.

90. Ibid., pp. 154–55.

91. Canada, Sessional Paper 13–1897, pp. 42–43.

92. International Boundary Commission, *Joint Report upon the Survey and Demarcation of the International Boundary between the United States and Canada . . . along the 141st Meridian from the Arctic Ocean to Mount St. Elias*, p. 236.

93. Canada, Sessional Paper 13–1897, pp. 43–44.

94. Ibid.

95. Public Archives of Canada, Constantine Papers, Volume 1, Diary for 15 May, 1896.

96. Ibid., and Canada, Sessional Paper 15–1897, Appendix DD, *Report on the Yukon Detachment*, p. 234.

97. Public Archives of Canada, Constantine Papers, Diary for 1 June 1896. A ten per cent royalty was later imposed by Canada, Privy Council No. 2326 of 29 July 1897.

98. Ogilvie, *Early Days on the Yukon*, pp. 245–48 and Alfred Hulse Brooks, *Blazing Alaska's Trails* (Caldwell, ID: Caxton Printers, 1953), pp. 509–11 both describe the miners' meeting and their role in the community.

99. Public Archives of Canada, Constantine Papers, Volume 4, Letter Book, pp. 126–29: Constantine to Commissioner, North-West Mounted Police, 13 July 1896.

100. Ibid., pp. 130–33: Strickland to Constantine, 13 July 1896.

101. Ibid., pp. 126–29: Constantine to Commissioner, 13 July 1896.

102. Canada, Sessional Paper 13–1897, p. 44.

103. Ibid., pp. 48–49.

104. Ogilvie, *Early Days on the Yukon*, pp. 131, 160–64.

105. Public Archives of Canada, Constantine Papers, Volume 1, Diary for 15 October 1896.

106. Ogilvie, *Early Days on the Yukon*, pp. 170–71.

107. Ibid., pp. 216–19.

108. In 1899, Ogilvie, at the time commissioner of the Yukon, conducted an enquiry into some of the miners' charges against the government officials. His investigation, circumscribed by the terms of reference that Ottawa set for it, accomplished very little (Canada, Sessional Paper 87–1899).

109. Public Archives of Canada, Constantine Papers, Volume 4, Letter Book p. 352; and Woodside Papers, Volume 48: Ogilvie to Woodside, 23 September 1909.

CHAPTER 3: STAKING A CLAIM TO THE PANHANDLE

1. HBC Archives B.226/b/35, fo. 368, George M. Dawson, *Report on an Exploration in the Yukon District, N.W.T. and Adjacent Northern Portion* of British Columbia, 1887, Geological Survey of Canada Report No. 629 (Ottawa: Queen's Printer, 1898), p. 60, gives the date as about 1863. Possibly

Alexander Choquette, one of the discoverers of gold on the Stikine, began acting as an independent trader at the earlier date.

2. R. M. Patterson, *Trail to the Interior* (Toronto: Macmillan of Canada, 1966), p. 81.

3. Great Britain, Colonial Office, *Memorandum on the Boundary between Canada and Alaska showing the Contention of the Canadian Government in Respect Thereto, 1899* (London: Colonial Office, 1899), pp. 7–10.

4. Dawson, *Report on an Exploration . . . 1887*, pp. 23, 76–83. Principal placer creeks were Dease Creek, flowing into Dease Lake, and Thibert and McDame Creek, flowing into Dease River. Gold production for 1874 and 1875 totalled about two million dollars, and at one time in 1876, about two thousand people were in the Cassiar. The principal settlement was Laketon at the mouth of Dease Creek.

5. Canada, Sessional Paper 125–1878, *Report with accompanying Map, of the Engineer employed last year in determining the probable boundary line between British Columbia and Alaska . . . and also such other papers as relate to the defining of the Boundary Line between Alaska and British territory, and the navigation of the rivers passing from Columbia, through Alaska to the Sea* (Ottawa: Queen's Printer, 1878), pp. 47–48. See also: Georgiana Ball, "The Peter Martin Case and the Provisional Settlement of the Stikine Boundary," *BC Studies* 10 (Summer 1971), pp. 35–55.

6. Ibid., pp. 102, 121.

7. Ibid., p. 105.

8. Ibid., p. 58.

9. Ibid., p. 104.

10. Ibid., pp. 116–18.

11. Ibid., pp. 144–45.

12. Ibid., pp. 150–51.

13. Ibid., pp. 151–52.

14. Ibid., pp. 153–54.

15. *Daily British Colonist*, 8 March 1878.

16. Great Britain, Colonial Office, *Memorandum on the Boundary between Canada and Alaska . . . 1899*, appendix No. V, p. 69.

17. United States, Alaskan Boundary Tribunal, *Counter Case Appendix* (Washington: Government Printing Office, 1903), p. 186.

18. Great Britain, Alaska Boundary Tribunal, *Various Documents bearing on the Question of the Alaska Boundary – Printed for convenience of Reference* (London: McCorquodale, 1903), I: 70, from a memo by George M. Dawson, 3 February 1890.

19. Ibid., pp. 13–43. A preliminary memo dated 9 April 1886 is printed in Great Britain, Foreign Office, *Confidential 5439, Correspondence respecting the Boundary between the British Possessions in North America and the Territory of Alaska – 1886* (London: Foreign Office, 1887), pp. 48–51.

20. Great Britain, Colonial Office, *Memorandum on the Boundary between Canada and Alaska . . . 1899*, p. 13.

21. Ibid., appendix No. VIII, pp. 74–75, George M. Dawson to Sir Charles Tupper, 11 February 1888.

22. Ibid., appendix No. XI, pp. 81–82, F. M. Thorn to E. Dewdney, 14 December 1888.

23. Great Britain, Alaska Boundary Tribunal, *Various Documents bearing on the Question of the Alaska Boundary*, pp. 47–69, Otto J. Klotz to A. M. Burgess, 11 December 1889.

24. Great Britain, Colonial Office, *Memorandum on the Boundary between Canada and Alaska . . . 1899*, appendix No. XII, pp. 83–93, W. F. King to E. Deville, 14 December 1891.

25. Great Britain, Alaska Boundary Tribunal, *Counter-Case* (London: Foreign Office, 1903), p. 9.

26. Great Britain, Colonial Office, *Memorandum on the Boundary between Canada and Alaska . . . 1899*, appendix No. XII, p. 91.

27. Ibid., p. 93.

28. Ibid., appendix No. XIV, p. 96, Convention between Great Britain and the United States, respecting the boundary between the two countries (Alaska and Passamaquoddy Bay) signed at Washington, 22 July 1892.

29. Ibid., appendix No. XV, pp. 98–101, Report of Messrs. Duffield and King, 31st December, 1895. Various names were used in referring to the project. "Alaska Boundary Commission" is the short title of Canada, Sessional Paper 74–1896. Others include: British Boundary Commission, Canadian Boundary Commission, United States Boundary Commission, and International Survey under Convention of 1892.

30. Depositions from the American and Canadian surveyors are among the Alaska Boundary Tribunal documents. They

concern the possible existence and location of "the summit of the mountains situated parallel to the coast" referred to in the 1825 treaty.

31. J. W. Taylor diary.

32. United States, Coast and Geodetic Survey, *Report of the Superintendent . . . showing the progress of the work during the fiscal year ending with June, 1893* (Washington: Government Printing Office, 1894), pp. 68–75.

33. International Boundary Commission (Canadian Section) papers, Folder 10, Field Correspondence 1893, Otto J. Klotz to W. F. King, 8 June 1893.

34. Ibid., H. H. Robertson to W. F. King, 11 December 1893. Robertson was the Canadian attaché on Tittmann's party.

35. Ibid.

36. United States, Coast and Geodetic Survey, *Report of the Superintendent . . . June 1894*, p. 67.

37. I.B.C. (Canadian Section) papers, Folder 10, H. H. Robertson to W. F. King, 11 December 1893.

38. Don W. Thomson, *Men and Meridians* (Ottawa: Queen's Printer, 1967), 2: 131–46.

39. J. W. Taylor diary and United States, Coast and Geodetic Survey, *Report of the Superintendent . . . June, 1893*, p. 72.

40. United States, Coast and Geodetic Survey, *Report of the Superintendent . . . June, 1894*, p. 65. Boat dimensions are for the ones used by MacArthur's party; presumably Brabazon's were the same.

41. J. W. Taylor diary, 15 May 1893.

42. Ibid., and United States, Coast and Geodetic Survey, *Report of the Superintendent . . . June, 1894*, p. 60.

43. Ibid., entries for 6–9 August and p. 61.

44. Great Britain, Colonial Office, *Memorandum on the Boundary between Canada and Alaska . . . 1899*, appendix No. XV,

p. 99, Report of Messrs. Duffield and King, 31st December, 1895.

45. United States, Coast and Geodetic Survey, *Report of the Superintendent . . . June, 1894*, p. 69.

46. Ibid., pp. 70–71; and National Archives of the United States, Coast and Geodetic Survey, RG23, Series 22: McGrath to Mendenhall, 12 July 1894 and 10 January 1895.

47. McGrath to Mendenhall, 10 January 1895, pp. 15–16.

48. McGrath to Mendenhall, 12 July 1894, p. 10.

49. I.B.C. (Canadian Section) papers, Folder 14, Index to photographic views.

50. Great Britain, Colonial Office, *Memorandum on the Boundary between Canada and Alaska . . . 1899*, appendix No. XV, pp. 99–100, Report of Messrs. Duffield and King, 31 December 1895.

51. Ibid., pp. 98–101.

52. I.B.C. (Canadian Section) papers, Folder 4, File 1301–5, W. F. King, 1 April 1898.

53. United States, *Messages and Papers of the Presidents*, pp. 6087–90.

54. T. C. Mendenhall, "The Alaska Boundary," *Atlantic Monthly* (April 1896).

55. Great Britain, Alaska Boundary Tribunal, *Appendix to the Case of His Majesty's Government* (London: McCorquodale and Co., 1903), pp. 300–304.

56. The storehouses were brought to the attention of Canada's minister of the interior by a letter from the Indian agent at Metlakatla, B.C., dated 29 July 1901. The United States' acting secretary of state acknowledged they had been built on disputed territory in a note dated 16 September 1902; ibid., pp. 293–96 and Great Britain, Alaska Boundary Tribunal, *Various Documents Bearing on the Question of the Alaska Boundary,* Volume 1, pp. 107–8.

CHAPTER FOUR: THE KLONDIKE RUSH AND TEMPORARY BOUNDARIES

1. Public Archives of Canada, Woodside Papers, volume 48, William Ogilvie Correspondence 1907–1909, Ogilvie to Woodside, 18 March 1907.

2. The estimate was conservative. A ton of impure placer gold valued at $17 a troy ounce would be worth close to $500,000

while the report describes $700,000 in gold in the captain's cabin alone. Archie Satterfield, *Chilkoot Pass* (Anchorage: Alaska Northwest Publishing, 1978), p. 37, puts the amount at more than two tons.

3. Tappan Adney, *The Klondike Stampede*

(New York and London: Harper and Brothers, 1900), pp. 31–34, 49–52, 134–37.

4. Canada, Sessional Paper 38B–1898, *Letters and reports . . . from Commissioner Walsh,* p. 8.

5. Canada, Sessional Paper 15–1899, *Annual Report of the North-west Mounted Police,* part III, Yukon Territory, appendix F, p. 81.

6. Canada, Sessional Paper 38B, p. 13.

7. In August 1897, Sifton had engaged W. T. Jennings, an engineer from Toronto, to examine the Stikine route. His report was published as Canada, Sessional Paper 30–1898.

8. House of Commons Debates, 8 February 1898, pp. 203–12.

9. Ibid., 7 March 1898, p. 1280.

10. British Columbia, *Statutes 1898,* chapter 30, and *Statutes 1899,* chapter 61.

11. *The Canadian Mining Review* (June 1898), p. 175, Klondyke Letter of 1 June 1898 by T. (A.N.C. Treadgold).

12. House of Commons Debates, 16 February 1898, pp. 619–20.

13. Samuel B. Steele, *Forty Years in Canada* (Toronto: McClelland, Goodchild and Stewart, 1915), p. 291.

14. Canada, Sessional Paper 15–1899, part III, appendix G, pp. 88–94.

15. Ibid., p. 89.

16. Ibid., p. 94.

17. Ibid., appendix F, pp. 80–87.

18. Steele, *Forty Years in Canada,* p. 293. Machine guns in the passes are not mentioned in contemporary police reports. Steele (Sessional Paper 15–1899, part III, p. 29) reports two Maxim guns, one at Tagish and one at Dawson plus one Nordenfelt gun at Tagish in January 1899. Walsh (Sessional Paper 38B–1898, p. 9) mentions two Gatling (Maxim?) guns brought in by his party.

19. Canada, Sessional Paper 13–1899, *Annual Report of the Department of the Interior,* Report of Major J. M. Walsh, 15 August 1898, p. 319.

20. John W. Dafoe, *Clifford Sifton in Relation to His Times* (Toronto: Macmillan, 1931), pp. 214–15, Sifton to Walsh, 1 April 1898.

21. National Archives of the United States, War Department, Records of the Adjutant General, RG94, Volume 488, No. 67221A-1. Acting secretary of war to commanding general, Department of Columbia, telegram of 9 February 1898.

22. Ibid., Volume 490, No. 73764 (filed with 67221).

23. Ibid., Walsh to Anderson, 17 March 1898.

24. Ibid., Anderson to Adjutant General, Department of Columbia, 20 March 1898.

25. Ibid., 1st Indorsement by Brigadier General H. C. Merriam, 1 April 1898.

26. Steele, *Forty Years in Canada,* p. 312.

27. Canada, Sessional Paper 15–1899, part III, appendix H, pp. 95–110.

28. Ibid., p. 97.

29. National Archives of the United States, War Department, Records of the adjutant general, RG94, Volume 489, No. 67221A-31, Jackson to secretary of war, 15 November 1898. In addition to the supplies to be moved by reindeer, supplies, pack-trains, and an escort were assembled at Dyea to freight supplies to Lake Laberge before the Yukon River opened in the spring of 1898 (Satterfield, *Chilkoot Pass,* pp. 83–85). This part of the expedition was abandoned on 5 March 1898 (Adjutant General to Merriam, Volume 488, No. 67221A–21) after it became obvious that the North-West Mounted Police had dealt with the problem.

30. Ibid., Jackson to the secretary of war, 15 November 1898. Jackson left Alaska on 10 April 1898, and in describing events after this date, his report is confusing on distances travelled and campsites used. If he had stayed a few more weeks he might have prevented the catastrophes that followed.

31. *The Klondike Nugget,* 11 January and 4 February 1899.

32. Canada, Sessional Paper 15–1899, part III, appendix H, p. 109.

33. Sheldon Jackson states that Mr. Redmeyer, in charge of the reindeer, gave the name (Jackson to the secretary of war, 15 November 1898, p. 8).

34. Canada, Privy Council No. 490 of 28 February 1898. This set out a claim to the head of Lynn Canal and, in the south, ran the boundary along Clarence Strait and Ernest Sound to the 56th parallel of latitude. The latter lay west of the claim put forward by British Columbia in 1885 (in United States, Alaskan Boundary Tribunal, *Counter Case Appendix* [Washington]: Government Printing Office, 1903], pp. 180–90).

35. Great Britain, Colonial Office, *Memorandum on the Boundary between Canada*

and Alaska showing the Contention of the Canadian Government in Respect Thereto, 1899 (London: Colonial Office, 1899), pp. 16–19 and appendix No. XVI, pp. 102–8.

36. United States, Annual Reports of the Department of the Interior for the fiscal year ended June 30, 1899 (Washington: Government Printing Office, 1899), Miscellaneous Reports, part II, appendix E of the report of the Governor of Alaska of 18 October 1899, pp. 58–59.

37. Norman Penlington, Canada and Imperialism 1896–1899 (Toronto: University of Toronto Press, 1965), pp. 209–10.

38. Canada, Sessional Paper 15–1899, part III, p. 6. Superintendent Steele of the N.W.M.P., together with a magistrate for British Columbia, travelled to Atlin in late July 1898.

39. British Columbia Placer Mining Act of 20 May 1898, Journals of the Legislative Assembly, Session 1898, pp. 133, 189.

40. Canada, Privy Council No. 302 of 20 February 1901.

41. United States, Alaskan Boundary Tribunal, Case Appendix (Washington: Government Printing Office, 1903), p.

539, Tittmann to the secretary of state, 21 June 1900.

42. To an extent, the court recognized the Chilkat custom, and only the leader was sentenced to be hanged. This was later changed to a life sentence (Annual Reports of the Department of the Interior for the fiscal year ended June 30, 1901 [Washington: Government Printing Office, 1901], Miscellaneous Reports, part II, Report of the Governor of Alaska, p. 32).

43. Archer Martin, Report under the Porcupine District Commission Act, 1900 (Victoria: King's Printer, 1901).

44. International Boundary Commission (Canadian Section) papers, Folder 14, File 1301, W. F. King, Alaska Boundary 1901–1903, White-Fraser to King, 4 December 1902.

45. Arthur O. Wheeler, "How I went to Alaska," Canadian Surveyor 3 (July 1929): 7–9.

46. Ibid., and I.B.C. (Canadian Section) papers, Folder 11, Wheeler to King, 23 May 1903.

47. Wheeler, "How I went to Alaska," p. 9.

CHAPTER FIVE: FORCED SETTLEMENT

1. International Boundary Commission, Joint Report upon the Survey and Demarcation of the Boundary between Canada and the United States from Tongass Passage to Mount St. Elias (Ottawa and Washington: International Boundary Commissioners, 1952), pp. 1–4.

2. Ibid., pp. 3–4.

3. Norman Penlington, The Alaska Boundary Dispute: A Critical Reappraisal (Toronto: McGraw-Hill Ryerson, 1972), p. 72.

4. Sir Wilfrid Laurier, House of Commons Debates, 13 March 1903, p. 44.

5. Ibid., p. 42.

6. Henry Cabot Lodge, ed., Selections from the Correspondence of Theodore Roosevelt and Henry Cabot Lodge, 1884–1918 (New York and London: Scribner's, 1925), 2: 4–5.

7. Elting E. Morison, ed., Letters of Theodore Roosevelt (Cambridge, MA:

Harvard University Press, 1951), 3: 529–31.

8. John A. Garraty, "Henry Cabot Lodge and the Alaskan Boundary Tribunal," New England Quarterly 24 (1951): 480.

9. Ibid., pp. 481–82. Tower, as secretary, was soon to learn the difficulties of working for two masters. Two sets of stationery were required, one titled "Alaska Boundary Tribunal" for dealing with the Foreign Office and another "Alaskan Boundary Tribunal" for the Americans. Comment in Geographical Journal 69 (January 1927), p. 60.

10. Ibid.

11. Maurice Pope ed., Public Servant: The Memoirs of Sir Joseph Pope (Toronto: Oxford University Press, 1960), p. 297.

12. Public Archives of Canada, Pope Papers, MG 30 E1, Volume 60, File 34, memorandum of 10 October 1903.

13. Captain George Vancouver, A Voyage

of Discovery to the North Pacific Ocean and Round the World in the Years 1790–95 (London: G.G. and J. Robinson, Paternoster-Row and J. Edwards, Pall-Mall, 1798), 2:344.

14. Ibid., p. 371. Bentinck, now Cavendish-Bentinck, is the family name of the Dukes of Portland.

15. Great Britain, *Alaska Boundary Tribunal. Protocols, Oral Arguments, with Index, Award of the Tribunal, and Opinions of its Members. September 3 to October 20, 1903* (London: Foreign Office, 1903), p. 82.

16. Pope, *Joseph Pope*, p. 155. Another instance was when King Edward VII wished to receive Lodge and Root as representatives of the United States government rather than as tribunal members, thus excluding ex-senator Turner and the Canadians. Lodge put his foot down over Turner, and the upshot was that the king received the Americans at noon and the Canadians later in the day (Garraty, "Henry Cabot Lodge and the Alaskan Boundary Tribunal," p. 493).

17. John W. Dafoe, *Clifford Sifton in Relation to His Times* (Toronto: Macmillan, 1931), p. 228.

18. Ibid., pp. 228–29.

19. Garraty, "Henry Cabot Lodge and the Alaskan Boundary Tribunal," p. 475ff., has numerous comments on the relationship between Lord Alverstone and the Canadian tribunal members.

20. Ibid., p. 489.

21. Ibid., p. 490.

22. Ibid., p. 491.

23. Charles Callan Tansill, *Canadian-American Relations, 1875–1911* (New York and Toronto: Yale University Press and Ryerson Press, 1943), p. 257.

24. Garraty, "Henry Cabot Lodge and the Alaskan Boundary Tribunal," p. 492.

25. Tansill, *Canadian-American Relations, 1875–1911*, pp. 257–58.

26. Ibid., pp. 258–59.

27. Douglas Cole, "Allen Aylesworth on the Alaska Boundary Award," *Canadian Historical Review* 52 (December 1971), p. 474.

28. Ibid., and John S. Ewart, *Kingdom of Canada . . . and Other Essays* (Toronto: Morang, 1908), pp. 299–347.

29. Garraty, "Henry Cabot Lodge and the Alaskan Boundary Tribunal," p. 493.

30. Dafoe, *Clifford Sifton in Relation to His Times*, p. 233.

31. Ibid.

32. W. F. King and J. J. McArthur were on Sifton's staff. The topography around Kates Needle (B.P. 70) is also sketched in. Gossip at the time was that O. H. Tittmann, who had named the peak after his wife, asked that it be part of the boundary line (Cole, "Allen Aylesworth on the Alaska Boundary Award," p. 476).

33. Garraty, "Henry Cabot Lodge and the Alaskan Boundary Tribunal," p. 493.

34. Cole, "Allen Aylesworth on the Alaska Boundary Award," p. 475.

35. International Boundary Commission (Canadian Section) papers, Atlas of the Award of the Alaska Boundary Tribunal.

36. The Alaska Boundary Tribunal Award in I.B.C., *Joint Report upon the Survey and Demarcation of the Boundary . . . from Tongass Passage to Mount St. Elias*, p. 6.

37. Cole, "Allen Aylesworth on the Alaska Boundary Award," pp. 475–76.

38. Richard Harrington, "The Fantasy of Tarr Inlet as a New Yukon Port," *Canadian Geographical Journal* 91 (November 1975): 12–17.

39. Public Archives of Canada, Pope Papers, Volume 48, diary for 20 October 1903.

40. I.B.C., *Joint Report upon the Survey and Demarcation of the Boundary . . . from Tongass Passage to Mount St. Elias*, p. 214.

41. Lord Alverstone's secretary told Pope that he did not know where the idea came from and had only heard of it a few hours before the award. On comparison, Alverstone's final opinion on the second question (Portland Channel) was found similar to the earlier one aside from the alteration of some sentences. In fact, the copy handed to Sifton gave two of the islands to Canada in the main text and all four in the conclusion printed in capital letters at the bottom. On learning of the mistake, Alverstone personally hunted up Sifton, got possession of the copy, and issued a new opinion (Pope, *Joseph Pope*, p. 299, and Cole, "Allen Aylesworth on the Alaska Boundary Award," pp. 474–75). For a slightly different version see Ewart, *Kingdom of Canada . . .*, pp. 323–43.

42. J. Castell Hopkins, *The Canadian Annual Review of Public Affairs, 1903*

(Toronto: Annual Review Publishing, 1904), p. 376.

43. Aylesworth expressed this opinion in an interview given in 1942, by which time some of Roosevelt's threatening letters had become public (Cole, "Allen Aylesworth on the Alaska Boundary Award," p. 477).

44. Frederick S. Wood, compiler, *Roosevelt As We Knew Him: The Personal Recollections of One Hundred and Fifty of His Friends and Associates* (Philadelphia and Chicago: John C. Winston, ca. 1927), pp. 119-21.

45. Ibid., pp. 121-22.

46. Lodge, *Selections from the Correspondence of Theodore Roosevelt and Henry Cabot Lodge, 1884-1918,* 2: 66-67, Roosevelt to Lodge, 5 October 1903.

47. *New York Times,* 2 November 1903.

48. United States, Congress, Senate, *Wales Island Packing Co. vs United States,* 72nd Congress, 1st Session, Senate Document No. 61, 1932, and *The Dawson News,* 25 June 1936.

CHAPTER SIX: MARKING THE PANHANDLE BOUNDARY

1. International Boundary Commission, *Joint Report upon the Survey and Demarcation of the Boundary between Canada and the United States from Tongass Passage to Mount St. Elias* (Ottawa and Washington: International Boundary Commissioners, 1952), p. 246.

2. Ibid., pp. 8-9. King's official title was "His Britannic Majesty's Commissioner" but, in conformity with present-day usage, he is referred to as the Commissioner for Canada.

3. Ibid., pp. 9-11.

4. Ibid., pp. 137-40. In the 1920 work in the Portland Canal and Blue River areas, twenty-five manganese-bronze posts, 7¼ inches high, were used as monuments. In other places, where it was impractical to carry in a conventional monument, copper and bronze bolts or bronze disks have been used in their place.

5. Ibid., pp. 33-38.

6. Ibid., pp. 38-39.

7. Ibid., pp. 39-42.

8. International Boundary Commission (Canadian Section) papers, Folder 9, G. R. White-Fraser's report on the 1904 season.

9. Ibid.

10. Quoted by permission Provincial Archives of British Columbia, T. F. Harper Reed papers, Add. MSS 516, Box 4.

11. I.B.C., *Joint Report . . . Tongass Passage to Mount St. Elias,* pp. 42-43.

12. Ibid., pp. 99-101, 104-5, 109-11.

13. Ibid., pp. 42-43, 53-55, 99-101, 112-15.

14. Ibid., p. 28.

15. I.B.C. (Canadian Section) papers, Folder 9, G. R. White-Fraser's report on the 1905 season, p. 4.

16. Ibid., p. 8.

17. Ibid., Folder 9, Fremont Morse's report on the 1910 season.

18. Ibid., Folder 9, J. D. Craig's report on the 1920 season.

19. Ibid., Craig to McArthur, 12 August 1920.

20. The surveys were done using metric units, but the final report gives horizontal distances in metres and vertical elevations in feet above sea level. Hence the use of the two systems in this instance.

21. I.B.C., *Joint Report . . . Tongass Passage to Mount St. Elias,* pp. 51-53, 81-85, 88-91, 116-19.

22. I.B.C. (Canadian Section) papers, Folder 9, O. M. Leland's report on the 1908 season.

23. I.B.C., *Joint Report . . . Tongass Passage to Mount St. Elias,* pp. 71-73, 79-80, 87-88.

24. I.B.C. (Canadian Section) papers, Folder 9, unsigned draft of J. D. Craig's report on the 1907 season.

25. Ibid.

26. Ibid. Craig may not have been in the camp when this incident occurred.

27. Ibid.

28. Ibid., Folder 10, F. H. Mackie's report on the 1909 season.

29. Ibid.

30. Ibid.

31. I.B.C., *Joint Report . . . Tongass Passage to Mount St. Elias,* pp. 39-42, 50-51, 108.

32. J. A. Flemer and Fremont Morse were

with the American section, the latter based at Sitka doing astronomical observations for longitude.

33. Alex G. Gillespie, *Journey through Life* (Victoria: privately printed, 1954), p. 39.
34. Ibid., pp. 33–34.
35. Ibid., p. 37.
36. Ibid., p. 40.
37. I.B.C. (Canadian Section) papers, Folder 9, scattered pages from W. M. Dennis's report on the 1912 season, dated 25 March 1919.
38. I.B.C., *Joint Report . . . Tongass Passage to Mount St. Elias*, pp. 39–42, 69–71.
39. Ibid., pp. 77–79, 86–87.
40. I.B.C. (Canadian Section) papers, Folder 9, Eberhardt Mueller's report on the 1908 season.
41. I.B.C., *Joint Report . . . Tongass Passage to Mount St. Elias*, pp. 64–65, 69–71.
42. I.B.C. (Canadian Section) papers, P. W. Green in W. F. Ratz's report on the 1907 season.
43. I.B.C., *Joint Report . . . Tongass Passage to Mount St. Elias*, pp. 45, 63–64, 69–71, 98–99, 106.
44. I.B.C. (Canadian Section) papers, Folder 9, W. F. Ratz's report on the 1906 season.
45. I.B.C., *Joint Report . . . Tongass Passage to Mount St. Elias*, pp. 68–69.
46. Ibid., pp. 38–39, 47–49, 61–63.
47. Ibid., pp. 33–38, 45–47, 60–61, 95–97.
48. Ibid., pp. 36, 43–45, 92–95.
49. I.B.C. (Canadian Section) papers, Folder 9, O. M. Leland's report on the 1910 season.
50. I.B.C., *Joint Report . . . Tongass Passage to Mount St. Elias*, pp. 66–68, 106–8.
51. I.B.C. (Canadian Section) papers, Folder 9, scattered pages from W. M. Dennis's report on the 1912 season, dated 25 March 1919.
52. I.B.C., *Joint Report . . . Tongass Passage to Mount St. Elias*, pp. 57–60, 74–77.
53. Gillespie, *Journey through Life*, pp. 42–43.
54. Ibid., pp. 45–46.
55. I.B.C., *Joint Report . . . Tongass Passage to Mount St. Elias*, pp. 56–59, 102–6.
56. I.B.C. (Canadian Section) papers, Folder 9, three loose pages from W. M. Dennis's report on the 1911 season, dated 31 March 1919.
57. Ibid., Folder 9, loose page from H. S. Mussell's report on the 1911 season.
58. Ibid., Folder 9, H. S. Mussell's report on the 1912 season.
59. I.B.C., *Joint Report . . . Tongass Passage to Mount St. Elias*, pp. 145–46, 181.
60. On 24 May 1910, the American ambassador in London wrote to the British government, retracting an earlier letter and disclaiming any British rights in Dixon Entrance and Hecate Strait beyond the three-mile limit around the islands. Personal communication from A. C. McEwen, international boundary commissioner for Canada.

CHAPTER SEVEN: THE 141st MERIDIAN

1. International Boundary Commission, *Joint Report upon the Survey and Demarcation of the International Boundary between the United States and Canada along the 141st Meridian from the Arctic Ocean to Mount St. Elias* (Ottawa and Washington: International Boundary Commissioners, 1918), pp. 15–16.
2. Ibid., p. 110. Otto Klotz observed at Vancouver and Edwin Smith of the USC & GS at Eagle.
3. Guy Lawrence, *40 Years on the Yukon Telegraph* (Vancouver: Mitchell Press, 1965), pp. 63–64.
4. I.B.C., *Joint Report . . . 141st Meridian from the Arctic Ocean to Mount St. Elias,* pp. 28, 231–38.
5. Ibid., pp. 29–36.
6. I.B.C. (Canadian Section) papers, Box 34, Thomas Riggs, Jr., report on the 1907 season, p. 2. Party chiefs had limited authority to hire labourers and cooks in the field and apparently to fix wages.
7. I.B.C., *Joint Report . . . 141st Meridian from the Arctic Ocean to Mount St. Elias,* pp. 118–24.
8. Ibid., p. 124.
9. Ibid., pp. 124–30.
10. Ibid., pp. 192–93.
11. Ibid., pp. 182–86.
12. Ibid., pp. 186–92.
13. Ibid., pp. 278–79.
14. I.B.C. (Canadian Section) papers, Box 34, Thomas Riggs, Jr., report on the 1907 season, p. 5.
15. Ibid., p. 8.

16. I.B.C., *Joint Report . . . 141st Meridian from the Arctic Ocean to Mount St. Elias*, pp. 34, 40, 50, 69.

17. Ibid., pp. 37–41.

18. I.B.C. (Canadian Section) papers, Box 34, Thomas Riggs, Jr., report on the 1908 season, p. 5.

19. Ibid., p. 8.

20. Ibid., p. 9.

21. I.B.C., *Joint Report . . . 141st Meridian from the Arctic Ocean to Mount St. Elias*, pp. 43–48.

22. I.B.C. (Canadian Section) papers, Box 34, Thomas Riggs, Jr., report on the 1909 season, p. 3.

23. I.B.C., *Joint Report . . . 141st Meridian from the Arctic Ocean to Mount St. Elias*, p. 46.

24. Ibid., pp. 49–57.

25. I.B.C. (Canadian Section) papers, Box 34, Thomas Riggs, Jr., report on the 1910 season, pp. 1–3.

26. I.B.C., *Joint Report . . . 141st Meridian from the Arctic Ocean to Mount St. Elias*, p. 55.

27. I.B.C. (Canadian Section) papers, Box 34, A. C. Baldwin in Riggs' report on the 1910 season, p. 41.

28. I.B.C. (Canadian Section) papers, Box 34, Thomas Riggs, Jr., report on the 1910 season, p. 10.

29. I.B.C., *Joint Report . . . 141st Meridian from the Arctic Ocean to Mount St. Elias*, p. 58–67. Douglas H. Nelles, "The Exploration and Survey of the 141st Meridian, Alaska," *Geographical Journal* 61 (January 1913): 48–55 gives a partial distribution of personnel for the season:
Projection party (Canadian):
Fore-heliograph sub-party: assistant surveyor, packer, and cook, with eight horses.
Observing sub-party: American and Canadian observers, packer, and cook, with eight horses.
Rear-heliograph sub-party: American and Canadian heliographers, with three horses.
Triangulation reconnaissance party (American?): surveyor, an assistant, cook, two packers, with fourteen horses.
Triangulation party (American): surveyor, a recorder, cook, two packers, with nine horses.
Topographic party (American): surveyor, an assistant topographer, two recorders, two traverse men, two rodmen, cook, two packers, with fourteen horses.
Line-cutting and monumenting parties (two, Canadian): chief, two assistants, two cooks, two rodmen, three packers, three labourers, with (?) horses.
Transportation parties (two American and two Canadian): pack-trains, with the numbers of men and horses not given.
In addition to the boundary surveys proper, the two governments took advantage of the activity to commence geological mapping of the boundary strip from the Yukon River north to the Arctic coast. D. D. Cairnes of the Geological Survey of Canada was assigned the area from the Yukon to the Porcupine Rivers and A. G. Maddren of the U.S. Geological Survey that from the Porcupine River north.

30. I.B.C., *Joint Report . . . 141st Meridian from the Arctic Ocean to Mount St. Elias*, pp. 60–61.

31. I.B.C. (Canadian Section) papers, Box 34, Thomas Riggs, Jr., report on the 1911 season, p. 6.

32. I.B.C., *Joint Report . . . 141st Meridian from the Arctic Ocean to Mount St. Elias*, p. 61.

33. Ibid., p. 62.

34. Thomas Riggs, Jr., "Running the Alaska Boundary," *The Beaver* Outfit 276 (September 1945), p. 43.

35. I.B.C. (Canadian Section) papers, Box 34, A. C. Baldwin in Riggs' report on the 1911 season p. 24.

36. Ibid., Thomas Riggs, Jr., report on the 1911 season, pp. 14–15. Riggs had used $3,000 worth of equipment and supplies in establishing the quarantine at Rampart House. Later, his government refused to reimburse him claiming that most of the Indians were Canadians. The amount, equal to a year's salary, was finally paid by the Canadian government after Craig presented Riggs' case to them.

37. I.B.C., *Joint Report . . . 141st Meridian from the Arctic Ocean to Mount St. Elias*, p. 68–79.

38. I.B.C. (Canadian Section) papers, Box 34, Thomas Riggs, Jr., report on the 1912 season, p. 4.

39. Ibid., p. 5.

40. Ibid., p. 6.

41. Ibid., p. 8.

42. Ibid., p. 9.

43. I.B.C., *Joint Report . . . 141st Meridian from the Arctic Ocean to Mount St. Elias,* pp. 72–73. Probably written by J. D. Craig, who prepared much of the report, Thomas Riggs, Jr., having resigned in May 1914 (ibid., pp. 200–201).
44. Ibid., pp. 80–98.
45. Ibid., pp. 93–97.
46. Ibid., p. 84.

47. I.B.C. (Canadian Section) papers, Box 34, Thomas Riggs, Jr., report on the 1913 season, p. 3.
48. Ibid., p. 6.
49. Ibid., p. 5.
50. Ibid., pp. 10–11.
51. I.B.C., *Joint Report . . . 141st Meridian from the Arctic Ocean to Mount St. Elias,* p. 8.

AFTERWORD

1. House of Commons Debates, 20 September 1971, pp. 8012–13. A Canadian boat fishing south of Cape Muzon was boarded by the U.S. Coast Guard on 7 June 1981. Since then, fishermen of both countries have staged "fishins" near the A-B line in hopes of provoking an incident that will force their respective countries to support their boundary claims (Vancouver *Sun,* 9, 20, 27 June and 2, 16, 17 July 1981)
2. International Boundary Commission, *Joint Report upon the Survey and Demarcation of the Boundary between Canada and the United States from Tongass Passage to Mount St. Elias* (Ottawa and Washington: International Boundary Commissioners, 1952), p. 110.
3. Ibid., pp. 16–20.
4. Ibid., pp. 134–35.
5. Erik B. Wang, "Canada-United States Fisheries and Maritime Boundary Negotiations: Diplomacy in Deep Water," *Behind the Headlines,* The Canadian Institute of International Affairs, Volume 38(6)/39(1) (April 1981), p. 4.
6. Ibid., p. 15.

Bibliographical Note

In preparation for the Alaska Boundary Tribunal of 1903, both Great Britain and the United States printed a great many documents intended to support their cause or dispute their opponent's. Much of this material is in the appendices to the Case and Counter-Case prepared by each side. It includes diplomatic correspondence leading up to the signing of the Anglo-Russian Treaty of 1825 and later claims to occupation of part of the disputed territory by one side or the other. Other, less relevant, material is there as well, perhaps included to avoid the government's being charged with concealing something. In total, it comprises an invaluable source of historical material on the Panhandle area.

Another useful source is the British Colonial Office's memorandum, North American No. 187. A copy of this among the Pope papers in the Public Archives of Canada is annotated:

> This is the memo prepared by me and which I took to England printed in Sept. 1899. On it was prepared the memo subsequently published by the C.O. in Oct. 1899, "North American 187."
> J. Pope.

Norman Penlington's *The Alaska Boundary Dispute: A Critical Reappraisal* is a concise, well-documented history of the dispute. In contrast to the former's dispassionate approach, something of Canadian feelings at the time can be gained from John A. Munro's, *The Alaska Boundary Dispute,* consisting mainly of contemporary material. Both make numerous references to other works dealing with the broader spectrum of British, Canadian, and American relationships during this period. In writing of the Tribunal, I have used contemporary accounts whenever possible. Perhaps unconsciously, later accounts by the participants are long on statesmanship and careful reasoning and short on manoeuvring and pressure tactics.

The two International Boundary Commission reports are the main source of information on the boundary surveys. In addition, there is a minor amount of published material plus the internal reports the surveyors made to their respective commissioners. Many of the latter are dry reading, little more than a chronology of the season's work. Fortunately, a few individuals such as Thomas Riggs, Jr., took the trouble to record some of the incidents that took place. Reading such snippets, one can imagine the tales told after the field men returned to headquarters each fall.

Selected Bibliography

Unpublished Sources

Diaries, privately held
    Robert Bryce Craig, 1893–94.
    J.W. Taylor, 1893.
International Boundary Commission (Canadian Section)
    Internal reports and correspondence.
National Archives of the United States
    War Department: Records of the Adjutant General.
    Coast and Geodetic Survey records.
Public Archives of Canada
    Papers of Charles Constantine.
    Papers of Otto J. Klotz.
    Papers of Sir Wilfrid Laurier.
    Papers of William Ogilvie.
    Papers of Sir Joseph Pope.
    Papers of Sir Clifford Sifton.
    Papers of Henry J. Woodside.

Published Sources

Adney, Tappan. *The Klondike Stampede,* New York and London: Harper and Brothers, 1900.
Alverstone, Right Hon. Viscount. *Recollections of Bar and Bench.* New York and London: Longmans, Green and E. Arnold, 1914.
Andrews, C.L. *The Story of Alaska.* Caldwell, ID: Caxton Printers, 1938.
Andrews, G.S. *Professional Land Surveyors of British Columbia, Cumulative Nominal Roll, 4th Edition, 1978.* Victoria: The Corporation of Land Surveyors of the Province of British Columbia, 1978.
Ball, Georgiana. "The Peter Martin Case and the Provisional Settlement of the Stikine Boundary." *BC Studies* 10 (Summer 1971): 35–55.
Bailey, Thomas A. "Theodore Roosevelt and the Alaska Boundary Settlement." *Canadian Historical Review* 18 (June 1937): 123–30; also in Sherwood, *Alaska and Its History,* 1967.
Beale, Howard Kennedy. *Theodore Roosevelt and the Rise of America to World Power.* Baltimore, MD: Johns Hopkins, 1956.
Begg, Alexander. "Notes on the Yukon Country." *Scottish Geographical Magazine* 12 (November 1896): 553–59.
⸻. "Review of the Alaska Boundary Question." *Scottish Geographical Magazine* 17 (January, February 1901): 30–40, 86–96.
Berton, Pierre. *Klondike.* Toronto: McClelland and Stewart, 1972.

Billman, Christine W. "Jack Craig and the Alaska Boundary Survey." *The Beaver,* Outfit 302 (Autumn 1971): 44–49.

Bishop, Joseph Bucklin. *Theodore Roosevelt and His Time, Shown in His Own Letters.* 2 vols. New York: Scribner's, 1920.

Bond, Courtney C.J. "Surveyors of Canada, 1867–1967." *Canadian Surveyor* 20 (December 1966).

Brooks, Alfred Hulse. *Blazing Alaska's Trails.* Caldwell, ID: Caxton Printers, 1953.

Brown, Robert Craig. *Canada's National Policy 1883–1900: A Study in Canadian-American Relations.* Princeton: Princeton University Press, 1964.

Burpee, L.J., ed. *Alexander H. Murray, Journal of the Yukon 1847–48.* Ottawa: Archives of Canada, 1910.

Bush, Edward F. "Policing the Border in the Klondike Gold Rush." *Canadian Geographic* 100 (October/November 1980): 70–73.

Cairnes, D.D. *The Yukon-Alaska International Boundary between Porcupine and Yukon Rivers.* Memoir 67, Geological Survey of Canada. Ottawa: Government Printing Bureau, 1914.

Campbell, A.E. *Great Britain and the United States, 1895–1903.* London: Longmans, 1960.

Campbell, Charles S., Jr. *Anglo-American Understanding, 1898–1903.* Baltimore, MD: Johns Hopkins, 1957.

Canada. Parliament. *House of Commons Debates.*

———. *Sessional Papers.* 125–1878: *Report . . . of the engineer employed last year in determining the probable boundary line between British Columbia and Alaska . . . and also, such other papers as relate to the defining of the Boundary Line. . . .*

———. 14–1888: Department of the Interior, No. 11, Report of William Ogilvie.

———. 15–1895: North-west Mounted Police (Constantine report).

———. 15–1896: North-west Mounted Police (Supplement with Constantine report).

———. 13–1897: Department of the Interior, No. 9, Extracts from reports of Wm. Ogilvie, D.L.S.

———. 15–1897: North-west Mounted Police, Appendix DD, Report on the Yukon Detachment.

———. 15–1898: North-west Mounted Police, Appendix LL (Constantine report).

———. 38–1898: Commission of and letters and reports from Commissioner J.M. Walsh.

———. 13–1899: Department of the Interior. Reports of Major J.M. Walsh.

———. 15–1899: North-west Mounted Police, Part III, Yukon Territory, 1898.

Classen, H. George. *Thrust and Counterthrust.* Don Mills, Ont.: Longmans Canada, 1965.

Cline, Gloria Griffen. *Peter Skene Ogden and the Hudson's Bay Company.* Norman: University of Oklahoma Press, 1974.

Cole, Douglas. "Allen Aylesworth on the Alaska Boundary Award." *Canadian Historical Review* 52 (December 1971): 472–77.

Coutts, R.C. *Yukon: Places & Names.* Sidney, B.C.: Gray's Publishing, 1980.

Dafoe, John W. *Clifford Sifton in Relation to His Times.* Toronto: Macmillan, 1931.

Dall, William H. *Alaska and Its Resources.* Boston, MA: Lee and Shepherd, 1870.

Davidson, George. *The Alaska Boundary.* San Francisco: Alaska Packers Association, 1903.

Dawson, George M. "Report on an Exploration in the Yukon District, N.W.T. and Adjacent Northern Portion of British Columbia, 1887," *Geological Survey of Canada,* Annual Report 1887–1888. New Series, Vol. III, Part 1, Report B. Later reprinted *as* Report No. 629, Geological Survey of Canada. Ottawa: Queen's Printer, 1898.

Dennett, Tyler. *John Hay, from Poetry to Politics.* New York: Dodd Mead, 1933.

Dennis, Alfred L.P. *Adventures in American Diplomacy, 1896–1906.* New York: E.P. Dutton, 1928.

Deville, E. *Photographic Surveying.* Ottawa: Government Printing Bureau, 1895.

Ewart, John S. *Kingdom of Canada . . . and Other Essays.* Toronto: Morang, 1908.

Filippi, Filippo de. *The Ascent of Mount St. Elias [Alaska] by H.R.H. Prince Luigi Amedeo di Savoia, duke of the Abruzzi.* Translated by Signora Linda Villari. New York: Frederick A. Stokes, 1900.

Foster, John W. "The Alaskan Boundary." *National Geographic Magazine* 10 (November 1899): 425–56.

———. *Diplomatic Memoirs.* Boston, New York and London: Houghton Mifflin and Constable, 1910.

Franklin, Captain John, RN, FRS. *Narrative of a Second Expedition to the Shores of the Polar Sea in the Years 1825, 1826, 1827.* London: John Murray, 1828.

Galbraith, John S. *The Hudson's Bay Company as an Imperial Factor, 1821–1869.* Berkeley and Los Angeles: University of California Press, 1957.

―――. *The Little Emperor: Governor Simpson of the Hudson's Bay Company.* Toronto: Macmillan of Canada, 1976.

Garraty, John A. "Henry Cabot Lodge and the Alaskan Boundary Tribunal." *New England Quarterly* 24 (December 1951): 469–94.

Gibson, James R. *Imperial Russia in Frontier America.* New York: Oxford University Press, 1976.

Gillespie, Alexander. *Journey through Life.* Victoria, B.C.: Privately printed, 1954.

Gordon, Hon. P.H. "An Arbitrary Boundary." *The Beaver,* Outfit 302 (Autumn 1971): 50–51.

Great Britain. Alaska Boundary Tribunal. London, 1903.

Case presented on the part of the Government of His Britannic Majesty . . . plus Appendix (3 Vols.).

Counter-Case presented on the part of the Government of His Britannic Majesty . . . plus Appendix.

Argument presented on the part of the Government of His Britannic Majesty. . . .

Alaska Boundary — Various Documents bearing on the Question of the Alaska Boundary — Printed for Convenience of Reference (3 Vols.).

Alaska Boundary Tribunal. Protocols, Oral Arguments, with Index, Award of the Tribunal, and Opinions of its Members. September 3 to October 20, 1903.

―――. Colonial Office. *Memorandum on the Boundary between Canada and Alaska showing the Contention of the Canadian Government in Respect Thereto, 1899, with Appendices.* North American No. 187.

Hamilton, Walter R. *The Yukon Story.* Vancouver: Mitchell Press, 1964.

Harrington, Richard. "The Fantasy of Tarr Inlet as a New Yukon Port." *Canadian Geographical Journal* 91 (November 1975): 12–17.

Hopkins, J. Castell. *The Canadian Annual Review of Public Affairs, 1903.* Toronto: Annual Review Publishing, 1904.

Hutchison, Bruce. *The Struggle for the Border.* New York, London, Toronto: Longmans, Green, 1955.

International Boundary Commission. *Joint Report upon the Survey and Demarcation of the International Boundary between the United States and Canada along the 141st Meridian from the Arctic Ocean to Mount St. Elias.* Ottawa and Washington: 1918.

―――. *Joint Report upon the Survey and Demarcation of the Boundary between Canada and the United States from Tongass Passage to Mount St. Elias.* Ottawa and Washington: 1952.

Jackson, C. Ian. "The Stikine Territory Lease and Its Relevance to the Alaska Purchase." *Pacific Historical Review* 36 (August 1967): 289–306.

Jessup, Phillip C. *Elihu Root.* 2 vols. New York: Dodd, Mead, 1938.

Johnson, Claudine O. "George Turner." *Pacific Northwest Quarterly* 34 (July and October 1943): 243–69, 367–92.

Kerr, F.A. *Lower Stikine and Western Iskut River Areas, British Columbia.* Memoir 246, Geological Survey of Canada. Ottawa: King's Printer, 1948.

Klotz, Otto. *Certain Correspondence of the Foreign Office and of the Hudson's Bay Company copied from Original Documents, London, 1898.* Ottawa: Government Printing Bureau, 1899.

Lambart, H.F.J. "The Ascent of Mt. Natazhat in Alaska." *Canadian Alpine Journal* 6 (1915): 1–10.

Lawrence, Guy. *40 Years on the Yukon Telegraph.* Vancouver: Mitchell Press, 1965.

Lodge, Henry Cabot, ed. *Selections from the Correspondence of Theodore Roosevelt and Henry Cabot Lodge, 1884–1918.* 2 vols. New York and London: Scribner's, 1925.

McConnell, R.G. "Report on an Exploration in the Yukon and Mackenzie Basins, N.W.T." *Geological Survey of Canada,* Annual Report 1888–1889, New Series, Vol. IV, Report D. Ottawa: Queen's Printer, 1891.

McQuesten, Leroy N. *Recollections of Leroy N. McQuesten of Life in the Yukon, 1871–1885.* Dawson: Yukon Order of Pioneers, 1952.

Maddren, A.G. *Geologic Investigations along the Canada-Alaska Boundary.* Bulletin 520-K, U.S. Geological Survey. Washington: Government Printing Office, 1912.

Martin, Archer. *Report under the Porcupine District Commission Act, 1900.* Victoria: King's Printer, 1901.

Martin, Edward Sandford. *The Life of Joseph Hodges Choate.* 2 vols. London: Constable, 1920.

Mendenhall, T.C. "The Alaska Boundary." *Atlantic Monthly* (April 1896).

———, McGrath, J.E., and Turner, J.E. "The Alaskan Boundary Survey." *National Geographic Magazine* 4 (1892): 177–97.

Morison, Elting E., ed. *Letters of Theodore Roosevelt.* 8 vols. Cambridge, MA: Harvard University Press, 1951.

Munro, John A. *The Alaska Boundary Dispute.* Toronto: Copp Clark, 1970.

Murray, Alexander H. *Journal of the Yukon, 1847–1848.* Edited by L.J. Burpee. Ottawa: Archives of Canada, Pub. No. 4, 1910.

Nelles, Douglas H. "The Exploration and Survey of the 141st Meridian, Alaska." *Geographical Journal* 41 (January 1913): 48–55.

Nesham, Major E.W. "The Alaska Boundary Demarcation." *Geographical Journal* 69 (January 1927): 49–61.

Nevins, Allan. *Henry White, Thirty Years of American Diplomacy.* New York and London: Harper and Brothers, 1930.

Ogilvie, William. *Exploratory Survey of Part of the Lewes, Tat-on-duc, Porcupine, Bell, Trout, Peel and Mackenzie Rivers.* Ottawa: Queen's Printer, 1890; also in Canada, Sessional Paper 14–1890.

———. *Early Days on the Yukon.* London and New York: John Lane, 1913.

Ormsby, Margaret A. *British Columbia: a History.* Toronto: Macmillan of Canada, 1958.

Patterson, R.M. *Trail to the Interior.* Toronto: Macmillan of Canada, 1966.

Penlington, Norman. *Canada and Imperialism 1896–1899.* Toronto: University of Toronto Press, 1965.

——— *The Alaska Boundary Dispute: A Critical Reappraisal.* Toronto: McGraw-Hill Ryerson, 1972.

Pike, Warburton. *Through the Sub-Arctic Forest.* London and New York: Edward Arnold, 1896.

Pope, Maurice, ed. *Public Servant: The Memoirs of Sir Joseph Pope.* Toronto: Oxford University Press, 1960.

Raymond, Captain Charles W. *Report of a Reconnaissance of the Yukon River, Alaska Territory.* Washington: Government Printing Office, 1871.

Riggs, Thomas, Jr. "Marking the Alaskan Boundary." *National Geographic Magazine* 20 (July 1909): 593–607.

——— "Surveying the 141st Meridian," *National Geographic Magazine* 23 (July 1912): 685–713.

——— "Running the Alaska Boundary." *The Beaver,* Outfit 276 (September 1945): 40–43.

Russell, Israel C. "A Journey up the Yukon River." *Journal of the American Geographical Society* 27 (1895): 143–60.

Satterfield, Archie. *Chilkoot Pass, the Most Famous Trail in the North.* Anchorage: Alaska Northwest Publishing, 1978.

Schwatka, Frederick. *Report of a Military Reconnaissance in Alaska Made in 1883.* Washington, DC: Government Printing Office, 1885.

——— *A Summer in Alaska.* St. Louis, MO: J.W. Henry, 1894.

Sherwood, Morgan B. *Exploration of Alaska, 1865–1900.* New Haven and London: Yale University Press, 1965.

———, ed. *Alaska and Its History.* Seattle and London: University of Washington Press, 1967.

Skelton, Oscar Douglas. *Life and Letters of Sir Wilfrid Laurier.* 2 vols. Toronto: Oxford University Press, 1921.

Stacey, C.P. *Canada and the Age of Conflict: A History of Canadian External Policies, Volume I: 1867–1921.* Toronto: Macmillan of Canada, 1977.

Steele, Samuel B. *Forty Years in Canada.* Toronto: McClelland, Goodchild and Stewart, 1915.

Tansill, Charles Callan. *Canadian-American Relations, 1875–1911.* New York and Toronto: Yale University and Ryerson, 1943.

Thomson, Don W. *Men and Meridians.* 3 vols. Ottawa: Queen's Printer, 1966–69.

Tittmann, O.H. "Marking the Alaskan Boundary." *National Geographic Magazine* 19 (March 1908): 176–89.

Tompkins, Stuart Ramsay. *Alaska: Promyshlennik and Sourdough.* Norman: University of Oklahoma Press, 1945.

———. "Drawing the Alaskan Boundary." *Canadian Historical Review* 26 (March 1945): 1–24, also in Sherwood, *Alaska and Its History,* 1967.

United States. Alaskan Boundary Tribunal. London, 1903. *The Case of the United States before the Tribunal . . . plus Appendix.*

———, ———. *The Counter Case of the United States before the Tribunal . . . plus Appendix.*

———, ———. *The Argument of the United States before the Tribunal. . . .*

———. Congress. *Congressional Record.*

———. Department of the Interior. Annual Reports. Washington: Government Printing Office.

———. Treasury Department. *Report of the Superintendent of the U.S. Coast and Geodetic Survey showing the Progress of the Work during the Fiscal Year ending June 1890 to June 1896.* Washington: Government Printing Office.

Vancouver, Captain George. *A Voyage of Discovery to the North Pacific Ocean and Round the World in the Years 1790–95.* London: G.G. and J. Robinson, Paternoster-Row and J. Edwards, Pall-Mall, 1798.

Wang, Erik B. "Canada-United States Fisheries and Maritime Boundary Negotiations: Diplomacy in Deep Water," *Behind the Headlines,* Canadian Institute of International Affairs, Volume 38(6) and 39(1) (1981): 1–47.

Washburn, Charles G. "Memoir of Henry Cabot Lodge." *Massachusetts Historical Society Proceedings* 58 (April 1925): 324–76.

Wheeler, Arthur O., D.L.S. "How I Went to Alaska." *Canadian Surveyor* (July 1929): 7–9.

White, James. "Henry Cabot Lodge and the Alaska Boundary Award." *Canadian Historical Review* 6 (December 1925): 332–47.

Whymper, Frederick. *Travel and Adventure in the Territory of Alaska.* London: John Murray, 1868.

Wilson, Clifford. "The Surrender of Fort Yukon." *The Beaver,* Outfit 300 (Autumn 1969): 47–51.

———. *Campbell of the Yukon.* Toronto: Macmillan of Canada, 1970.

Wood, Frederick S., compiler. *Roosevelt As We Knew Him: The Personal Recollections of One Hundred and Fifty of His Friends and Associates.* Philadelphia and Chicago: John C. Winston, ca. 1927.

Wright, Allen A. *Prelude to Bonanza.* Sidney, B.C.: Gray's Publishing, 1976.

Zaslow, Morris. *The Opening of the Canadian North, 1870–1914.* Toronto: McClelland and Stewart, 1971.

Abbreviations

ABC	Alaska Boundary Commission (1893–95)
ABT	Alaska Boundary Tribunal (1903)
DLS	Dominion Land Surveyor (Canada)
DTS	Dominion Topographical Surveyor (Canada)
GSC	Geological Survey of Canada
HBC	Hudson's Bay Company
IBC	International Boundary Commission (since 1904)
NWMP	North-West Mounted Police
141st	141st Meridian
RAC	Russian-American Company
RN	Royal Navy
USA	United States Army
USC&GS	United States Coast and Geodetic Survey
USGS	United States Geological Survey
USN	United States Navy

Index